PENGUIN B[...]

RENAISSANCE D[...]
GENERAL EDITOR: J[...]

THREE TRAGEDIES BY RE[...]

The Renaissance Dramatists series is designed to produce a scrupulously prepared text, with a minimum of interference, in an attempt to preserve the integrity of the original editions. Therefore the texts of these plays follow the original spellings, reproduce the punctuation of the early editions and manuscripts and are accompanied by extensive explicatory Notes. Where appropriate, the volumes will also include a Glossary and List of Historical and Mythological Names.

JANE, LADY LUMLEY was born in 1537, the daughter of Henry Fitzalan, Earl of Arundel, and Katherine Grey, the aunt of Lady Jane Grey. Given an outstanding humanist education in both Greek and Latin by her father (one of the leading peers of the realm under Edward VI, Mary and Elizabeth), she married John, first Baron Lumley, around 1550, and helped him to collect the largest private library in England. Lady Lumley's wide interests included medical and scientific writings as well as moral exposition, and she translated several works by Isocrates as schoolroom exercises. Her family's political fortunes waned when their loyalty to the Catholic Church began to isolate them. She died in 1576.

Lady Lumley's translation of Euripides' *Iphigeneia in Aulis* was made in the early 1550s, probably in 1553. She does not merely translate Euripides; she adapts him to the protocols of Renaissance moral and political concerns.

MARY, COUNTESS OF PEMBROKE was born Mary Sidney in 1561, daughter of Sir Henry Sidney and Mary Dudley, herself the daughter of John Dudley, Duke of Northumberland, the powerful and over-ambitious leader of extreme Protestants under Edward VI. As a member of one of the most cultured and well-regarded families of the era, she was educated well, learning Latin, Hebrew, Greek, French and Italian. Married at fifteen to the middle-aged Henry Herbert, Earl of Pembroke, she was in many ways an icon of Renaissance womanhood: a loyal and dutiful wife and mother, but also a cultured and intelligent woman.

One of the best-known and most respected patrons of the era, Lady Pembroke was also a gifted editor, translator and author. After the death of her brother, Philip Sidney, she did a gr[...] deal of work on the texts he left unfinished, completing his translation of the *Psalms*, and revising his *Arcadia*. She also translated Petrarch's *Triumph of Death* and Philippe DuPlessis-Mornay's *Discourse of Life and Death*, as well as composing original verse of her own, including an elegy for her brother and a pastoral dialogue. Her translation of Robert Garnier's *Tragedie of Antonie* (1592) inspired a vogue for Senecan tragedy and influenced Shakespeare's *Antony and Cleopatra* – testimony to her literary powers and wide influence. She died in 1621.

ELIZABETH CARY was born about 1585, the only daughter of Lawrence and Elizabeth Tanfield. She was given an excellent education in ancient and modern languages, and was praised by her tutors for her commitment to learning. She married Sir Henry Cary, later created Viscount Falkland, in 1602. The latter part of their marriage was marred by conflict over religion, and on her eventual conversion to Catholicism in 1626 Henry Cary not only withdrew his wife's financial support, but had her children removed, and, for a while, had her physically confined. After legal wrangling her husband was forced in 1627 to begin supporting her again, but by the time of his death in 1633 they had only effected a partial reconciliation. She died in 1639.

Elizabeth Cary began to write in the early days of her marriage and seems to have written and translated widely. *The Tragedie of Mariam* (1613) was preceded by another tragedy, on Tamburlaine, which is now lost, and she was the first woman to write a history play, *The History of the Life, Reign and Death of Edward II* (1625). After her conversion she wrote several saints' lives in verse, and translated Jacques Davy du Perron's *Replye* to James I, dedicating her translation to Queen Henrietta Maria.

DIANE PURKISS is Lecturer in English at the University of Reading. She has published widely on women's writing in the early modern period, and is the author of a study on witchcraft, *The Witch in History* (Routledge, 1996). She has recently completed *Broken Men: Masculinity and the Irrational in the English Civil War*, and is now working on a study of fairies.

JOHN PITCHER is Vice President of St John's College, Oxford, and Visiting Research Professor at the University of Ulster at Coleraine.

Three Tragedies by Renaissance Women

The Tragedie of Iphigeneia
IN A VERSION BY JANE, LADY LUMLEY

The Tragedie of Antonie
TRANSLATED BY MARY, COUNTESS OF PEMBROKE

The Tragedie of Mariam
BY ELIZABETH CARY

Edited with an Introduction and Notes by
DIANE PURKISS

PENGUIN BOOKS

PENGUIN BOOKS

Published by the Penguin Group
Penguin Books Ltd, 27 Wrights Lane, London w8 5tz, England
Penguin Putnam Inc., 375 Hudson Street, New York, New York 10014, USA
Penguin Books Australia Ltd, Ringwood, Victoria, Australia
Penguin Books Canada Ltd, 10 Alcorn Avenue, Toronto, Ontario, Canada m4v 3b2
Penguin Books (NZ) Ltd, 182–190 Wairau Road, Auckland 10, New Zealand

Penguin Books Ltd, Registered Offices: Harmondsworth, Middlesex, England

This edition first published 1998
1 3 5 7 9 10 8 6 4 2

Set in 9.5/12 pt PostScript Monotype Garamond
Typeset by Rowland Phototypesetting Ltd, Bury St Edmunds, Suffolk
Printed in England by Clays Ltd, St Ives plc

CONTENTS

SERIES STATEMENT

All editions are compromises, especially perhaps editions of drama. Dramatic speeches in verse or prose, entrances and exits of characters, stage directions, scene divisions, are communicated to us in manuscripts, typescripts and printed books. From these we receive a whole range of impressions: what the dramatist hoped to achieve, how his or her play was performed, last year or four centuries ago, and how a director and actors might present it to us again. The text of a play is a record, a memory, sometimes even a monument to what has been written and played, and adapted by actors, but it is also the ground from which that play may return to the special life of the theatre, where written or typeset words become speech, and where the book, with its conventions of silent reading, gives way to the space and sounds of the auditorium, and the spectacle of performance.

Editors of drama in English have to choose the best way of passing on play texts to modern readers, who may also be actors and audiences. One choice is to modernize or normalize the texts. With older plays (written before 1700), this involves changing the format as well as the spellings of the original texts, and the punctuation, capitals and italics, so that the words and sentences and phrases look modern. The intention is to reduce what is taken to be too difficult in these older texts for modern readers. This compromise is largely rejected in this series, as for the most part unnecessary, but also because it may impair what the past has to tell us. The punctuation and spelling we encounter in older play texts may of course come from compositors or scribes, rather than from the dramatist, but still their additions and idiosyncrasies bear the imprint of the past. Even where we judge them to be wrong in the way they printed or copied a text, a Renaissance compositor or a scribe is likely to be more interestingly and informatively wrong than a twentieth-century editor who changes the texts to make them easier for us.

For these reasons, the texts of the plays in this series reproduce, wherever possible, the spelling and punctuation of the first printed editions and manuscripts. Original readings are modified only where this is essential (type damaged during printing, turned letters, patently impossible punctuation), and there is a record of significant modifications of spelling and punctuation included in the Textual Notes at the back of each volume. Until the late seventeenth century, the modern distinctions between the letters *i* and *j*, and *u* and *v* were not observed in the printing house, and printers still used *vv* for *w*, a long *s* letter shape for our *s*, and so forth. All these forms are modernized in this series. Speech prefixes are expanded, regularized, and set in small capitals, and abbreviations are silently expanded, except those still in modern use, such as ampersands and *etc*. Where necessary, the act and scene divisions of the original texts are regularized and expanded, as are stage directions, entrances and exits, which are printed in italic, with the names of speaking parts in small capitals. Any words added to the original texts are enclosed within square brackets. Other changes, for example to the lineation of prose and verse, and to the divisions of the verse, are left to the discretion (and arguments) of the volume editors. Details of how specific plays have been edited are given in Textual Procedure. In all of this, the aim of the series is to produce a standard textual frame, within which there is a scrupulously prepared version of the text, minimally interfered with, but accompanied by adequate explicatory Notes, a Glossary and a List of Historical and Mythological Names.

John Pitcher

ACKNOWLEDGEMENTS

I would like to thank the British Library for permission to reproduce the manuscript of Lady Lumley's *Iphigeneia*, and the manuscript librarians fro their help.

A number of people helped substantially with the preparation of this edition: Ivan Dowling, as always, generously lent his keen eyes to the proceedings; Alexandra Bennett, Danielle Clarke, Helen Cooper, Elizabeth Heale, Lorna Hutson, John Pitcher and Marion Wynne-Davies discussed the Introduction with me and made useful suggestions. Adam Smyth produced the Glossary and the List of Historical, Geographical and Mythological Names and helped in the preparation of the texts; his heroic labours are greatly appreciated. The series editor, John Pitcher, diligently strove to extract copy from me and to elevate it to the level his own high standards demanded. Any errors are, of course, my own.

One further debt remains; this volume owes its existence to Julia Briggs. Her perseverance in defending women's writing to publishers initially not enthusiastic about the production of anything so *outré* is a heartwarming sign of dedication in an academic world increasingly lacking in such fidelity to ideals. This volume is doubly her doing, for she is responsible for encouraging me to persevere with this and other earlier projects. In dedicating this volume to her, I am only giving her back what is hers already.

CHRONOLOGY

1534 Birth of Henry Herbert, later Earl of Pembroke.

1537 Birth of Lady Jane Fitzalan, later Lady Lumley. Birth of Lady Jane Grey.

1547 Death of Henry VIII; accession of Edward VI.

c. 1550 Lady Jane Fitzalan married to John, first Baron Lumley.

1553 Death of Edward VI; failed coup attempts to make Lady Jane Grey queen; accession of Mary Tudor; restoration of Catholicism; arrest of Cranmer. Probable translation of *The Tragedie of Iphigeneia* by Lady Lumley.

1554 Execution of Lady Jane Grey and Guildford Dudley. Birth of Sir Philip Sidney.

1558 Death of Mary Tudor; accession of Elizabeth I.

1561 Birth of Mary Sidney, later Countess of Pembroke.

1563 Publication of John Foxe's *Acts and Monuments*.

1572 St Bartholomew's Day massacre of Huguenots in Paris.

1576 Death of Lady Lumley. Mary Sidney marries Henry Herbert, second Earl of Pembroke.

1580 Birth of Lady Pembroke's son William Herbert, later third Earl of Pembroke and Shakespeare's patron.

1581 Tightening of laws against Catholicism.

c. 1585 Birth of Elizabeth Tanfield, later Elizabeth Cary, Viscountess Falkland.

1586 Death of Sir Philip Sidney.

1588 Spanish Armada. Death of Robert Dudley, Earl of Leicester.

1590 Lady Pembroke completes *The Tragedie of Antonie*.

1590s Lady Pembroke translates Petrarch's *Triumph of Death*.

1591 Lady Pembroke issues a corrected edition of Sir Philip Sidney's works.

1592 Lady Pembroke publishes *The Tragedie of Antonie*, with her translation of Philippe DuPlessis-Mornay's *A Discourse of Life and Death*.

1595 Lady Pembroke publishes revised editions of *The Tragedie of Antonie* and of her brother's works.

1601 Death of Henry Herbert; William Herbert becomes the new Earl.

1602 Elizabeth Tanfield marries Henry Cary, later Viscount Falkland; she moves in with his mother.

1603 Death of Elizabeth I; accession of James I.

1603–4 Elizabeth Cary probably writes *The Tragedie of Mariam*.

1610 Birth of Lucius Cary, eldest son of Elizabeth Cary.

1612 John Davies, *The Muse's Sacrifice or Divine Meditations*, dedicated to Lady Pembroke, Elizabeth Cary and Lucy, Countess of Bedford.

1613 Printing of *The Tragedie of Mariam*.

1619 Birth of Elizabeth Cary's daughter Lucy, probable author of her mother's life.

1621 Death of Lady Pembroke.

1622 Elizabeth and Henry Cary arrive in Ireland.

1625 Death of James I; accession of Charles I. Marriage of Charles and Henrietta Maria. Scribal MS of *The History of the Life, Reign and Death of Edward II*, by Elizabeth Cary.

1626 Elizabeth Cary received into the Catholic Church.

1630 Publication of Elizabeth Cary's translation of Jacques Davy du Perron's *The Replye of the Most Illustrious Cardinal of Perron to the King of Great Britaine*, printed at Douai, dedicated to Henrietta Maria.

1633 Death of Henry Cary. Elizabeth Cary receives dedication of Marston's *Collected Plays*.

1639 Death of Elizabeth Cary.

INTRODUCTION

It has become customary to begin any discussion of women's writing in the Renaissance by mentioning Judith Shakespeare, one of Virginia Woolf's most memorable fictions.[1] In Woolf's moving, melodramatic narrative, the Bard's brilliant sister must battle her own family in her struggle for recognition, but is doomed to obscurity by the harshness of sixteenth-century patriarchy. She writes nothing, and she meets a sticky end, lying buried where the omnibuses stop outside the Elephant and Castle. Those omnibuses are the key to the utility of this narrative for those who cannot seem to stop citing it. They represent the modernity that will not mark the grave of Judith Shakespeare, that will not recognize that she was 'as talented as himself'. They bury her in obscurity. Thus they form the strongest possible contrast to the critic citing the story, who can congratulate herself on *not* burying Judith, on erecting a monument to her, undoing the cruelties of patriarchies past and present. It is obligatory to differ somewhat from Woolf's narrative, to say something like 'See? It wasn't so bad. Judith didn't die without a word. Here she is, with a whole lot of plays by her, available for us to read.' Cue feeling of smugness in relation to the dark patriarchal barbarity of the past.

If we approach the plays in this volume with Judith Shakespeare or someone like her at the forefront of our minds, we will fail to understand them or even to read them. Judged against the standards set by Woolf and those who cite her, these plays will be a great disappointment. Woolf's Judith Shakespeare is a genius; *if* we had her writings, Woolf implies, we would instantly see them as extraordinary, without having to adjust our ideas of 'greatness' by one jot. This is not true, by a long chalk, of any of the surviving plays by Renaissance women writers, a problem which many critics have not managed to bring themselves to confront directly. Another problem is Woolf's proposed relationship between Judith's life and her work, or lack thereof. Judith's life is simply that which impedes her work: she faces unremitting opposition from her father; her brother is no help at all; the marriage proposed for her is 'hateful' to her because it will prevent her from writing. The women whose plays are collected here, on the other hand, were not so wholeheartedly victimized. If we adopt the Judith Shakespeare paradigm, we will be forced to conclude that they do not have the same excuses for failing to be geniuses. Lady Lumley, for instance, wrote *in order* to please her father, and probably her husband.[2] Lady Pembroke and Elizabeth Cary were encouraged to write by positively fawning overtures from other poets, and Elizabeth Cary's first work, now lost, was dedicated to her new husband.[3] Though certainly not hailed as geniuses on every side, these women probably had to face less savage criticism than did Shakespeare, certainly less than Keats.

And yet these works are unlikely to strike the reader as 'great literature'. Many have tried to pre-empt this attack by seeing these plays as oppositional writing, writing which finds and establishes 'feminine' values and interests in masculine spheres. We do not find these texts great, the argument goes, because they are voicing a gendered opposition to the male mainstream that we have come to know and love. Once again, Judith Shakespeare is a figurehead here; her defiant refusal of conformity in life stands as a symbol of the unruly femininity that some have been eager to find in the texts of women writers. This feminist argument itself *appears* oppositional, while actually recycling some fairly familiar and widely shared notions. For we now value Renaissance writers on very post-Romantic grounds. Take the recanonization of Sir Walter Ralegh, dropped from the canon when he began to seem too lickspittle and British Empire. Then Stephen Greenblatt created a Ralegh for the 1980s: careerist, but cynical, master of deception and disguise, comprehensively disillusioned with everyone, not least himself, sexually unruly, ultimately unsuccessful, highly original, pretty much like Christopher Hampton's Valmont from *Dangerous Liaisons*.[4] This new Ralegh conforms exactly to the Romantic stereotype of authorship: he is solitary, 'different', implicitly rebellious. The same qualities can be located, fortuitously, in his work. Thus, ironically, he has been brought into line with more stalwart malcontents such as Marlowe, Nashe, Shakespeare and Donne. Other figures, including even such unlikely candidates for Romantic martyrdom as Spenser and Sir Philip Sidney, have been brought into Romantic line, not without a titanic effort.[5]

This Romanticization is one reason why women writers have been assumed into the Renaissance canon with little fuss; far from subverting its current criteria, they have confirmed them, or rather they have been read as if they do. For this Romantic myth, we need biography, hence the remarkable overuse of women writers' biographies in setting the critical agenda of late.[6]

The spadework involved in producing these biographies is commendable. But certain features of authorial biographies are overused: any features which will allow us to see these women as Romantic outsiders. A wish to find the woman in the text might lead us to assume that Lady Lumley's choice of *Iphigeneia in Aulis* for translation from the Euripides canon was because *Iphigeneia* is 'about' Lumley.[7] However, the reason for Lumley's choice of play was almost certainly that Erasmus had translated both *Iphigeneia* and *Hekabe* from Greek into Latin, with the result that for the whole of the sixteenth century these two plays were the most performed, adapted and read of Euripides' work.[8] That Lumley chose *Iphigeneia* instead of the more popular *Hekabe*, which was later to move Hamlet to tears, is not without biographical significance, but it cannot have been due solely to the gender of the protagonist. If we were in search of biographical signs of rebellion on Lumley's part, we would find *Hekabe* a much more 'readable' choice. Elizabeth Cary's conversion to Catholicism has been resolutely mapped on to her play *The Tragedie of Mariam*, despite the fact that her reunion with Rome occurred some twenty years after the play was written, and despite the impossibility of identifying any remote trace of Romishness in the play's Protestant orthodoxy. Lady Pembroke's supposed incestuous passion for her brother is mentioned surprisingly often, though it is usually dismissed as unkind gossip; the gossip itself furnishes a reason for her oppositional status, a status not very visible in her play text.

However, other aspects of these authors' biographies have been relatively neglected. We hear far less about the political and social standing of the families of which these women were members (even the Sidneys) than we do about their more personal commitments.[9] Lady Lumley was the daughter of Henry Fitzalan, Earl of Arundel, one of the principal peers of the realm under Edward VI, Mary and Elizabeth. Lady Pembroke, less elevated, was nevertheless the daughter of Mary Dudley, who was the sister of the Earl of Leicester, and the sister-in-law of Lady Jane Grey. Elizabeth Cary's father and husband were both paradigms of the career-gentleman with a title. These facts have all been acknowledged, but far less weight has been given to them than to the women's marital difficulties. Yet it was these facts which made the women who they were, and set the limits of what they could or wanted to write.

A misplaced insistence on seeing these women apart from their families is reflected in the names literary criticism has bestowed on them. Feminist literary criticism has chosen to call these women Jane Lumley, Mary Sidney,

Elizabeth Cary: these are names which harmonize with our assumptions about *modern* women writers, women for whom, as Foucault observed, the whole name stands simply as a synecdoche for a row of books.[10] However, few contemporaries would have thought of the translator of *The Tragedie of Antonie* as plain Mary Sidney, or even as plainish Mary Sidney Herbert. To them, she would have been Lady Pembroke, Pembrokeana, a name which is synecdochical not only of a row of book spines, but money, acres, a great house, political influence, a place in the social hierarchy, a position within national, economic and familial hierarchies. It is as if she were known as Mrs Microsoft or Madame Sony. The false egalitarianism and individuation of 'Mary Sidney' covers over the way Lady Pembroke's identity was a composite of complex associations redolent of class privilege and power. This edition tries to reconstruct the creation of these women's identities in families by using their alien, alienating titles: Lady Lumley, Lady Pembroke, though Elizabeth Cary remains unadorned because at the time of writing *Mariam* her husband had not yet been elevated to the peerage.

Admittedly, naming women writers is always a problem, because in literary tradition writers are signified by their surnames and women inconveniently change theirs upon marriage; the seventeenth-century prophetess Lady Eleanor Davies is the worst-case scenario, having three husbands as well as her maiden name for the critic to choose from. This in itself points to the relative instability of women's individual identities, the extent to which those identities are inseparable from the identities of their families. This contingency of identity can be illustrated by the confusing repetition of similar names in family circles. Both Lady Pembroke and her even more prolific niece Lady Mary Wroth were at one time in their lives Mary Sidney, so that the name 'Mary Sidney' does not refer securely to a Romantic individual but points at efforts to transfer family prestige, perhaps even to reproduce identities in a new generation. All these women had Christian names which echoed the names of ruling queens, and as a result their names – Jane, Mary, Elizabeth – are the same as those of many other noblewomen of the same generation. There were no fewer than three Elizabeth Carys active in the literary world of early modern England; the author and dedicatee of *Mariam* are both called Elizabeth Cary. Such names do not separate the individual from society, but connect her to it.

Feminist family biography often represents the woman writer as opposed to her family, struggling to assert individuation in the face of coercion. Prone as we are to understand literary works as individual self-expression, we need to remind ourselves constantly that the Renaissance understood literature and identity as more collaborative familial and social projects. Plays by Renaissance women dramatists were produced as part of the self-fashioning and dynastic establishment of families rather than individuals. This is very visible in Lady Lumley's case. Jane Fitzalan Lumley was the daughter of Catherine Grey, sister of Lady Jane Grey's father Thomas Grey, which placed Lady Lumley close to the royal family, almost – though not quite – within the royal circle. Her father, the Earl of Arundel, was an exceptionally ambitious and important career-politician and noble. In giving his daughter a strong classical education, he was not giving her a voice so that she might embark on a career as a writer or express herself fluently. He was buying a commodity, or, rather, he was following the standard practice of Renaissance nobles in turning his daughter into a sign of his own wealth, prestige, power and fashionableness. Lady Lumley's facility in Greek and Latin seemed to both her father and her husband not an unfeminine eccentricity, but the very vanguard of fashion, ornaments which enhanced her own status and therefore theirs. Perhaps the very fact that a girl could not *use* an elaborate humanist education enhanced its value as conspicuously useless, like buying a banquet in order to throw it away uneaten. Arundel was also emphasizing Lady Lumley's resemblance to her cousin, Lady Jane Grey, born the same year as herself and like her named for Jane Seymour, one of Henry VIII's queens and Edward VI's mother. Although he was Lady Jane Grey's political enemy, the Earl of Arundel recognized in her the fashionable education of a princess. Similarly, the princesses Mary and Elizabeth had received humanist learning in thick slabs. To have a daughter able to read Greek was figuratively to stand near the throne. The play Lady Lumley produced is itself both a display of that wealth and prestige invested in her – a profitable return on her father's investment – and an ornament, a display of classical learning which signifies her father's wealth. It is more than that, in the context of the family, as we shall see. But that is why it exists at all.

By contrast, the Tanfield family into which Elizabeth Cary was born, were on the make. They were not nobles, but represented an alliance between old and new gentry. Though Elizabeth Cary, like Lady Lumley, was named for a queen, she did not stand near the throne. Her father Lawrence Tanfield was a smart lawyer, a rising professional man with strong links to the court, who financed his ambitions by oppressing his tenants, and part of his programme involved his daughter's marriage into the nobility. Henry Cary, though not yet a viscount when Elizabeth was married to him, had noble connections through his mother which made his promotion to a peerage highly likely. Significantly, Elizabeth moved in with his mother while he was away in the Netherlands, so that she was at the heart of his family household, rather than her own, and identified with the Carys: her first two plays were dedicated to her husband and to his sister. Rather than interpreting these dedications in terms of Elizabeth Cary's personal affections, it might be worth looking at the way they connect her dramatic output with her new family. Despite the fact that her mother-in-law apparently punished her by depriving her of books, Elizabeth Cary seems to have connected books with becoming a Cary. One reason for this might be Lady Pembroke, praised as the exemplary Protestant noblewoman and wife by her own coterie, and translator of Robert Garnier's trendsetting Senecan drama *The Tragedie of Antonie*:[11] a possible role-model of female self-fashioning for a bookish young wife who was later to try so hard to advance her husband's prestige that he had to beg her to stop, embarrassed. On marrying into the upper classes, Elizabeth Cary sets out her stall as a noblewoman by writing two Senecan dramas of her own, dramas which display the education she brings to her new circumstances and her appropriateness for them. Far from signalling her rebellion against her husband's family, her plays signal the change of position wrought by her marriage and imply that she is fitted by education to occupy it. They are part of her self-fashioning, not as a Romantic individual, but as a member of a noble household.[12]

And as a member of a political faction, too; despite an ever-growing interest in the political allegiances of Renaissance writers, we still hear little about the factions of which these families formed a part, because the production of these women's writings as part of political projects involving dozens of people interferes with our Romantic notions of authorship. Lady Lumley's father was a conservative whose position did not change, but who found himself beached by receding tides of religion until he linked himself with conscious Catholic rebellions like the Ridolfi plot. Lady Lumley's translation of *Iphigeneia* was probably produced to mark – perhaps even to celebrate – the zenith of his career under Mary's reign. The Sidneys were committed to the ardent Protestantism of their grandfather Northumberland's political programme; Lady Pembroke was the niece of Leicester, the Protestant leader under Elizabeth, and the mother of William Herbert, third Earl of Pembroke, who inherited his mantle as tough-talking Protestant at court. Lady Pembroke's interest in Senecan tragedy reflects and forwards those concerns; it is part of a family interest in moral reformation and political commitment. The Carys were among those dragged to the top in Buckingham's faction; when Elizabeth Cary wrote *The Tragedie of Mariam*, however, her father and husband were just beginning their careers, and so her play is part of that struggle for notice in its efforts to compliment the Sidneys by tactful imitation.

Least of all do we hear admissions that one reason these women's actual writings, as opposed to their lives, are not conformable to the canon as usually understood is because those writings fail to adhere to standards set by writers from a completely different social class. We do not want to hear in detail about houses like Nonesuch, Wilton House and Burford Priory, because to do so would be to sound as if we were wallowing in a class status that embarrasses our absurd notion that the literary canon and its counter-canons are meritocracies. The most cursory glance at these women reveals that their class status was what made it possible for them to write at all. The Lumley library, for instance, twenty-six hundred volumes in 1609, was not available to middling women, or middling men for that matter. Judith Shakespeare is a female version of her brother; she is middle class; and so her wish is to write for the public stage. (With characteristic delicacy, Woolf does not point out that Shakespeare's motivation was partly financial.) The women represented here, all members of the nobility by birth or marriage, did not write for the public stage or for money, no matter how much financial hot water they were in. Elizabeth Cary may have hoped for some small returns on her published works, but she would not have anticipated living on her earnings. Given how small fees for printed books were, such hopes would have been unrealistic. These women were nobles themselves: they could hardly expect to be financially patronized by other nobles. They would have hoped for indirect financial benefit from the acknowledgement of their presence in a faction; they may have used their works as gifts to cement social alliances, as a successful hostess today might use well-chosen gifts of flowers.

Their social position closed to them the chance of making money by writing for the commercial theatre. They probably never thought of doing so, though one of them was a patron of public drama. Their plays were almost certainly not 'performed' at all, at any rate not displayed to a paying public. If 'performed', they might have been read aloud by a circle of friends. These women's lack of interest in public drama is routinely related to the equation between women actors and notorious whores made many times by godly moralists. Yet men from a similar social background also refrained from writing for the public stage, despite strong interests in the theatre and the authorship of a number of private or closet dramas: Philip Sidney and Fulke Greville both come to mind. The public stage bulked less large in the minds of Elizabethan and Jacobean nobles than it does in our own; our view is deformed by the primacy of Shakespeare. Lady Pembroke did not sit at home feeling stifled because writing a comedy for the Globe would make her appear whorish, any more than A. S. Byatt might today feel cheated because no one has invited her to write an episode of *Neighbours* or *ER*.

The modern assumption that public equals public stage, and the concomitant idea that private drama is a secluded space for delicate and publicity-shy flowers, was not always shared by the upper classes. Senecan 'private' drama could be much more dangerously 'public' or political than plays for the public stage, because it did not have to pass the scrutiny of the Revels office. Both *Antonie* and *Mariam* are more explicitly engaged with questions of good rule and resistance to tyranny than most historical dramas produced on the public stage, while *Iphigeneia* reflects and comments on the anxieties of humanists like Erasmus and More, concerned about the rise of opportunistic nobles unwilling to sacrifice themselves for the state. In these ways, all these dramas are not exceptional just because their authors are women; men contributed to the trends for humanist translations and Senecan tragedies.

Entangled in dynasties, marriages, coteries, factions, these women were not alone or isolated. Their writing sprang from a sense of involvement with such local worlds, and from a sense that microcosms mattered to the macrocosm. In different ways, at different moments, all were part of struggling, self-fashioning families where men were scrambling rapidly up the glassy pyramid of class. Women's role was to contribute to and sympathize with these masculine struggles. The result was to focus women's attention on the class position of the family rather than gender ideology within it. These plays illustrate strikingly similar preoccupations to those written by men from similar family circumstances. The plays presented here are historical tragedies with clear political overtones, part of a genre initiated by humanists, revived by Lady Pembroke, and produced by men like Samuel Daniel, Greville and Thomas Kyd. All these plays reshape gender boundaries, but often unconsciously, in the service of their tormented relations with an overt political agenda and a covert and anxious figuration of the self.

The sex of these women did give their writings an ambiguous position in the political groupings of which they were members. Philip Sidney, Greville and even James I himself wrote as part of the humanist self-display which constituted the courtier's identity. Writing was a form of advertising, a way of circulating ideas, a means of influencing the great and their hangers-on. As women, none of these writers could hope for real preferment in their own right. This did not render their self-fashioning pointless, however. One idea behind dynastic marriages of the kind made by all these women was that they would bring loyalty to their parents and siblings into their new family; as patrons, or members of court circles. For upper-class women, writing was an extension of the normal female role of 'carrying' a family's reputation at court or in a new family. Any writing which formed part of these projects advertised its links to the writings of the family. The chains of association visible in women's lives are also visible in their writings; Lady Pembroke advertises her links to the Sidney family, just as Elizabeth Cary makes a feature of her new husband's family while imitating the Sidneys.

There was nothing peculiarly feminine about this connectedness; the literature of clientage involved showing signs of loyalty in choice of style and theme. Writings were not judged by the criteria that we use; proficiency came from careful imitation of worthy models, not from flagrant individuality. Lady Pembroke's willingness to figure as her brother's sister should be seen less as a prop for a woman unable to throw off the shackles of an oppressive male relative than as a sign of her knowledge of her own entanglement in family and patronage networks. Later, her niece Lady Mary Wroth also imitated her illustrious uncle, and she may have helped to ensure his reputation, and to ensure his further imitation by a new generation of women, including Anna Weamys and the Restoration romancers Aphra Behn and Delarivier Manley.

The connectedness of women's writing is illustrated by the fact that two of these plays are only 'by' women in the sense that they are translated by women. The distinction between translation and original work was blurrier in 1600 than it is now. To a Renaissance writer, translation was a vital exercise in imitation, a kind of acting or role-playing, whereby the imitator became imbued with the qualities of what was imitated, and at the same time signalled a willingness to be identified with it. All writing is translation in that it draws upon and imitates the writings of others; the Renaissance knew this and celebrated it. The texts Lady Lumley and Lady Pembroke chose to translate are highly significant in themselves, and we need not confine our attention to changes made by them or rewritings of the originals. Lady Lumley's choice of *Iphigeneia* is an attempt to correlate a variety of themes important to her family and her faction. Lady Pembroke's choice of *Antonie* is part of her self-fashioning as the sister, image and literary heir of her brother Philip Sidney, a process of imitation which elevates him by portraying him as worthy of imitation. It deals with mourning and loss, but also takes up the political themes which had absorbed the attention of the whole faction; in giving them new significance, Lady Pembroke at once glorified and replaced her brother.

Writing could also be a way of dealing with the crushing disappointments and insults which the career of a courtier entailed. All three of these women were disappointed. Lady Lumley and her family were sidelined by increasingly Protestant regimes and by the death of her brother and children. Lady Pembroke was shut out of all that being Pembrokean meant when her son died. Elizabeth Cary was unable to maintain her position as a woman of letters while becoming a Catholic, though she may have gained a position of influence later under Charles I's queen, Henrietta Maria. These disappointments are undoubtedly marked by gender, especially Lady Pembroke's, yet they boil down to falling from favour, power and importance, something which also overtook their male relatives. Sidney and Greville had used writing as a means of working off anger and uniting a sympathetic audience around them, so their female relations were able to do the same. Still other men never dreamed of rising to the heights of power and prestige occupied by these women. Nashe and Shakespeare might have laughed hollowly if it had been suggested that they were oppressing the Countess of Pembroke.

In this respect, it is not surprising that the central preoccupations of the three plays are shared with men, writing in the same genres at the same time. All three are preoccupied with politics, in the broadest sense. They interest themselves in contemporary events, and in their ethical and theoretical consequences. They describe politics and they actively intervene in them. All were written by women who saw themselves as close to the centre of power and able to affect it. Looking at families means noticing why these particular women, rather than other noblewomen, might have chosen to write dramas. We must be cautious, because many manuscript archives remain to be explored, some of which have already produced surprises (however, some works are undoubtedly lost for good). Initially we might begin by considering the particular constellation of women here. What unites this group *apart* from gender? Why these women, and not others?

These women had families who actively supported their educations, not because the women were seen as exceptional in any way, but because education made women more adept at the arts of courtiership. The Sidney family is an obvious instance. They united faith in courtly acts of pleasing with strong Protestantism. The idea was to use the former to advance the latter, and the daughters of that family were taught courtly and humanist skills so that they might help in the family's larger private and public causes. Such a programme is explicable in the light of the family's Dudley ancestry, which united them not only to the Duke of Northumberland but, through the marriage of his son Guildford, to Lady Jane Grey. Lady Jane, educated to be a suitable wife and queen to her cousin Edward VI, is one of the original role-models for all these women.[13] Through Lady Jane Grey, too, the Sidney women are connected to Lady Lumley. Lady Lumley was related to Lady Jane, and we have seen how Arundel's ambitions expressed themselves in both his daughters' expensive education.

What had been acutely fashionable in Lady Lumley's childhood had become something else by Lady Pembroke's adolescence: the symbol of an almost-lost cause. Lady Jane Grey had been mythologized by Protestant hagiographer John Foxe and by the play *The Famous History of Thomas Wyatt* as *the* Protestant martyr: beautiful, modest, quiet, deferential. Yet her cult began with the publication of her works in 1555.[14] As a writer, and a decidedly unfeminine disputant, Lady Jane Grey became known to the Protestant reading public: she exemplified the woman who could use her learning and resolution in the cause of God. Philip Sidney was inspired by Lady Jane Grey: Katherine Duncan-Jones plausibly suggests that she was one inspiration for the courage and eloquence of the imprisoned Pamela in the *New Arcadia*.[15] The Sidneys' mother, too, was a kind of Protestant martyr, having sacrificed her appearance for the sake of nursing Elizabeth I through smallpox. The Sidneys *inherit* (almost literally) the notion that writing, education, learning are ways to serve the Protestant cause.

Philip Sidney's enthusiasm for Lady Jane Grey is interesting given his own future role as Protestant martyr and figure of the combination of high culture and Protestant virtue. Sidney's effort to reanimate and rewrite Lady Jane Grey's virtues in turn inspired his sister and niece: he imitated Lady Jane Grey, and they him. They in turn were imitated by others, notably the young Elizabeth Cary. Philip Sidney's writings always had a lot to do with women and femininity: he wrote a prose romance dedicated to his sister, was a sonneteer, and in both cases created genres friendly to women which his niece Lady Mary Wroth and his imitator Anna Weamys would later exploit. Sidney was able to inspire women writers in and outside his family to follow him in a way that an author of humanist treatises on hunting would not have done.[16]

Lady Pembroke maintained Sidney's uneasy fusion of courtiership and Protestant earnestness, but his other female successors did not. Elizabeth Cary did in *Mariam*, but later turned to the rather different intellectual notions of the Counter-Reformation when she was reconciled with the Roman Catholic Church in 1626, while Sidney's niece Lady Mary Wroth encouraged a different politics of style from that of the original Sidney circle, one where political issues were understood through love and romance. Combining the roles of courtier and Protestant activist came to seem impossible to Greville too, and it is hard to think of a mid or late Jacobean figure who exemplifies both. Henrietta Maria eventually came to explore, through *préciosité*,[17] a position in which once again courtly arts could serve political ends rather than existing to please and to allow for social interaction. Through Henrietta, Elizabeth Cary is linked to later writers of politicized histories and romances, including Aphra Behn and Delarivier Manley. But by this time, the genre was highly feminized. These plays revel in an era before politics became as gendered, as masculinized, as the English republic made them.

That moment, however, was full of other kinds of tension, which these plays explore. All have politics as their main theme. All concern marital conflict. The emphasis on marriage in these plays springs not from the authors' personal circumstances but from its centrality as a political metaphor. The relationship between monarch and subject was frequently understood in terms of the relationship between husband and wife; the monarch was a husband to the subject wife. Just as the husband was to rule the wife, so the monarch was to govern the subject. For some thinkers, as the wife could in exceptional circumstances rebel against the husband, so the subject could sometimes differ from the prince. The marriage metaphor was used by political theorists to explore the issues which preoccupied Renaissance political thinkers: allowable and intolerable levels of resistance to tyranny, and questions of rebellion and tyrannicide and their justifications. The unruly wives who have been seen as proto-feminist might be better understood as proto-democratic, since wifely rebellion could signify the subject's resistance to political tyranny, and its limits. What might to us seem like gender politics is often a metaphor drawn from political theory. Elizabeth Cary's Salome, for example, misread by early feminists as a feisty feminist foresister, is also a duplicitous courtier and rebellious subject who undermines the stability of the realm by seeking her own good at the expense of others. Elizabeth

Cary unselfconsciously uses the image of the promiscuous woman to signify courtly corruption, just as John Webster does.

Political dramas were not just quarries for abstractions; they were political in another, more immediate sense too. Thanks to the survival of histories and dramas with annotations by sixteenth- and seventeenth-century readers, we know that histories were interpreted as guides to contemporary political events. While reading Livy, Gabriel Harvey carefully connected the main characters in the history with his contemporaries, while Philip Herbert, younger brother of William and son of Lady Pembroke, read Chapman's *The Conspiracie and tragedie of Charles, Duke of Byron* (1608) in terms of the fall of Buckingham.[18] Although these are late instances, there is no reason to suppose that this method of reading developed late. Lady Lumley's *Iphigeneia* might be understood not only in terms of abstract issues of rule and subordination, public and individual good, but also through the more personal stories of her family's political engagements. The play is usually seen as a companion to Lord Lumley's translation of Erasmus' *Institutio Principis Christiani*, or *The Institution of a Christian Prince* (1550), and *Iphigeneia* shares that work's concern with the notion that corruption stems from the people's wilful ignorance of the good of the community in favour of their own interests. Anyone who governs for his own benefit, and not that of the commonwealth, is not a prince but a man-eater and a tyrant. Similarly, at the end of More's *Utopia* (1551), Hythlodaeus speaks of 'a certain conspiracy of rich men procuring their own commodities under the name and title of a commonwealth'.[19] Such anxieties about self-fashioning, whether or not actually endorsed by More, were certainly abroad. And if More, self-fashioner *par excellence*, could entertain them, why not Henry Fitzalan, Earl of Arundel, whose political biography epitomizes the career-politician? In Iphigeneia's speech of acceptance, these political concerns are reiterated:

> remember how I was not borne for your sake onlie, but rather for the
> commodite of my countrie, thinke you therfore that it is mete, that
> suche a companie of men beinge gathered together to revenge the
> greate injurie, whiche all grece hathe suffered shoulde be let of their
> journye for my cause.   (808 – 13)

Here Iphigeneia asserts a value beyond and yet analogous to her use-value as a marriageable daughter, a value as a commodity item to be used by her country.

To understand the familial concerns which this play might stage, and to identify in doing so the moment when it may have been written, we need to look in more detail at the career of Lady Lumley's father in the late 1540s to mid 1550s. Arundel's power was essentially regional and territorial; he represented a noble tradition whereby powerful barons managed locales on behalf of the monarch and therefore had to be included in government, placated and managed themselves. As a result, he was free to form his own alliances, offensive and defensive, and can be seen doing both during the short reign of Edward VI. One of the Catholic traditionalists on Edward's council, he disliked and helped to overthrow the Duke of Somerset, allying himself with Warwick to do so. They first solicited Mary's support in August 1549, but she may have refused to be drawn in. Later, and predictably, Arundel seems to have fallen out with the increasingly mighty Warwick, now Duke of Northumberland, and was alleged to have plotted with Somerset to assassinate his fellow councillors at a banquet. Somerset was executed, but Arundel never came to trial: he was fined and set free in December 1552, after he had confessed to being party to the conspiracy. He was back in the council in 1553. If Lady Lumley really produced her translation in 1550 or thereabouts, it may be a graceful allusion to her father's efforts to serve the state at his own risk.[20] It might even allude to his imprisonment in the *stasis* of the windless Greek ships.

If, on the other hand, it was produced later, which seems much more likely, then it may have had another kind of meaning.[21] There is reason to think it must date from after Mary's accession and the overthrow of Thomas Cranmer, since Lady Lumley appears to have used his copy of Euripides if she consulted a Greek text at all; with characteristic rapacity, Arundel snaffled Cranmer's library upon the confiscation and sale of his goods. Lady Lumley's translation may have been intended to celebrate these events, and to exalt her father's restoration to the political centre as a sacrifice of leisure for the interests of the state. Arundel's behaviour under Queen Jane, formerly Lady Jane Grey, illustrates his capacity for theatricality, and (depending on one's point of view) his ability to put this quality at the service of the public good. Arundel was part of Jane's council; he attended Jane on her progress from Syon House to the Tower, and was among those who urged Northumberland to take personal command of the force sent to capture Mary. On Northumberland's departure, however, Arundel was foremost among those who removed the council from the Tower, met at Baynard's Castle and proclaimed Mary queen. He arrived first of the council at Mary's side, and was duly rewarded. Mary gave him the incomplete but magnificent Nonsuch Palace on her death.[22] When Mary died, his services were retained by Elizabeth, and it was a crucial part of the legitimation of her government that she kept the likes of Arundel, Shrewsbury and Pembroke on board.[23] It would be hard to see all this as self-sacrifice for the state, but Lady Lumley may have been transforming the sharp fears and uncertainties of mid Tudor politics into an elevated moral platform: those who seemed to lose such battles, even those who seemed to lose their lives, are really immortalized in the state they serve and the events they set in motion. However, this seems two-edged in the face of Arundel's role in Jane's overthrow. Jane was, after all, Lady Lumley's cousin, and Arundel's niece by blood. If *Iphigeneia* was written after her execution on 12 February 1554, it might have made very uncomfortable reading for Arundel, and raised questions about just who had been sacrificed and how willingly. This reading is so far against the grain of the text that it suggests a date of no later than 1553 for the play.

Such political readings of dramatic action were the outcome of the Renaissance system for interpreting playscripts through the lenses of Cicero and Quintilian. Scripts were an exchange between an actor speaking with all the devices of persuasion to convince listeners of a moral argument, generally one with political implications, and an audience. Renaissance editions of classical scripts come with prefatory treatises, indexes of memorable quotations or aphorisms marked in the text with quotation marks and other materials which ensure that the text will be read in certain ways. Michael Neandrus's anthology *Aristologia Euripidea Graecolatina* offers a plot summary of every Euripides play, followed by a numbered collection of memorable speeches, or *sententiae*.[24] Lady Lumley's sister Mary compiled a number of such *sententiae* from Greek drama and orations to present to her father, translated into Latin.[25] Years later, Lady Lumley asked for and obtained a copy of the Latin *sententiae* on the walls of the library at Gorhambury.[26] Such maxims were invariably general, best understood in Shakespeare's brilliant parody of them in Polonius' advice to Laertes.

The emphasis on *sententiae* probably explains why Lady Lumley did not translate the lyrical choruses of *Iphigeneia*, an absence usually explained as a lapse of literary taste. *Iphigeneia*'s first dialogue, between Agamemnon and his old servant, illustrates this tendency to interpret the text as a series of *sententiae*: Agamemnon opines, for instance, that 'trulie I do thinke that mortall man to be verye fortunate, whiche beinge witheout honor dothe leade his life quietlye' (19–20). *Sententiae* also have the effect of flattening out the class differences in the play; what matters is not Agamemnon and Senex, master and servant, but the moral maxims both enunciate. Dropping the chorus – dropping the commoners, in fact – has the same effect, leaving the nobles onstage with their maxims. The same impulse animates Lady Pembroke, though the *sententiae* of *Antonie* are more carefully worked into narrative and dialogue. Here, rather than being the kind of maxim you might inscribe on a library wall, the *sententiae* are an integral part of a rhetorical event, one persuasive device among many that the speaker might draw on in order to create a moral argument. When Cleopatra explains that the gods are not responsible for human misery, for instance, she says that

> If we therein sometimes some faults commit,
> We may them not to their high majesties,
> But to our selves impute; whose passions
> Plunge us each day in all afflictions.   (II.240–43)

This is not just a philosophical statement, but a political one: Cleopatra is throwing out the notion that the fall of rulers is due to providential inter-ference, and suggesting that instead it is caused by their own failures of self-control. Elizabeth Cary follows the same line: the frequently quoted chorus on matrimony in *Mariam* is a mass of *sententiae*, not least the uncomfort-able couplet: 'For in a wife it is no worse to finde,/ A common body, then a common minde' (III.3.128–9).

The emphasis on *sententiae* alerts us to the difficulty of leaping to conclusions about these women's investment in tragedy as a genre; before we eagerly conclude that they are disrupting its masculinity, we should ask what they are likely to have meant by tragedy, whether reading and writing tragedy was the same for the writers of closet drama as it was for those who wrote for the popular stage. Oddly, the principal influence for the development of both is the same: the Roman dramatist, moralist, politician and essayist Seneca, but at first sight the high and popular meanings of the term 'Senecan tragedy' seem absolutely different. Popular Senecan tragedy is characterized by crimes and vengeances gorily enacted; closet Senecan drama takes up Senecan stoicism and couples it with Seneca's excessive, hyperbolic rhetoric, extending the set-piece and the moral maxim while rigidly excluding the lyrical. Yet these two 'Senecan tragedies' have more in common than might be supposed; in closet Senecan dramas, as in *Titus Andronicus* and Kyd's *The Spanish Tragedie*, violence is central to the plot. For if tragedy as a whole signifies the helplessness of the individual enmeshed in uncontrollable events, that process of enmeshing or getting caught is most often signified by violence, by the body's entanglement in death and dissolution. Both kinds of Senecan tragedy also share intense awareness of a world sensing the beginning of its own dissolution; the world of the empire, Seneca's world, becomes in both kinds of Senecan tragedy an apt signifier for the Renaissance's engagement with corruption, degeneracy and death.

Unlike us, the early sixteenth century saw tragedy as a feminine genre with female protagonists; the Erasmian translations of Euripides and the distribution of Seneca's plays saw to that. A glance at the proliferation of classicizing dramas based on Seneca and Euripides, the many Medeas and Trojan women and Hekabes and Iphigeneias, illustrates the way the Renaissance found it possible and even necessary to explore the tragic eclipse of an individual through violence through a female protagonist.[27] This perception was always available to dramatists even as late as Webster and Middleton.[28] Women like Lady Lumley, Lady Pembroke and Elizabeth Cary were able to write tragedy because it was always potentially or partially dominated by female images. The gendering of the protagonists of these three plays reproduces gendered signifiers common to men's as well as women's work. If Erasmus were a woman, we would be hailing his choice of Euripides' texts for translation as signs of his own life story and experience in the text. Since he is not one, we need an alternative explanation, and we might want to ask if it applies to Lady Lumley too. On the other hand, if *Mariam* were by a man, we would see Mariam's death as the punishment of her rebelliousness and interpret the play in the light of pleasure in the disfigurement of the outspoken woman; Elizabeth Cary may have been just as caught up in these representations, these discourses (though perhaps *differently* caught up in them), as Webster or Shakespeare.[29]

As tragedies, the plays forge a series of connections between the death of a woman, sacrifice and marriage, helping to explain an alternative understanding of tragedy as a feminized genre. The new historicist Leonard Tennenhouse writes angrily that 'it is difficult to think of a Renaissance tragedy in which at least one woman is not threatened with mutilation, rape or murder', yet this applies fully to the plays here. So, why do Iphigeneia, Cleopatra and Mariam have to die? And why are their deaths (or in Iphigeneia's case, death without actual slaying or dying) understood as redemptive, even necessary? Why do women writers embark on the tragic ways of killing a woman which characterized tragedy in antiquity and in early modern England?

It is in this context that we can begin to understand the handling of the question of marriage in both Lady Lumley's and Elizabeth Cary's work. It is important to note that their plays in this volume were produced by women who had *just* been married; without mistaking them for epithalamia, their relation to the women's biographies is remarkable in its parallelism. And yet that parallelism looks odd, even bewildering, if we read it as autobiography. Both women sit down to write plays about the deaths of women at the hands of their patriarchal representatives at the very moment when their own fathers had handed them over to husbands. If we were incautious, we might leap to interpret this in a post-Romantic light, to see these plays as crying out, Judith Shakespeare-like, that marriage was hateful. However, we should pause. The proposed deaths of Iphigeneia and Mariam are hardly subtle aspects of the subtext; if we were to read the plays in this way, we would have to assume the authors knew that they were performing an extraordinary act of defiance.

In Greek tragedy, as both Nicole Loraux and Helena Foley point out, the sacrifice of the maiden for the public good is often described as marriage; it is a taking of virginity, a shedding of pure blood.[30] This figure is common to the deaths of both Iphigeneia and Polyxena, daughter of Priam and Hekabe, sacrificed across the tomb of Achilles by his son Neoptolemus. It dominates *Iphigeneia in Aulis* completely, for Iphigeneia comes to Aulis to be married to the best of the Achaeans, Achilles, while the preparations for the sacrifice are masked as wedding celebrations: 'Tell me, O kinge, I praye the, to whom shall she be maried?' begs the messenger sent to tell Agamemnon of his daughter's arrival (286). Her mother Clytemnestra is told that she is to marry Achilles, and it is only when Achilles denies it that Clytemnestra discovers the truth. The sacrifice of Iphigeneia is equated with her prospective marriage to Achilles by both Iphigeneia and Achilles himself. The homologous relation between marriage and death, enacted in ancient Greek prenuptial rituals, arose through the notion that all virgins must die to or in their virginity for Artemis (or Diana, as Lady Lumley translates it), and by dying to her, be free of her.[31] A vivid sense of the violent change of identities required by marriage, the loss of one persona as member of a birth family and the assumption of another, is enacted in these rites, which may seem incomprehensible to us precisely because we see identity as continuous across the line of marriage, and reject the gender asymmetry implied in the ancient Greek practice. But to Lady Lumley or Elizabeth Cary – both known now, even to feminist literary critics, by their married names, both part of large-scale familial schemes for dynastic advancement and above all both less given to the notion of the self as individual and more given to the notion of the self as a plastic element in larger structures of society and family, the motif of marriage as death might well have seemed comprehensible, even natural.[32]

In the noble families of sixteenth-century England, dynastic marriage was often the way in which a woman could contribute to the future well-being of her family, as Iphigeneia does by dying. Marriage involved a different kind of bloodshed, and a different kind of blood flow; not the *sphage* or cut-throat blood poured out on the altar, but the flow of blood between two noble families; not the blood of the neck vein, but the blood of the opened hymen and the blood of childbearing. As Jean-Pierre Vernant argues, marriage is to sexual consummation what sacrifice is to the consumption of meat; the sacrificial meat ensures bodily continuance, while the consummation ensures the continuity of the family, and specifically the male identities held within it.[33] The publicity of Iphigeneia's death is the publicity of marriage, enacted in the public view. In this context, what might otherwise seem the very odd dedication of a play by a daughter to a father about a daughter killed by a father seems more explicable: that daughter had just been married dynastically herself. We might also want to see this play as celebrating Arundel's dynasty-building. He was to be frustrated by the deaths in infancy of all three of Lady Lumley's children and the death of his own son in 1556, but no one knew this in 1553.

At the same time, the trope of sacrifice as marriage gives meaning to the idea of marriage as a moment of dynastic creation. Iphigeneia's sacrifice – her bloodshed – is overtly necessary not just to save another marriage, that of Helen and Menelaus, but also to allow for empire-building and exploration on a lavish scale. Iphigeneia's sacrifice recalls the 'founding sacrifices' of chaste women such as Lucretia and the pre-Virgilian or chaste Dido, all of whom died to prevent the loss of an empire or to create a new one. As Stephanie Jed has demonstrated, these chaste women's deaths were crucial founding myths of republican political theory, representing in their dead forms the terrain of empire and the limits of imperial power.[34] And yet Lucretia, and to some extent Dido too, represent the nobility as opposed to – as very much opposed to – the ruler. Lucretia's and Dido's fidelity to their husbands, which confers on them a kind of virginity, allows them to be understood as martyrs to the ideal of patrilineality, which requires female chastity and underpins noble identity and dynastic creation. In this sense, the attempts of upstart kings to disrupt that lineage are ideal figures for the increasing power of the monarch and the consequent removal of power from the nobility. That is, their deaths enhance empire, but at the expense of curtailing the ruler's powers. And at this point we must recall that the sacrifice of Iphigeneia is always haunted by the tyranny of Agamemnon, and also and more importantly by his murder, and the trail of revengeful murders which follow. Despite appearances, her sacrifice does not really fit the Lucretia–Dido model of reconciliation and protection; rather, it initiates the process by which the family is destroyed by internal violence. There is no hint in the play that Lady Lumley knew what became of the house of Atreus, but if she did, its fate must have looked plausible and terrifying during the 1550s, when the ambitions of nobles could still cost them their lives, and when royal families tore themselves apart for the sake of ambition or religion.

What this tradition allowed was a noble, heroic role for the female protagonist of tragedy, one both firmly gendered and equal to the significantly masculine roles of the heroes of chronicle plays and other political tragedies. If Henry V or Caesar could create a state, a woman's death could safeguard one. Yet in this case it is not Lady Lumley who is the belated rewriter; rather, it took all Shakespeare's genius to naturalize the masculinity of the abject body that founded the state, understood in the Roman world as inevitably feminine. In 1553 Lady Lumley would have read the ending of her play, the substitution of animal for girl, in the light of another founding national myth: Abraham's sacrifice of his son Isaac. Abraham's willingness to kill his patrilineal identity and future paradoxically guarantees that identity, always already threatened by his wife's barrenness. This makes God's sacrifice of Christ both justifiable and understandable, is reciprocation for it. By showing himself willing to *give* his son away, Abraham creates a future for his family, his nation and humanity. Yet the phrase 'give away' draws our attention to the oddity of this narrative when it takes a son as its object, and its naturalness when it involves a daughter, for giving away a daughter is what a father does in marriage. The substitution of hind for girl signifies the restoration of the future the father was willing to sacrifice. At the same time, the analogy with Christ implies a heavenly future as well as an earthly one.

The ultimate sacrifice, and the ultimate martyr, is always Christ, who

unites both roles. Caroline Walker Bynum, and many others, have pointed
to the medieval feminization of Christ as wounded victim, the figuration of
his body in suffering as the body of a loving mother and nurturer, a girl
victim, a deflowered bride.[35] Christ is also a figure for the redemptive power
of pain and death, the ability of bloodshed to create something new, to give
life rather than take it away. In this sense, and in its productiveness, Christ's
shedding of blood resembles the blood-letting of a fertile marriage. Lady
Lumley understands Iphigeneia as a Christ figure; the fact that a *white* hart
is substituted for her is significant, for the white hart or unicorn as beast of
the chase was often a figure for Christ, and his death a representation of
the crucifixion. But she also signifies the prince or statesman, and his
willingness to abandon the personal for the general. If we look at the play's
argument, for example, Iphigeneia's political motivation is stressed:

> Then Iphigenia her selfe chaunged hir minde, and perswadethe hir
> mother, that it is better for her to dye a glorious deathe, then that for
> the safegarde only of hir life, either so many noblemen shoulde fall
> out within them selves, or else suche a noble enterprise, beinge taken
> in hande, shulde shamefullye againe be let slippe.   (47–52)

This politicization of Iphigeneia's tragedy cites the most obvious reasons
an early modern person might give for avoiding civil strife: the division of
the nobility and the loss of foreign prestige. These are ruling-class concerns,
of course, especially the anxiety for the nobility, but they are also public,
political concerns. If we turn to Iphigeneia's speech of acceptance, these
essentially political concerns are reiterated in her argument that she is a
'commodite' of her country, and when she is sacrificed, the messenger
reports, she comforts her father's grief by saying:

> O father, I am come hether to offer my bodie willinglie for the wellthe
> of my countrie: Wherfore seinge that I shall be sacraficed for the
> commodite of all grece, I do desier you, that none of the grecians may
> slaie me previlie: for I will make no resistance ageinste you.[36]

>   (926–30)

The first clause ('I . . . offer my bodie willinglie') reminds us of the sacrifice
of Christ, but the remainder of the speech reminds us that Iphigeneia's
sacrifice is a public act, *pro bono publico*, and hence performed in the public

sight. There were other communities for whom to sacrifice oneself too. Lady Lumley rewrites Iphigeneia's end in the light of saints' *vitae* and plays of saints' lives. When the chorus comment on Iphigeneia's appearance on the morning of her sacrifice, it is in the discourse of the representation of saints like Agnes and Barbara in the *Legenda Aurea*:[37] 'Beholde yonder goethe the virgine to be sacraficed withe a grete companye of souldiers after hir, whos bewtifull face and faire bodi anone shalbe defiled withe hir owne blode' (908–10). When she offers to die willingly, the messenger reports that her determination to suffer made all those present grow 'wonderfullye astonied at the stoutenes of her minde' (932), a common remark about virgin martyrs who remain resolute and fearless even after incredible sufferings. At this point we might recall not only that Lady Lumley is writing under Mary, within a rather militantly Catholic framework, but also that for a devout Catholic ancient times were not just a source of learning, but the moment when innocent young girls were routinely put to the sword to appease pagan gods and goddesses slighted by their loyalty to Christ. But we might also notice that the imagery is not only sanctified but sexualized. Iphigeneia is beautiful, and her beauty is about to be defiled, despoiled, ruined. This figures death as rape, a trope oppressively common in Golden Legend stories. The opening of Iphigeneia's body is a form of defloration.

After her conversion, Elizabeth Cary composed poems on the lives of three saints; sadly, none has as yet been recovered from the archives, but one is about Agnes, a virgin martyr and type of Christ because her name means 'lamb' (*agnus*), and she also recalls Iphigeneia because her name also means she is a virgin set apart (*hagne*). Agnes's martyrdom – which involves plunging a sword into her throat – is likened to marriage with Christ, and opposed to earthly marriage, though it must be emphasized that Elizabeth Cary did not produce these saints' lives until many years after *Mariam*.

The same mixture of family and public politics, and the same logic of death as marriage, animates in different ways the tragedies of Lady Pembroke and Elizabeth Cary. In *Antonie* and *Mariam*, the trope of woman as sacrifice is intertwined with factional politics and the nobility's concern with what might legitimately be expected of a subject. By the 1590s, the debate had deepened and darkened, even as the likelihood of being literally killed in the course of courtiership receded. *Antonie* resonates with DuPlessis-Mornay's treatise *A Discourse of Life and Death*, with which it was originally published, dealing with the futility of worldly ambition, the need to curb worldly desires as part of the preparation for death and the mutability of worldly success.

By the time the DuPlessis-Mornay appeared, all this had acquired resonance with the death of Sir Philip Sidney at the battle of Zutphen, but DuPlessis-Mornay's original may have been aimed at pleasing the living Sidney with an account of the unimportance of the little deaths he had suffered: frustrated ambition, family decline.

Politically, *Antonie* is also about these little deaths. But in the light of Zutphen, such little deaths necessitate physical death. Antonie remarks grimly that 'I must a noble death,/ A glorious death unto my succour call' (III.378−9). Like Sir Philip Sidney, slain for the Protestant cause, and like Iphigeneia, Antonie must become a martyr in order to continue to signify. The spectacle of Cleopatra dying, with which the play closes, turns mourning into memorialization; by dying, Cleopatra can signify the importance of Antonie's death:

> A thousand sobbes I from my brest will teare,
> With thousand plaints thy funeralls adorne:
> My haire shall serve for thy oblations,
> My boiling teares for thy effusions,
> Mine eies thy fire: for out of them the flame
> (Which burnt thy heart on me enamour'd) came.   (V.199−204)

The extreme, almost baroque image in which Cleopatra turns her body into grave goods and then a funeral pyre for Antonie goes with her notion that her death is a self-forgetting or self-loss, an absolute abjection to love which promises − ineluctably − the marriage union:

> No, no, most happie in this happles case,
> To die with thee, and dieng thee embrace:
> My bodie joynde with thine, my mouth with thine,
> My mouth, whose moisture burning sighes have dried
> To be in one selfe tombe, and one selfe chest,
> And wrapt with thee in one selfe sheete to rest.   (V.185−90)

Cleopatra's body is already lost to grief; her mouth is dry with sighs instead of moist with kisses, and her character becomes nothing more than a vehicle for the mourning process, a place from which grief can speak. Her identity has already been lost. It is logical, then, for her to understand her own death as the self-loss or self-sacrifice implied in marriage, to see herself as losing only an unwanted solitude to gain the unity of the tomb, where 'My bodie joynde with thine' she may 'in one selfe sheete' rest.

As well, *Antonie* deals with a theme also present in more vestigial form in *Iphigeneia*, and dominant in *Mariam*: when does it become lawful for the subject to resist? The horrors of civil war are graphically portrayed in a manner which, for the author of the original, Robert Garnier, commented on events in France, but for Lady Pembroke may have signified the division in Christendom as well as in England:

> Our hands shall we not rest
> > to bath in our owne brest?
> > and shall thick in each land
> > our wretched trophees stand,
> > to tell posteritie,
> > what madd Impietie
> > our stonie stomacks led
> > against the place us bred?   (IV.383–90)

Here the division which Iphigeneia's sacrifice was to prevent is vividly signified. The polity is a body divided against itself, stomach pitted against maternal womb. This metaphor of the dismembered body of the state seems to resemble, but in fact opposes, the workings of the sacrificed body. The sacrifice of the soldier is opposed to rather than equated with the stoical, self-abnegating deaths that Antonie and Cleopatra wish to die.

Elizabeth Cary and Lady Pembroke are linked in John Davies's dedication of his *Muse's Sacrifice* to them, while Jonson, who wrote for Lady Pembroke's son William Herbert, also composed an epigram on Henry Cary's imprisonment which must date from roughly the same period as the composition of *Mariam*.[38] There is no evidence that the two women knew each other, but Lady Pembroke is Elizabeth Cary's obvious source of inspiration for the kind of plays she chose to write at the time she chose to write them; the long reference to Antony and Cleopatra in *Mariam* may be intended as a complimentary allusion to Lady Pembroke's play.[39] Nevertheless, most criticism has insisted on reading *Mariam* as a Catholic or proto-Catholic play. *Mariam* is entirely orthodox and Protestant, with virtually no hint of Elizabeth Cary's later conversion. She had read the works of Martin Luther, John Calvin, Hugh Latimer and John Jewel, according to her daughter, and she had also read More. Her Protantism was inflected by a sense of religious conflict, one especially natural in a woman whose husband had just been posted to Holland and had been taken prisoner in October 1605 by the enemy, but it was not always already Catholic.

As well as rebellion and its just limits, Elizabeth Cary was interested in the way a woman's sacrifice in either death or marriage might prevent bloodshed by the effusion of her own blood. Like Lady Lumley, Elizabeth Cary had herself just been the subject of a dynastic marriage, and *Mariam* is addressed to a sister-in-law who might have said the same. In her mind, too, was the image of the woman martyr of religion, a group of whom Lady Jane Grey is again an instance, as were the Protestant martyrs under Mary, a group which included women like Anne Askew. The sixteenth-century Catholic Margaret Clitherow is described as a blood sacrifice by John Mush. Drawing on the early modern medical notion that semen is a blood product, Margaret Clitherow's blood is a seed:

> as she cast the seed of her blood to the generation of many, so now she fighteth with blood to save those that she hath borne, that the lily roots being watered with the fruitful liquor of blood, may keep still and yield new branches hereafter with so much more plentiful increase by how much more abundantly such sacred streams flow among them.[40]

Her martyrdom is a dynastic marriage furnishing children of blood. To us, it might seem a radical critique of marriage to suggest that it is somehow like martyrdom, but not to Elizabeth Cary. Far from being a private affair of the heart, marriage could be understood as part of a political process. Mariam's marriage to Herod, as well as her death at his hands, is intended to reconcile warring factions: Herod is a usurper who has married the granddaughter of the hereditary king Hircanus. We do not see the marriage, only the beheading that finally overthrows the tyrant's reason, if not his rule.

Faced with the chance to obey a secular authority's laws on religion, the martyr sacrificed herself, not only to maintain her own integrity, but also as a way of enabling her dead body to become an ethical text, or witness (the literal meaning of martyr), readable by others as a sign of what is and is not good.[41] This is in Elizabeth Cary's mind when she emphasizes the way the dead Mariam can speak as a loyal subject, and be heard by Herod when the living Mariam could not. The martyr's body could also be read as a sign of state oppression, as in the myth of Lucretia discussed earlier. Mariam's death is a signifier of tyranny and also a sign that a more just state may ensue. The marks of state power on the body of the martyred were not affirmations of that power, but signifiers of tyranny, an idea deployed by John Foxe on behalf of the Marian martyrs and also by Catholic martyrology. When the messenger, Nuntio, makes explicit mention of Mariam's execution, and tells us that 'Her body is divided from her head' (V.1.90), we should read this too as emblematic: the state (body) is divided from its ruler (Herod, the head) by Mariam's death. The execution of the wife is a violent signifier of tyranny because she represents the conquered people.

And yet the whole purport of the messenger scene implies a *public* execution, like the execution of a martyr rather than a queen; Nuntio speaks of himself as one chosen from a crowd: 'Was none so haples in the fatall place,/ But I, most wretched, for the Queene t'chuse' (V.1.5–6). He has, by his own account, turned up on the spur of the moment to see a show:

> I went amongst the curious gazing troope,
> To see the last of her that was the best:
> To see if death had hart to make her stoope,
> To see the Sunne admiring *Phoenix* nest.   (V.1.22–5)[42]

The troop which assemble are understood by the messenger to be actuated by the desire to see, to know; they are 'gazing', 'curious'. These desires are shared by the messenger, and also by the audience, whose desire to know is indulged by the messenger's narration. Only Herod does not want to look, does not want to know. What these gazes are directed at is the taming of a falcon; death has the courage to make Mariam, the falcon, stoop to his lure, the power to end her flight and bring her under his control. 'Hart' could refer to death's inner resources, or it could be far more visceral and disturbing, referring to the piece of offal a falconer might tie to a lure to attract a straying falcon; the image suggests Herod's wish to tame Mariam by appealing to her worse side, since the figure of falconry was already saturated by gender imagery because falcons are female. However, 'hart' might also mean 'deer', and thus recall Iphigeneia: almost allude to her, in fact. The image of death as falconer, taming the wayward Mariam with a piece of another's dead body, opposes the figure of Mariam as the triumphant phoenix who dazzles even the sun, the phoenix who makes her own nest and is reborn from it. Here, it seems, Elizabeth Cary is alluding directly to the life-in-death of

Mariam's end, and to the significance of death as a metaphor for marriage, procreation and birth.

We might also note that the phoenix image echoes Herod's immediate wish to reanimate Mariam, to have her alive again: this reminds us of Othello, another jealous husband who kills for adultery mistakenly. It might also remind us of Iphigeneia, and of Christ, both sacrificed, both saved; Mariam's dying speech implies the parallel when she says, 'By three daies hence if wishes could revive,/ I know himselfe would make me oft alive' (V.1.79–80), as does the suicide by hanging of her betrayer, which recalls the death of Judas. It might also remind us that Mariam's death, though tragic, is reconciliatory; when dead, she can be fully alive to Herod in a way impossible in life, and thus fully married to him. Herod uses the marriage imagery when he says that her calumny 'did *Mariam* from her selfe divorce' (V.1.118); the death has reconciled the couple. Herod's mad ramblings also draw heavily on imagery which contrasts his now-barren state with the blood of Mariam and its issue. He mourns not an individual but a bloodline: 'Within her purer vaines the blood did run,/ That from her Grandam *Sara* she deriv'd,/ Whose beldame age the love of Kings hath wonne,/ Oh that her issue had as long bene li'vd' (V.1.184–7), and 'My word though not my sword made *Mariam* bleed,/ *Hircanus* Grandchild died at my command' (V.1.194–5). These figures, while they draw attention to Mariam's loss, also point to the reconciliatory function of her marriage to Herod, now 'consummated' in the death which finally makes him love and trust her.

At the same time, this imagined future is presented as a tragic delusion (just as it is in *King Lear*). We might notice how close some of the rhetoric in this final scene comes to the more familiar commentary on the beautiful dead woman as apocalypse which characterizes the public stage's utterances. We cannot evade hearing Herod's outburst 'Shee's dead, hell take her murderers, she was faire' (V.1.153), and the speech beginning 'Ile muffle up my selfe in endles night' (V.1.252) through ears primed by the agonized guilt of Othello and Antonio in *Othello* and *The Duchess of Malfi*, even though both plays are probably later than *Mariam*.[43] Envisaging the death of a woman as the end of the world, and seeing a dead female body as a figure for the undoing of creation, is already complex and polysemic in these male-authored texts. Although Elizabeth Cary's careful moralizations of Herod's madness give her work a different flavour, we should not overlook the hints of the sensational and apocalyptic which peep through the decorum of her homily on tyranny and rashness. Those interpolations of more sensational figurations do not undo the solemnity of her moralizations, but they gloss her political and ethical musings. For if the dead woman is apocalypse, a promised end, then her meaning as a figure for sacrifice, marriage, martyrdom and Christ is also transfigured, albeit momentarily. The death of a woman can only be understood in terms of the engulfment of all possible futures rather than their instantiation. We might be tempted to understand this in psychoanalytic terms if it were indeed Shakespeare or Webster we were dealing with; in terms, say, of the metaphor of decapitation as a figure for woman's not-oneness or not wholeness; in Elisabeth Bronfen's splendid phrase, 'the castration of castration' that both reassures and terrifies.[44] Here, however, such a reading might seem to be immediately stymied by Elizabeth Cary's gender, by our problematic awareness that these are not *her* fantasies voiced through Herod. This illustrates just how accustomed we are to reinstating the author of a drama by way of their assumed inscription in characters. Instead, we might wish to see Elizabeth Cary's use of the discourses of apocalypse and oblivion as just as readable and mainstream as her use of the metaphor of sacrifice as marriage. Receiving a male education, as those of us who can still remember a relatively feminism-free upbringing might testify, means absorbing male values. In effect, it means learning to think like a man. The expensive humanist education Lady Lumley and Elizabeth Cary received, which was gendered exactly in as much as it turned them into marriageable commodities, is what made their dramas possible and conceivable; indeed those dramas exist to display that education. But that education also made it impossible for us to hear the authentic female voices we yearn for in these plays. There are no real women here, only more figurations, and the textuality of the past remains as inescapable as ever.

Although I have been emphasizing the links between these women, it is vitally important to recognize their differences. All are involved in politics, but there is a gap between Lady Lumley's idea of a profitable set of *sententiae* and the later mode of Lady Pembroke and Elizabeth Cary, eager to weave morality together with persuasive speeches. All may be preoccupied with death and with the dead woman martyr who can witness and be heard, but what is heard is different. Although *Iphigeneia* and *Mariam* are both concerned with marriage, its meaning as a dynastic and personal event is subordinate to its significance as a way of understanding the political relations between ruler and subject. Though linked by the haunting figures of Sir Philip Sidney and Lady Jane Grey, these women interpret and enact them differently. The ghosts of the past are continually transformed, remade inside the bodies of the living, and the bodies of their texts.

Notes

1 Judith Shakespeare appears in Woolf's *A Room of One's Own* (1929; Harmondsworth: Penguin, 1945), pp. 48 – 50.

2 *The Tragedie of Iphigeneia* is dedicated to Lady Lumley's father, Henry Fitzalan, Earl of Arundel, and forms a companion piece to her husband's translation of Erasmus. See Notes to the play. For my decision to refer to these authors by title rather than by the conventional formulation of forename and surname, see pp. xiii–xiv.

3 John Davies, for instance, urges Lady Pembroke and Elizabeth Cary to write and reform the age in *The Muse's Sacrifice or Divine Meditations* (1612), with no sense that he was flouting any gender norms. The poem is also addressed to a third woman, Lucy, Countess of Bedford. Elizabeth Cary makes it clear that the play, set in Syracuse, was dedicated to her husband in the dedication to *Mariam*: 'My first was consecrated to *Apollo*', while *Mariam* is dedicated to her sister-in-law under the pseudonym Diana (Apollo and Diana are twins).

4 Stephen Greenblatt, *Sir Walter Ralegh: The Renaissance Man and His Roles* (Berkeley: University of California Press, 1973).

5 The finest analysis of the causes of this trend is in Jonathan Crewe, *Hidden Designs: The Critical Profession and Renaissance Literature* (New York: Methuen, 1986), pp. 73 – 88, in the context of a discussion of Sidney family romances.

6 Stephanie Wright, 'The canonization of Elizabeth Cary', in *Voicing Women: Gender and Sexuality in Early Modern Writing*, ed. Kate Chedgzoy, Melanie Hansen and Suzanne Trill (Keele: Keele University Press, 1996), pp. 55 – 68.

7 See, for instance, Margaret Arnold's suggestively titled paper, 'Jane Lumley's *Iphigeneia*: self-revelation of a Renaissance noblewoman to her audience', presented at the 1990 Shakespeare Association Annual Meeting during a special session on Renaissance women.

8 See the Notes on the text of *Iphigeneia*, p. 168. See also Bruce R. Smith, *Ancient Scripts and Modern Stages from the Renaissance to 1699* (Princeton: Princeton University Press, 1988). I am indebted to Edith Hall for this reference.

9 A trend increasingly corrected in recent criticism: see Margaret Patterson Hannay, *Philip's Phoenix: Mary Sidney, Countess of Pembroke* (Oxford: Oxford University Press, 1990); Lewalski, *Writing Women in Jacobean England*; Schleiner, *Tudor and Stuart Women Writers*; Karen Raber, 'Gender and the political subject in *The Tragedy of Mariam*', *Studies in English Literature* 35 (1995), 321 – 43.

10 'What is an author?', in *The Foucault Reader*, ed. Paul Rabinow (Harmondsworth: Penguin, 1981), p. 54.

11 For an analysis of the relation between Lady Pembroke and Elizabeth Cary, see Marta Straznicki, ' "Profane Social Paradoxes": *The Tragedie of Mariam* and Sidneian closet drama', *English Literary Renaissance* 24 (1994), 104–34.

12 Elizabeth Cary's conversion to Catholicism might also be seen as an attempt to advance her standing which went disastrously wrong; it's significant that she is one of the major 'catches' of the 1620s Counter-Reformation mission, which explicitly targeted the wives of the nobility and greater gentry, but this was also a moment when becoming a Catholic came close to being fashionable owing to the centrality of Queen Henrietta Maria to court culture. On the conversion programme, see John Bossy, *The English Catholic Community 1570–1850* (London: Darton, 1975), and Anne Somerset, *Ladies in Waiting: From the Tudors to the Present Day* (London: Weidenfeld and Nicolson, 1984).

13 Edward may never have intended to accept Lady Jane Grey, but she was plainly in the running for him and so received a princess's education. On her, see Carole Levin, 'Lady Jane Grey: Protestant queen and martyr', in *Silent but for the Word*, ed. Margaret Patterson Hannay (Kent, Ohio: Kent State University Press, 1985), pp. 92–106. Jane had, of course, in turn been influenced by her mentor Catherine Parr, Protestant queen and author.

14 Thomas Dekker and John Webster, *The Famous History* (1599), in *The Dramatic Works of John Webster*, ed. William Hazlitt (London: Smith, 1897). Lady Jane Grey's writings first appeared in 1555 in *A most fruitefull, pithe, and learned treatise, how a Christian man ought to behave himself in the daunger of death*, trans. Miles Coverdale (reprinted 1582 and 1615, as well as repeatedly in Foxe).

15 Duncan-Jones, *Sir Philip Sidney*, p. 6.

16 Philip Sidney had many male imitators too, not least Greville, who was instrumental in ensuring the promulgation of his cult, but he is unusual in acting as role-model for both sexes with seeming impartiality. Like Lady Pembroke, Greville began his poetic career as a process of mourning for Sir Philip Sidney and also imitating him. Sidney represented a fusion of aristocratic courtliness and Protestant conscience which later came to seem impossible to Greville, who began with a sonnet sequence, *Caelica* (1633), in imitation of Sidney, and like Lady Pembroke wrote a drama of Antony and Cleopatra, which he burned after Essex's rebellion in case it was seen as a sign of support for Essex.

17 A cultural movement which emphasized the feminine power to civilize and to influence politics through cultural representations and through virtue. Elizabeth Cary, of course, eventually appears to have joined Henrietta's circle.

18 Lisa Jardine and Anthony Grafton, 'Studied for action: how Gabriel Harvey read his Livy', *Past and Present* 129 (1990), 32–73; A. H. Tricomi, 'Philip, Earl of Pembroke, and the analogical way of reading political tragedy', *Journal of English and Germanic Philology* 85 (1986), 332–45. See also Annabel Patterson, *Censorship and Interpretation* (Madison: University of Wisconsin Press, 1984), pp. 44–58.

19 Thomas More, *Utopia*, trans. Ralph Robinson (London: Dent, 1951), p. 132.

20 For an accessible summary of these events, see Williams, *The Later Tudors.*

21 For a full discussion of the date of *The Tragedie of Iphigeneia*, see Notes, pp. 167–8.

22 Nonsuch had been Henry VIII's attempt to create an English version of French and Medici splendours. During Mary's reign, Arundel was believed by the Spanish ambassador to be planning to wed his son Henry, Lord Maltravers, to Princess Elizabeth; when his son died, he took on the role of suitor himself (*Calendar of State Papers, Foreign Series, of the reign of Mary, 1553–1558*, ed. W. B. Turnbull (London: Longman, 1861), vol. 12, pp. 267, 231; vol. 13, p. 438; 'Life of Henry Fitzalan'). See also David Loades, *The Reign of Mary Tudor*, 2nd edn. (London: Longman, 1991), pp. 19–20.

23 Arundel's subsequent career under Elizabeth was distinctly rocky. Initially, he tried to persuade Elizabeth to marry him, but the two did not get on well. He once told her that if she continued to try to rule the nation by her caprices, the nobility would take action; in 1566, a group of nobles held a meeting on the succession at Arundel's house, to the fury of the queen. He hated what he called 'new-fangled and curious tearmes', and also loathed foreign languages (George Puttenham, *The Arte of English Poesie*, ed. Gladys Doidge Willcock and Alice Walker (Cambridge: Cambridge University Press, 1936), pp. 271–2); eventually he became involved in the Ridolfi plot to marry Mary Queen of Scots to the Catholic Duke of Norfolk, and with John Lumley was one of the principal Catholics who stuck after Leicester had drifted away; he was allowed to retire gracefully from politics, probably owing to his age and lack of a male heir.

24 Michael Neander, *Aristologia Euripidea Graecolatina* (Basle: 1559).

25 *Sententiae quaedam ingeniosae ex variis Grecorum authoribus collectae* and *Sententiae quaedam acutae ex variis authoribus collectae, atque a graecis in latina versae.* Both are manuscripts in the British Library (MS Royal 12. A. I, II, III, IV), and both were completed after Mary's marriage. They contain numerous quotations from Euripides, but since they also cite Greek dramatists known only through quotations in others' works (Agathon, for example) this may not imply wide acquaintance with the plays.

26 Nicholas Bacon, Lord Keeper of the Great Seal, sent 'at her desire' an illuminated manuscript of the classical *sententiae* which decorated the long gallery at Gorhambury (BL MS Royal 17 A 23). See E. McCutcheon, 'Sir Nicholas Bacon and the Great House *Sententiae*', *English Literary Renaissance*, Supplement No. 3 (1977), which contains a transcript. This suggests that Lady Lumley knew the Bacon family: 'Mrs Cooke the queens woman' was one of the chief mourners at Lady Lumley's funeral; this was Ann Cooke Bacon, one of the 'learned ladies' of Tudor England, a writer herself and also Francis Bacon's mother.

27 On Medea and Iphigeneia alone, see, for example, George Buchanan's *Medea* (1544) and Jean-Bastier de la Péruse's *La Médée* (1553), both based on Euripides and Seneca, Maffeo Galladei's *Medea* (1558); Lodovico Dolce's *Medea* (1566), after Euripides, and his *Iphigenie in Aulide* (1543–7); and Thomas Sébillet's *Iphigenie à Aulis* (1549) after Erasmus. There were also numerous Dido plays, including John Ritwise's

The play of Dido (Latin; lost), which was said to have been performed before Cardinal Wolsey, perhaps at Christ Church in 1527. Dolce's drama *Didone* was printed in 1547. William Croston's play of *Aeneas and Queen Dido* (1567) is also lost. William Gager's neo-Latin play of Dido was produced at Christ Church on 12 June 1583.

28 See Posthumus' speech in *Cymbeline*: 'It is the woman's part. Be it lying, note it,/ The woman's; flattering, hers; deceiving, hers;/ Lust and rank thoughts, hers, hers; revenges, hers;/ Ambitions, covetings, changes of prides, disdain;/ Nice longing, slanders, mutability' (*Cymbeline*, II.v.22–6). See also Dymphna Callaghan, *Gender in Renaissance Tragedy* (Brighton: Harvester, 1989), and see Hamlet on Hecuba (*Hamlet*, II.ii.513).

29 For this thesis in relation to Webster and Shakespeare, see among others Leonard Tennenhouse, 'Violence done to women on the Renaissance stage', in *The Violence of Representation: Literature and the History of Violence*, ed. Nancy Armstrong and Leonard Tennenhouse (London and New York: Routledge, 1990), pp. 77–97.

30 Loraux, *Tragic Ways of Killing a Woman*, and Helena Foley, *Ritual Irony: Poetry and Sacrifice in Euripides* (Ithaca, N.Y.: Cornell University Press, 1985). I am grateful to Edith Hall for the reference to Foley.

31 Jean-Pierre Vernant, 'Artemis and rites of sacrifice, initiation, marriage', in *Mortals and Immortals: Collected Essays* (Princeton: Princeton University Press, 1991).

32 On this theme, see Hufton, *The Prospect before Her*, and Christiane Klapisch-Zuber, *Women, Family and Ritual in Renaissance Italy*, trans. Lydia C. Cochrane (Chicago and London: Chicago University Press, 1985).

33 Jean-Pierre Vernant, *Myth and Society in Ancient Greece* (New York: Zone Books, 1990), p. 149.

34 Stephanie Jed, *Chaste Thinking: The Rape of Lucrece and the Birth of Humanism* (Bloomington: Indiana University Press, 1989).

35 Caroline Walker Bynum, *Jesus as Mother: Studies in the Spirituality of the High Middle Ages* (Berkeley: University of California Press, 1982); Miri Rubin, *Corpus Christi: The Eucharist in Late Medieval Culture* (Cambridge: Cambridge University Press, 1994).

36 This is of course part of the ending usually seen as 'specious' by modern classicists. The Greek translates fairly literally as 'I am here at your command, and I give my body willingly to be sacrificed for my country'. The noun 'wellthe' (profit, good) is Lumley's.

37 Jacobus de Voragine, *The Golden Legend*, trans. William Granger Ryan, 2 vols. (Princeton: Princeton University Press, 1993); on saints' lives in pre-Reformation England, see Eamon Duffy, *The Stripping of the Altars* (New Haven, Conn.: Yale University Press, 1994).

38 Ben Jonson, 'To Sir Henry Cary', *Epigrams*, no. 66, in *Ben Jonson*, ed. Ian Donaldson (Oxford: Oxford University Press, 1985), p. 244, which commemorates an event that took place in October 1605.

39 I.2.85ff. See also III.3.58. These may be allusions to Daniel's *Cleopatra* (1601) as well as Lady Pembroke's *Antonie*.

40 Claire Cross, 'An Elizabethan martyrologist and his martyr: John Mush and Margaret Clitherow', *Studies in Church History* 30 (1993), 278.

41 On martyrdom, see John Ray Knott, *Discourses of Martyrdom in English Literature 1563–1694* (Cambridge: Cambridge University Press, 1993), and on the martyr's body as witness against tyranny, see Elizabeth Hanson, 'Torture and truth in Renaissance England', *Representations* 34 (1991), 53–84.

42 Most editions print as 'phoenix's', but I read 'nest' as a verb rather than a noun, in which case the line means 'to see Mariam die' rather than 'to see her dead body'.

43 The dates of all three plays are conjectural; Webster's *Duchess of Malfi* is almost certainly the latest. Elizabeth Cary did enjoy going to the public theatre, according to her daughter: 'after her husband's death she never went to masques or plays, not so much as at the court, though she loved them very much, especially the last extremely' ('The Lady Falkland Her Life, by one of her daughters', in *The Tragedy of Mariam, The Fair Queen of Jewry, with The Lady Falkland Her Life*, ed. Barry Weller and Margaret W. Ferguson (Berkeley: University of California Press, 1994), p. 224). See also Lucy Brashear, 'A case for the influence of Lady Cary's [sic] *Tragedy of Mariam* on Shakespeare's *Othello*', *Shakespeare Newsletter* 26 (1976), 31.

44 Elisabeth Bronfen, *Over Her Dead Body: Death, Femininity and the Aesthetic* (Manchester: University of Manchester Press, 1992), p. 34.

FURTHER READING

Amussen, Susan, *An Ordered Society: Gender and Class in Early Modern England* (Oxford: Blackwell, 1988)

Brennan, Michael, *Literary Patronage in the Renaissance: The Pembroke Family* (London: Routledge, 1988)

Cerasano, Susan P. and Marion Wynne-Davies, *Renaissance Drama by Women* (London: Routledge, 1995)

Duncan-Jones, Katherine, *Sir Philip Sidney: Courtier Poet* (London: Hamish Hamilton, 1991)

Farrell, Kirby, Elizabeth H. Hageman and Arthur F. Kinney (eds.), *Women in the Renaissance: Selections from English Literary Renaissance* (Amherst: University of Massachusetts Press, 1991)

Fletcher, Anthony, *Gender, Sex and Subordination in Early Modern England* (New Haven, Conn.: Yale University Press, 1996)

Haselkorn, Anne, and Betty Travitsky, *The Renaissance Englishwoman in Print* (Amherst: University of Massachusetts Press, 1991)

Hendricks, Margo, and Patricia Parker (eds.), *Women, 'Race', and Writing in the Early Modern Period* (London and New York: Routledge, 1994)

Hufton, Olwen, *The Prospect before Her: A History of Women in Western Europe, Volume I: 1500–1800* (London: HarperCollins, 1995)

Knott, John Ray, *Discourses of Martyrdom in English Literature 1563–1694* (Cambridge: Cambridge University Press, 1993)

Lewalski, Barbara, *Writing Women in Jacobean England* (Cambridge, Mass.: Harvard University Press, 1992)

Loraux, Nicole, *Tragic Ways of Killing a Woman*, trans. Anthony Forster (Cambridge, Mass.: Harvard University Press, 1987)

Schleiner, Louise, *Tudor and Stuart Women Writers* (Bloomington: Indiana University Press, 1994)

Sommerville, Johann P., *Politics and Ideology in England 1603–1640* (London and New York: Longman, 1986)

Williams, Penry, *The Later Tudors: England 1547–1603*, The New Oxford History of England (Oxford: Clarendon Press, 1995)

TEXTUAL PROCEDURE

This edition of *Three Tragedies by Renaissance Women* conforms to the aims of the Renaissance Dramatists series: to present the original spellings and punctuation of the earliest texts with a minimum of editorial interference; see pp. vi–vii. In particular, the conjectural and sometimes venturesome emendation attempted in most modern-spelling editions of Elizabeth Cary's *The Tragedie of Mariam*, including my own previous, has been avoided. Each text follows the readings of a single copy of the play (the base text) specified in the Notes. The Textual Notes contain a record of all differences between the base texts and the ones printed here, and a list of interesting and important instances where early versions of the plays differ from the base texts.

The plays in this edition are recent rediscoveries. Lady Lumley's version of *The Tragedie of Iphigeneia* has been edited only once this century, Lady Pembroke's *The Tragedie of Antonie* only twice – although a full-scale edition is in progress. This is the sixth edition this century of Elizabeth Cary's *Mariam*, but a flurry of activity does not imply an advance in scholarship; after the Malone edition, prepared by Dunstan and Greg, the three subsequent editions were published without reference to each other, each editor working from scratch, so that the same information has often been rediscovered by each successive editor, without adding to our knowledge or understanding of this text. Moreover, all the editions after Malone are in modern spelling, which presents different problems and limitations for readers. Before this century, only Lady Pembroke's play was edited at all, in 1890. Where other volumes in the Renaissance Dramatists series are able to draw on centuries of meticulous editing and commentary, this volume on the whole rests on a mere ten years of scholarship. It may be fifty years before these texts become as settled as even Shakespeare's or Ben Jonson's, so the reader's indulgence is unapologetically sought; these texts are new, and it will take time for us to discover the value of every comma they contain – or omit. On the other hand, these texts are not completely uncharted territory. Critical and editorial customs have grown up around them. Emendations have been established in successive editions and in critical and historical studies; this is especially true of *The Tragedie of Mariam*, so that one cannot simply reproduce the 1613 quarto without comment, without apology, as one might for an unknown play. There has been an understandable urge among modern editors to make these women's texts look smoother, more canonical perhaps, more accessible certainly, but this edition follows a different course, preferring to allow readers to experience rougher versions. The idiosyncrasies and inconsistencies of a text may or may not be the author's own; but it seems wrong to homogenize them away when we are only at the beginning of knowing about what it might mean to write as a woman in the English Renaissance. For example, among other characteristic spellings, Lady Lumley repeatedly writes 'nwes' for 'news'. This version has been retained; it may be an abbreviation, but may also be an interesting idiosyncrasy.

One of these plays is taken from a single authorial manuscript; the second from a carefully printed text, almost certainly one overseen by the author; while the third is from a printed quarto almost definitely *not* overseen by the author, and fraught with minor errors, misreadings and omissions. These different texts require different editorial strategies. Lady Lumley's *The Tragedie of Iphigeneia* is taken from a unique authorial manuscript; few changes are justified, and all that has been done is some regularization of punctuation and a very few corrections of scribal errors. *The Tragedie of Antonie* was seen through the press by its author; the printer did his job well, and few changes have been needed for this edition. *The Tragedie of Mariam* does require more intervention, but the temptation to go beyond a few obvious corrections into more conjectural alterations has been resisted.

In all three plays, stage directions have been greatly expanded, with the expansions indicated in square brackets. Lady Lumley's manuscript provides no stage directions at all except speech prefixes (following Euripides, of course), and the others few, in part because none of these plays was destined for performance. These women drew on classical drama, and normally classical texts do not contain stage directions. Modern editors of Euripides in translation usually add them, however, as has been done here. The modern reader not familiar with closet drama may need help from stage directions in order to turn the brain into the stage, as Margaret Cavendish was to put it in relation to her own closet dramas, and imagine who is on, who off and who is speaking.

The Tragedie of Iphigeneia

IN A VERSION BY

JANE, LADY LUMLEY

The Tragedie of Euripides called Iphigeneia
translated out of Greake into Englisshe.

The Argument of the Tragadie.

After that the captaines of the grecians withe the navye and the other preparacions of battell, did come together unto the haven of Aulida, that from thens they mighte saile towardes Troye: ther came sodenly suche a calme wether, that for wante of wynde they coulde have no passage. Wherfore the hooste beinge greved that they spent there their time idlelye, asked cowncell of the wisemen, to whom Calchas the propheciar awnswered, that if Iphigeneia the daughter of Agamemnon weare sacraficed to the goddes Diana of Aulida, that then the grecians shulde have a fortunate passage to Troye. Wherfore the hooste beinge called together, Menelaus did perswade his brother Agamemnon to 10 agree that his daughter might be sente for. And bicause that Clytem-nestra her mother shulde be the willinger to let hir goo, they fained that she shulde be maried to Achilles one of the chefeste noble men of grece. This excuse none knewe but only Agamemnon, Menelaus, Calchas, and Ulysses. But Agamemnon after that he had written unto his wife of this matter, repented greatly that whiche he had done, lamentinge moche the deathe of his daughter. Wherfore in the nighte he wrote other letters prevely unto his wife, declaringe that she shulde not nede to sende the virgine hir daughter unto Aulyda: for hir mariage shulde be deferred unto a nother time. Thes letters he delivered afore 20 daye unto an olde man his servante, that he mighte carye them into grece, declaringe unto him, what they conteined. But Menelaus waitinge afore daye for the comminge of the virgine, toke the olde man carienge the letter, and did reprove Agamemnon verye vehementlye, for his unconstantesie. In the meane time one of Clitem-nestras company tolde Agamemnon, Menelaus beinge ther present, that Iphigeneia withe her mother Clitemnestra, and yonge Orestes hir brother was come unto Aulida, and that all the hooste knewe of their comminge. Menelaus then perceivinge that Agamemnon colde not sende his daughter home againe, began fainedlye to perswade him 30 not to sley the virgine for his sake. In the meane time whilste they are resoninge of this matter, Clitemnestra commethe in withe Iphigenia hir doughter, thorowe whos comminge Agamemnon is wonderfully trobled, bycause he purposed to keape secrete the cownsell of his daughters deathe. Wherfore whilste he goethe about to aske counsell

of Calchas, Achilles commethe in the meane time to chide withe him. Whom Clitemnestra hearinge, she dothe salute him as thoughe he sholde have bene hir sonneinlawe. Achilles beinge ignorante of this matter dothe wonder at it. Then Agamemnons servante the olde man
40   to whom the letters weare delivered, dothe bewray Agamemnons counsell, and declarethe to them the hole matter. Then Achilles beinge angrie that under the cooler of his name, they had determined the deathe of the virgine, he dothe defende hir in the cowcell of the grecians, that she shulde not be slaine, but he is overcomed withe the voice of the common people. Wherfore whan the matter was broughte to suche a troble, that the whole hooste required the virgine, and Achilles onlye was redie to contende againste them all. Then Iphigenia her selfe chaunged hir minde, and perswadethe hir mother, that it is better for her to dye a glorious deathe, then that for the safegarde
50   only of hir life, either so many noblemen shoulde fall out within them selves, or else suche a noble enterprise, beinge taken in hande, shulde shamefullye againe be let slippe. Wherfore she beinge brought to the aulter of the goddes, was taken up to the countrie of Taurus, and in hir place was sente a white harte. And whan the sacrafice was thus finisshed the grecians sailed to Troye.

The ende of the

Argument.

The names of the spekers in this Tragedie.

1. AGAMEMNON, the kinge.
2. SENEX, an olde man his servante.
3. CHORUS, a companie of women.
4. MENELAUS, *Agamemnons* brother.
5. CLYTEMNESTRA, *Agamemnons* wife.
6. IPHIGENEIA, the daughter of
   Clitemnestra and *Agamemnon*.
7. ACHILLES, her fained husbande.
8. NUNCIUS, the messenger.

Here beginnethe the tragedie of Euripides called Iphigeneia.

[*Enter* AGAMEMNON *and* SENEX.]

AGAMEMNON Come hether O thou olde man.

SENEX I come, but what is the matter O kinge?

AGAMEMNON Thou shalte knowe anone.

SENEX I make haste to come, for my oulde age is verie quicke and redie, for bothe the strengthe of my limmes, and also the sighte of mine eyes dothe yet continue.

AGAMEMNON But what meanethe this, me thinkes I see a starre shoote?

SENEX It maye be so in dede: for it is not yet midnighte, as it may be judged by the course of the seven starres.   10

AGAMEMNON I thinke so too, for I heare no noise of birdes, neither of the seae, nor yet of the winde, all thinges nowe are quiete and at reste.

SENEX What is the cause, O kinge, that at this time of nighte, thou commeste abrode? for all they that be of this haven take their reste still: yea and the Watchemen as yet are not come from the walles: wherfore I thinke it mete to goo in.

AGAMEMNON O thou oulde man thou semeste unto me to be verye happie: for trulie I do thinke that mortall man to be verye fortunate, whiche beinge witheout honor dothe leade his life quietlye: for   20
I can not judge their estate to be happie, whiche rule in honor.

SENEX In thes thinges the glorie and renowne of mans life dothe chefelye consiste.

AGAMEMNON But this renowne is verye brickle, for to wisshe for dignitie, it semethe verye plesant, but it vexethe them that obtaine it: for sometimes the goddes not trulye honored take vengance of mans life, and otherwhiles againe mens mindes withe care and thoughte to bringe their matters to passe are wonderfully troubled.

SENEX I do not praise this opinion in a noble man, for O Agamemnon, thou waste not borne to have all thinges chaunce happely unto   30
the: for seinge thou arte a mortall man, thou muste sometime rejoyse, and sometimes againe be sorie; for whether you will or no, this muste nedes happen, bycause it is so appointed by the

goddes. But me thinkes you are writinge a letter by candle lighte: what is this writinge? that you have in your hande? whiche sometime you teare, and then write againe: otherwhiles you seale it, and anone unseale it againe, lamentinge, and wepinge. For you seme to make suche sorowe, as thoughe you weare out of your witte: What is the matter, O kinge, what is the matter? If you will shewe it me, you shall tell it to a trustie man and a faithefull: for thou knoweste me to be one that Tindarus thy wives father sente withe hir, as parte of hir dowrie: bicause he thoughte me to be a messenger mete for suche a spouse.

AGAMEMNON Thou knoweste that Leda Thyestes daughter, had thre daughters: Phoebes, and Clytemnestra, whom I maried, and Helena whom manye noble men desired to have to their wives: But hir father Tindarus consideringe what greate destruction was thretened to them that obtained hir: doughted longe, whether he shulde give hir in mariage to any of them, or noo. Wherfore bycause he desired to have all thinges to happen prosperousely, he caused all the younge men that desired to marie his daughter, to come all together into the temple, and ther to make a promise eche to other before the goddes, that yf any man either grecian or els barbarian woulde goo about to take Helena from him, whom she choose to be hir husbande: that than they all wolde withe cruell battell take vengance of that man. And this beinge thus brought to passe, Tyndarus gave her free libertie to chose amonge them all, whom she liked beste: and she choose Menelaus: but I wolde to god it had not happened: for w-ithein a while after, Paris, whoo, as the common voice saithe was judge betwene the goddes of their bewtie, came to Lacedemon and he beinge a goodlie yonge man, and of noble parentage, began to fall in love withe her and so takinge hir privelye awaye, broughte hir to a litle village, uppon the hill Ida. But as sone as thes nwes weare broughte to Menelaus, he beinge as one halfe out of his witte for anger, began to reherse the covenante, whiche he and divers other noble men had made betwixte them at the desire of Tindarus: sainge that it was mete that they than shulde helpe him, seinge he was oppressed withe suche a manyfeste injurye. And the grecians beinge wonderfully moved withe his petefull complainte decreed, that they all wolde withe battaile invade the Trojanes, whiche so wrongefully had taken awaye Hellen. Wherfore after

that they had prepared weapons, horses, charettes, and all other thinges necessarie for the battell they choose me to be their captaine, bicause I was Menelaus brother. But I wolde that this honor had happened to some other in my place: for nowe we havinge gathered together our hooste, and prepared our selves ready to battell, are constrayned to tary here idle at this haven, bicause the windes beinge againste us, we can saile no further. And Calchas the prophesier studienge longe what shulde be the cause of it and occasion, at lengthe hathe answered that if my   80
daughter Ephigeneya be slaine and sacrafised to the goddes Dyana, that then the whole hooste shall not onlye have free passage to Troye, but also victoriously conquer it: But witheout the dethe of my daughter, none of all thes thinges can be broughte to passe. As sone as I harde of this, I commanded that the hooste shulde be sente home agayne. For I answered that my daughter shulde never be slayne throughe my consent. But I usinge all maner of meanes to perswade my brother to the contrarie, yet notwithstand-inge I was so moved with his ernest desire, that at lengthe, I agreinge to his cruell requeste, wrote a letter to my wife, that she   90
shulde sende my daughter hether. And bicause she shulde be the better willinge to let hir goo, I fained that she shulde be maried to Achilles: bicause he was so desirous of her, that he denied to goo to battell, witheout he might have hir to his wife; Soo that nowe I have determined the deathe of my daughter, under the color of mariage, and none knoweth of this, save only Menelaus, Calchas, and Ulisses. But nowe I repentinge me of the message whiche I wrote to my wife of, have here in this letter denied all that I saied before. So that if you will carie this letter unto greace, I will declare unto you all that is conteined in it, bicause I knowe   100
you to be a faithefull servante, bothe to my wife and me.

SENEX Shew me I praye you, what answere I shall make to your wife agreable to the letter?

AGAMEMNON Tell hir that she shall not nede at this time to sende my daughter hether: for her mariage shall be differred unto a nother time.

SENEX Will not Achilles thinke you be angerie, for that under the color of him you have determined the deathe of your doughter?

AGAMEMNON Achilles bearethe the name onlye: but he is not partaker

110   of the thinge. Neither knowethe he what crafte we goo aboute.

SENEX Thou haste prepared grevouse thinges, O kinge, for thou
haste determined to sacrafice thy owne childe, under the colour
of mariage.

AGAMEMNON Alas, I was than wonderfully disceived, for the whiche
I am nowe mervelousely trobled. Wherfore I praie thee make
haste, and let not thy oulde age hinder the in this journey.

SENEX I make haste to goo, O kinge.

AGAMEMNON Do not staie by the plesante springes, and tarie not
under the shadoinge trees, neither let any slepe hinder the.

120   SENEX Do not you thinke any suche slouthefulnes in me O kinge.

AGAMEMNON I praie you marke well the waye, and loke aboute it
diligentely, leste that my wife preventinge you, happen to come
hether withe my daughter in the meane time.

SENEX It shalbe done even so.

AGAMEMNON Make haste I praie the, and if thou mete my wife, turne
hir backe againe.

SENEX But what shall I do that your wife and your daughter may
beleve me?

AGAMEMNON Deliver them this token, whiche is enclosed in this
130   letter: go quickely, for the daye beginnethe to apeare: I pray the
helpe me nowe in this matter: for ther is no man to whom all
thinges have chaunsed happelye.

> [*Exeunt* AGAMEMNON *and* SENEX, *separately.*]
> [*Enter* CHORUS.]

CHORUS What is this? me thinkes I see Menelaius strivinge withe
Agamemnons servante.

> [*Enter* SENEX *and* MENELAUS.]

SENEX Darest thou O Menelaus committe so grevous an offence in
takinge awaye thos letters, whiche is neither mete, neither lawfull
that thou shuldest see.

MENELAUS Goo thy waye thou arte to faithefull to thy master.

SENEX Truly you have objected to me a good reproche.

140   MENELAUS Thou haste deserved ponisshement.

SENEX It is not mete that thou shuldeste open thos letters, whiche
I carie.

MENELAUS Neither oughtest thou to bringe suche a mischefe uppon
all grece.

SENEX Thou striveste in vaine, Menelaius, for I will not deliver my
letters to the.

MENELAUS Thou shalte not passe withe them.

SENEX And I will not leve them behinde me.

MENELAUS If thou wilte not deliver them to me I will breake thy
hede withe my mace.   150

SENEX I passe not for that: for I thinke it a good thinge to dye for
my masters cause.

MENELAUS O thou frowarde felowe deliver me thi letters and make
no more busynes heare.

SENEX Helpe O Agamemnon I suffer injurie heare of Menelaus: for
withe stronge hande, he hath taken awaie your letter and he
passethe not of honestie nor yet of righte.

   [*Enter* AGAMEMNON.]

AGAMEMNON Howe, what busines, and contention is ther amongste
you?

SENEX I oughte rather to tell the matter then you Menelaius.   160

AGAMEMNON What have you to do Menelayus withe my servante?
or what cause have you to strive withe him, and to take awaie that
whiche pertainethe to me?

MENELAUS Turne towarde me I praye you that I maye tell you all
the matter.   [*Exit* SENEX.]

AGAMEMNON Thinke you, that I the sone of Atreus am afraide to
loke uppon the Menelaus?

MENELAUS Seeste thou O Agamemnon thes thy letters whiche con-
teine thy craftye counsell?

AGAMEMNON I see them very well, but thou shalte not keape them   170
longe.

MENELAUS Suerlie I will not deliver them to the before that I have
shewed them unto the whole hooste.

AGAMEMNON Wilte thou desire to knowe that whiche dothe not
becomme the, and darest thou open the seales of my letters?

MENELAUS As sone as I had opened thy letter I merveyled what
mischefe had put thos thinges in thi mynde, whiche thou haste
prively declared in this letter.

AGAMEMNON Wheare diddest thou get my letter?

MENELAUS I toke them from your servante, for I watchinge by the   180

hooste to heare of your daughters comminge, bi chaunce met
withe him.

AGAMEMNON Do you thinke it mete, that you shulde knowe of
my matters, I praye you, is not this a token of a naughtie and
unshamefaste man?

MENELAUS It was my pleasure so to do: for I owe no dutie to the.

AGAMEMNON Thinke you that I can suffer this so grevous a thinge,
that I shulde neyther do my busines, nor yet rule my nowne house
after my fansye?

190   MENELAUS Suerlye you chaunge your minde oftentimes, for sometime you thinke one thinge, and by and by ageyne you are in a
nother minde.

AGAMEMNON In dede you file your wordes well: but a lerned tonge
disposed to evell is a naughtie thinge.

MENELAUS Yea, and an unconstante, and a divers minde is as evell.
But nowe I will overcome you withe your owne wordes if you will
not denie them for anger: for I will not speake them gretlye for
your prayse. Do not you remember that whan you desired to be
made captaine over the grecians you semed to refuse it? althoughe
200   in deade you wisshed for it? Howe lowlie than did you shewe
your selfe, takinge everie man by the hande, and kepinge open
householde, and salutinge everie man after his degree, as thoughe
you wolde have bought your honor withe the good will of the
people. But as sone as you had obtained this honor, you began to
change your condicions: for you refused the frendshipe of them,
whiche had shewed them selves frindly to you afore, and then you
waxed proude, kepinge your selfe secretly within your house. But
it dothe not become a good man to chaunge his fassions after that
he is in honor. For he oughte than to be more faithefull to his
210   frindes, when that he is in place to do them pleasure. I have
objected this reproche unto you, bicause I my selfe have had profe
of it. After that you withe the whole hooste weare come to this
haven, you weare careles: but whan you coulde have no passage
over the see, and the grecians desired license to goo home, refusinge
to spende their time idelly heare, Then you beinge wonderfully
trobled, fearinge leaste an evell reporte shulde rise of you, bicause
you beinge captaine over a thousande shippes shulde not overcome
Troie, you asked counsell of me what you mighte do, that you

mighte neither loose dignite, nor yet dishonor your name. Wherfore
as sone as Calchas the proficier had answered that the grecians   220
shulde bothe passe the see quiately, and also conquer Troye, if
your daughter weare sacrafised to the goddes Diana, then you
weare verye gladde, and promised of your owne accorde to give
your daughter to be sacrafised: and beinge not compelled by any
power, you sente unto your wife for your daughter, faininge that
she sholde be maried to Achilles. But nowe sodenly you have
chaunged your minde, and have written other letters: saienge that
you will not agree to the deathe of your owne childe: take hede
that you do not denie this, for the heaven it selfe can beare witnes
of your saienges. Truly this same dothe happen to divers other   230
men, whiche in the beginninge whan they take any weightie matter
in hande, do labor verie diligentlie till they have obteyned it, and
then they leve it of shamefullye: whiche shame dothe chance
sometimes throughe the fearfulnes of the subjectes, and sometimes
whan they do rule the common welthe whiche are unmete for it.
But nowe I do chefelye lamente the state of the unfortunate
grecians, whiche whan they toke in hande a noble enterprise
againste the barbarians, are constrained throughe your occasion,
and your daughters, withe grete dishonor to leave the same.
Wherfore truly I thinke that no captaine ought to be chosen for   240
dignite, nor yet for favor, but rather for witte: for he that shulde
rule an hooste, oughte in wisedome to excell all other.

CHORUS Suerly it is a grevous thinge that one shulde fall out withe
an other: but speciallie that any contention shulde be amonge
brethren.

AGAMEMNON Nowe I will tell you of your fautes, Menelaus, but in
fewe wordes, leste I shulde seme to be unshamfaste. Wherfore I
will speake to you as it becummethe one brother to an other. Tell
me I praye you, why you do sighe so? who hathe done you any
injurye? Do you lament the takinge awaye of your wife? But we   250
can not promise you to get hir againe for you. For you your selfe
have bene the occasion of your owne troble. Wherfore seinge I
have not offended you: ther is no cause that I shulde suffer
ponisshement for that, whiche I am not giltie of. Dothe my
preferment troble you? or els dothe the desier of your bewtifull
wife vexe you? for evell men divers times have suche like desiers.

And althoughe truly I am to blame, for that I have not better
determined my matters, yet I feare me leste you are moche more
to be reprehended, for that you beinge delivered of an evell wife,
260   can not be contented.

CHORUS Thes saienges truly do not agree withe that whiche was
spoken before. Yet notwithestandinge they do teache us well, that
we oughte not willingly to hurte our children.

AGAMEMNON Alas I wretche have never a frinde.

MENELAUS Yes you have divers frindes, excepte you will neglecte
them.

AGAMEMNON But it dothe becomme frindes to lamente one withe
an other.

MENELAUS If you wolde have frindes, you weare beste to love them,
270   whom you desier to helpe: and not them whom you wolde hurte.

AGAMEMNON Why, do you not thinke that grece nedethe helpe in
this matter?

MENELAUS Yes, but I thinke that bothe you, and grece also are
bewitched of some god.

AGAMEMNON Brother me thinkes you are to proude of honor: wherfore I muste seake some other waie, and get me other frindes.

[*Enter* NUNCIUS.]

NUNCIUS O Agamemnon, thou valiant captaine, I have broughte to
the Ephigeneya, thy daughter, whom thou diddeste sende for: and
withe hir is come Clitemnestra thy wife, and Orestes, that thou
280   mightest be comforted withe the sighte of them. I have made
haste to bringe you this nwes: bicause I see all the grecians waitinge
for the comminge of your daughter as it weare for some strange
thinge, and some of them saye, that you have sente for hir bycause
you are desirous to see her, other judge that she shulde be maried,
and some thinkethe that she shulde be sacraficed to the goddes
Dyana. Tell me, O kinge, I praye the, to whom shall she be maried?
But nowe let us leave to speake of suche thinges, for it is nede
and time to prepare that whiche shalbe necessarie for the weddinge.
Wherfore I praye you Menelaius, also be merie, for this day as I
290   truste shall be verie fortunate to Iphigeneya.

AGAMEMNON Thou haste saied well, wherfore goo thou in, for all
thinges will chance happely to the. [*Exit* NUNCIUS.] But what shall
I saye whiche am thus in troble, and yet may not bewaile my owne

miserye? For this occasion they whiche are of meane estate seme unto me verie happie: for they may complaine of their miserie, and bewaile withe teares the deathe of their children but to noble men no suche thinge is graunted, for I dare not lament my unfortunate chaunce, and yet it grevethe me that I may not shewe my miserie. Wherfore I knowe not what I shulde saie unto my wife, nor withe what face I shulde loke uppon her. Alas she hathe 300 undone me bicause of her comminge, althoughe in dede she thinkethe she hath a good occasion, for she belevethe that hir daughter shalbe maried, in whiche thinge she shall finde me a liar. Againe I have pitie of the litell gerle, for I knowe she will speake thus unto me, O father will you kill me? if you forsake me, of whom shall I aske remedie? Alas what answer shall I make to this, suerly nature oughte to move me to pitie, and if that wolde not, yet shame shulde let me. Alas, Alas: What a greate reproche is it, the father to be an occasion of his owne childes deathe. Howe therfore am I trobled? On this parte pitie and shame, on the other 310 side honor and glorie dothe moche move me.

CHORUS We also lamente your chaunce, so moche as it becommethe women to lamente the miserie of princes.

MENELAUS I praye you brother let me see your hande.

AGAMEMNON I give you libertie: for I will put all the victorie in your hande.

MENELAUS I will not flatter you brother, but I will shewe you faithefully my opinion. Suerly when I sawe you in suche miserie I was moved withe brotherly pitie, and lamented moche your chaunce. Wherfore nowe I cownsell you, not to sleye your daughter, neyther 320 to do your selfe any domage for my cause. For it is not mete, that thorowghe my occasion you shulde hinder either your selfe, or any of your children. For I waienge the matter, consider what a grevous thinge it is to kille your owne childe. And besides this I pitie moche hir, bycause I do consider she is my kinswoman and hathe not deserved to dye for Helen's cause. Wherfore I will councell you not to sacrafice your daughter, but rather to sende home againe the whoole hooste. And as for my parte, I will agre unto you. For I consideringe howe a father oughte to love his childe, have chaunged clene my opinion: for I knowe a good man 330 ought to folowe that whiche is good.

CHORUS O Menelayus, you have spoken lyke a noble man.

AGAMEMNON I praise you Menelaus bicause you have chaunged your minde so gentlelye.

MENELAUS Suerlye ambition and desire of welthe hathe caused moche strife betwene bretherne, howbeit I do abhorre soche cruell brotherhoode.

AGAMEMNON Althoughe you are agreed, yet I am compelled to slee my daughter.

340 MENELAUS Whie, no bodie will compell you.

AGAMEMNON Yes trulye the whole hooste will requier hir of me.

MENELAUS If you will sende her home againe, you neade not deliver her to the grecians.

AGAMEMNON If I shulde deceive them heare, then they wolde ponisshe me, whan I come home.

MENELAUS You oughte not trulie to feare so moche the hooste: for they knowe not of this matter.

AGAMEMNON But I doute leste Calchas shewe them of it.

MENELAUS You may remedie that in ponisshinge him.

350 AGAMEMNON Brother do you not feare Ulisses?

MENELAUS Yes trulye, for it dothe lie in his power to hurte either you or me.

AGAMEMNON I doughte that for he studiethe verye moche to get the good will and favor of the people.

MENELAUS He is desirouse in dede of ambition and honor.

AGAMEMNON If he shulde gather the people together, and declare unto them what Calchas hathe saied of my daughter, suerlie he might quickelye perswade them to sleye you and me, that thay might get her the easelier. But if it shulde chaunce that I shulde flie, then truly they wolde not onlie seke to destroie me, but also my children. Nowe therfore seinge that I am in soche troble that I knowe not what to do, I shall desier you, O Menelaius, not to shewe this nwes unto my wife, before that Iphigeneya be all redie sacrafised, that I may be lesse moved withe hir pitious complainte. And I praye you also, O ye women, not to open this matter.

360

[*Exeunt* AGAMEMNON *and* MENELAUS.]

CHORUS Truly we may see nowe, that they are mooste happie, whiche beinge neither in to hye estate, nor yet oppressed withe to moche povertie, may quietly enjoye the companie of their frindes. But

beholde heare commethe Clytemnestra the quene and Iphigeneya
her daughter, beinge adorned withe all nobles, Let us therfore   370
mete hir withe moche mirthe, leste she shulde be abasshed at hir
comminge into a strange countrye.

    [*Enter* CLYTEMNESTRA *and* IPHIGENEIA.]

CLYTEMNESTRA This trulye is a token of good lucke that so manye
    noble women meate us. Let us therfore comme downe from our
    charet, that they may bringe us to Agamemnons lodginge.

    [*Enter* AGAMEMNON.]

IPHIGENEIA I praye you mother be not offended withe me, thoughe
    I do embrace my father.

CLYTEMNESTRA O kinge Agamemnon I am come hether to fulfill
    your commaundement in that you sente for me.

IPHIGENEIA And I also, O father, am come beinge not a litle joyous   380
    that I maye see you.

AGAMEMNON Neither am I sorie of your companye daughter, for of
    all my children I love you beste.

IPHIGENEIA What is the cause father, that you seame to be so sadde,
    seinge you saye, you are so joyfull at our comminge?

AGAMEMNON You knowe daughter, that he whiche rulethe an hooste
    shall have divers occations to be trobled.

IPHIGENEIA Althoughe in dede a captaine over an hooste shall be
    disquieted withe sondrie causes, yet I praye you set aside all soche
    trobles, and be merie withe us whiche are therfore come unto   390
    you.

AGAMEMNON I will folowe your councell daughter, for I will rejoyse
    as longe as I may have your companie.

IPHIGENEIA But what meanethe this father that you do lament so?

AGAMEMNON I have good cause to morne: for after this daye I shall
    not see you ageine of a greate while.

IPHIGENEIA I do not understande, O father, what you mene by this.

AGAMEMNON Trulye daughter the more wittely you speake, the more
    you troble me.

IPHIGENEIA If it be so father, then will I studie to seme more folisshe   400
    that you may be delited.

AGAMEMNON Suerly I am constrained to praise gretlye your witte,
    for I do delite moche in it.

IPHIGENEIA I praye you than father set awaye all other busines, and
tarie amongste us your children.

AGAMEMNON Indede I am desirous so to do, althoughe I can not as
yet have libertie.

IPHIGENEIA What is the matter father that you tarie heare so longe
in this haven?

410 AGAMEMNON Trulye wc are desirous to goo hens, but we can have
no passage.

IPHIGENEIA Where I praye you dwell thos people whiche are called
the trojans?

AGAMEMNON They are under the kyngdome of Priamus.

IPHIGENEIA I wolde to god I might goo withe you into thos parties.

AGAMEMNON I will graunte you your requeste daughter, for I am
determined to take you with me.

IPHIGENEIA Shall I goo alone, or els with my mother?

AGAMEMNON No trulie you shall neither have the companie of me,
420 nor yet of your mother.

IPHIGENEIA Whie? will you set me in a strange house?

AGAMEMNON Leave to enquier of suche thinges, for it is not lawfull
that women shulde knowe them.

IPHIGENEIA Make haste O father to goo unto Troye, that you may
come quickely ageine from thens.

AGAMEMNON So I do daughter, but I muste sacrafice firste.

IPHIGENEIA Shall I be at the sacrafice father?

AGAMEMNON Ye daughter, for you muste be one of the chefeste.

IPHIGENEIA Why? shall I dawnce aboute it?

430 AGAMEMNON Truly I counte my selfe more happie bicause you do
not understande me, goo your waye therfore and make you redie
withe the other virgins. But let me firste take my leave of you, for
this daye shall seperate you and me farre asonder; althoughe this
your mariage shalbe verie noble, yet truly it dothe greve me to
bestowe you so farre of, whom withe suche care I have brought
up.   [*Exit* IPHIGENEIA.]

CLYTEMNESTRA Althoughe you are somewhat trobled yet I am not
of so slender a wit, but that I can easely be perswaded, seinge that
bothe the custome and also time dothe require. But tell me I praye
440 you shall not Achilles be my daughters husbande?

AGAMEMNON Yes trulie.

CLYTEMNESTRA He is a mete mariage in dede, but I am desirous to knowe wher he dwellethe.

AGAMEMNON His dwellinge is aboute the flode Aphidna.

CLYTEMNESTRA Whan I praye you shall the weddinge be?

AGAMEMNON Trulie verie shortelie, for we make haste to goo hence.

CLYTEMNESTRA If it be so, then you have nede to sacrefice that whiche muste be done before the weddinge.

AGAMEMNON I will goo about it therfore, that the mariage may be done the quickelier.   450

CLYTEMNESTRA Wher I pray you shall the feste be?

AGAMEMNON Heare bicause of the hooste.

CLYTEMNESTRA Shewe me I praye you the place, that I may be partaker of it.

AGAMEMNON I praye you wife obey me in this matter.

CLYTEMNESTRA What cause have you, O kinge, to saie so, for whan did I ever disobey you?

AGAMEMNON I am determined to marie my daughter here.

CLYTEMNESTRA Shall not I beinge hir mother be at the weddinge?

AGAMEMNON No trulie: for she shalbe maried amongste the grecians.   460

CLYTEMNESTRA Wheare then shall I tarie?

AGAMEMNON It is beste for you to goo againe to grece.

CLYTEMNESTRA If I leave my daughter behinde me, who shall than be in my steade?

AGAMEMNON Trulie I will do your office: for it doth not become you to be amongste suche a companye of men.

CLYTEMNESTRA Althoughe that it be not mete in dede: yet the mother ought to be at the mariage of the daughter.

AGAMEMNON But I thinke you have more nede to be amongste your other daughters at grece: make you redie therfore to go home.   470

CLYTEMNESTRA I will not goo home yet, for you oughte to do sacrafice onlie: but I muste see all thinges made redie for the mariage.   [*Exit* CLYTEMNESTRA.]

AGAMEMNON I have labored in vayne: for althoughe I have used deceite and crafte, yea unto my dearest frindes: yet I can not fulfill my purpose.   [*Exit* AGAMEMNON.]

          [*Enter* ACHILLES.]

ACHILLES Wher is Agamemnon, the captaine of the grecians, or who of his servantes will call him unto me? For I beinge moved withe

480   the pitious complaintes of the people, am compelled to enquire of their captaines the cause, whi they beinge constrayned to forsake bothe their wives, their children, and also their countrie, nowe lie heare idlely without any valiant dedes doinge?

[*Enter* CLYTEMNESTRA.]

CLYTEMNESTRA As sone as I harde your voice, O Achilles, I came out hastely to meate you.

ACHILLES What woman is this that semeth so bewtifull?

CLYTEMNESTRA I do not mervell thoughe you knowe not me, whom you never sawe: Yet nevertheles, I muste nedes praise your shame-fastenes.

ACHILLES Who are you I pray you, that you beinge a woman dare
490   come amongste suche a companie of men?

CLYTEMNESTRA My name is Clitemnestra, and I am the daughter of Leda and the wife of Agamemnon.

ACHILLES You have declared verie well in few wordes what you are, and althoughe you be a noble woman, yet is it not lawfull for me to tarie heare.

CLYTEMNESTRA Whether goo you I praye you let us shake handes to gether: for I truste this mariage shalbe verie fortunate unto you.

ACHILLES It is not lawfull that I shulde be so familiar withe Agamem-nons wife.

500 CLYTEMNESTRA Yes trulie you may well inoughe, seinge you shall marie my daughter.

ACHILLES I do not knowe what mariage you meane, excepte you have harde some nwes, whiche bicause you knowe to be untrue, you reporte as a false tale.

CLYTEMNESTRA I do not mervell, allthoughe you will not be ack-nowen of this mariage: for it is the fassion of all younge men to kepe it secrete for a time.

ACHILLES No trulie I will not dissemble withe you for in dede I never desired the mariage of your daughter.

510 CLYTEMNESTRA Yf it be so in dede, then I marvell as moche of your saienges as you did of mine.

ACHILLES Tell me I praye you wherfore you have spoken thes thinges: for it may happen that bothe of us are deceived.

CLYTEMNESTRA Thinke you that it is not a grete shame unto me,

that I have tolde suche a lye, but I will nowe goo, and knowe the
truthe of all this matter.

ACHILLES Tell me I praie you, or you goo hence, wher your husbande
is? for I am verie desirous to speake withe him.

    [*Enter* SENEX.]

SENEX Tarie I praie you, O Achilles, for I muste speake bothe withe
you, and also withe Clitemnestra.   520

CLYTEMNESTRA Who dothe call me so hastelye?

SENEX It is even I the servant of Agamemnon.

CLYTEMNESTRA If you have any thinge to saie to us come neare,
and tell it quickelie witheout any circumstance, for you neade not
to doughte us, for I knowe you have ever served diligentlye bothe
me and also divers of myne awnciters.

SENEX Bicause I have bene ever faithefull unto you, therfore nowe
I muste open unto you a verye secrete thinge, trulie Agamnon
hathe determined to sleye Iphigeneya his daughter in sacrafice.

CLYTEMNESTRA Suerlie I thinke either you be madde to tell suche   530
an unlikelie tale, or els if it be so in dede, Agamemnon to be halfe
out of his witte to agree to suche a cruell murther.

SENEX No trulie he is not madde thoughe in dede he hathe plaied
the madde mans parte.

CLYTEMNESTRA Wherfore I praye you hathe he pretended to do so
cruell a dede.

SENEX Trulye he is compelled to do so: for Calchas the propheciar
hath answered that the grecians can not sayle to troie without the
deathe of your daughter.

CLYTEMNESTRA If this be true, wherfore than did he faine, that she   540
shulde be maried.

SENEX That was bicause you shulde be the better willinge to let hir
come.

CLYTEMNESTRA Howe I praye you, do you know this?

SENEX Agamemnon him selfe shewed me of this thinge: for once
he did repente him selfe so moche of the consentinge to his
daughters deathe, that he was determined to sende you a nother
letter by me, whiche was contrarie to the firste.

CLYTEMNESTRA Whie did you not deliver them to me?

SENEX As I was bringinge them, I happened to mete withe Menelaus, 550
who withe violence toke them from me.   [*Exit* SENEX.]

CLYTEMNESTRA Heare you this O Achilles?

ACHILLES Yea truly I heare it well, and I pitie you moche: for I do
even abhorre this cruell dede of your husbande.

CLYTEMNESTRA Nowe therfore seinge this thinge is chaunsed so
unfortunately unto me, I shall moste ernestelie desier you O
Achilles, to helpe me nowe in this miserie: for the reproche shalbe
yours, seinge my daughter beinge sente for under the color of your
name, shall nowe be slaine. Besides this yf you do not helpe us,
we can bi no meanes avoide this mischefe: for I alone beinge a
woman can not perswade Agamemnon: And if you forsake us,
none shall dare to take our parte.

CHORUS Truly it is a verie troblesome thinge to have children: for
we are even by nature compelled to be sorie for their mishappes.

ACHILLES My minde is trobled more and more, for I am wonderfullie
moved withe your pitious complainte: Wherfore seinge you have
required helpe at my hande I will promise you to deliver bothe
you, and your daughter from this miserie, if by any meanes I maye
withestande the cruell pretence of Agamemnon and his brother.
For this matter pertainethe unto me also, bicause that if she beinge
sent for in my name shulde be slaine, then truly it wolde turne to
no small dishonor to me. Wherfore I am compelled to helpe your
daughter so moche as shall lie in my power: not onlye for that I
am moved withe pitie, but also bicause it shoulde sounde to no
litell reproche to me, if that throughe my occasion your daughter
shulde be slaine.

CLYTEMNESTRA Suerlie you have spoken verie well and like a noble
man.

How therfore I praye you shall I give you thankes worthie your
desertes: for if I shulde prayse you to moche, I feare leste I shulde
move you to hatred, rather then to pitie, for then you wolde judge
me to be a flatterer, whiche of all noble men is to be abhorred,
Againe if I shulde give you fewer thankes, than you deserve, then
I may well be counted unthankefull: so that now I doughte what
to do: but seinge you so gentlely have promised me your helpe, I
will submit bothe me, and my daughter under your rule: Wherfore
if it please you I will sende for her hether, that she hir selfe may
require helpe at your hande.

ACHILLES No trulie I thinke it not mete, that she shulde come abrode, for suerly men wolde judge evell of hir, if she shulde come moche amongste companie. It is beste therfore that you kepe hir at home, and as for my parte trulie I will do as moche for hir as shall lie in my power. But I thinke it beste, that you shulde prove firste if you can perswade her father not to deliver her.

CLYTEMNESTRA Suerlye I shall not prevaile withe him: for he is so fearfull, that he dareth do nothinge witheout the consent of the whoole hooste.

ACHILLES Althoughe you thinke you shall not perswade him, yet it is mete that firste you shoulde shewe him, what a grevous thinge it is to be called a destroyar of his owne children, and if he be   600 nothinge moved withe that, then you may lawfully seke helpe at other folkes handes.

CLYTEMNESTRA You have spoken verie well. Wherfore I will folowe your counsell. But tell me I praye you wher shall I finde you, that I may shew you what answer he dothe make me?

ACHILLES I will tarie heare till you come againe, for suerly if I shulde goo with you, you shoulde be sclandered by me.

CLYTEMNESTRA In all this matter I will be ruled by you, wherfore if I obtaine my swte the thankes shall be yours and not mine. But nowe heare commeth Agamemnon, shew me I praye you therfore   610 what I shulde answer him if he aske for my daughter, seinge that she maketh soche mone.   [*Exit* ACHILLES.]

[*Enter* AGAMEMNON.]

AGAMEMNON I am gladde that I have met withe you O Clitemnestra: for I have divers thinges to talke withe you of.

CLYTEMNESTRA If you have any thinge to saie to me, tell me I pray you, for I am redie to heare.

AGAMEMNON Firste call out my daughter that she maye goo withe me to the temple of the goddes Diana, for I have prepared all thinge redie for the sacrafice.

[*Enter* IPHIGENEIA *and an attendant carrying Orestes.*]

CLYTEMNESTRA You have spoken well, thoughe in dede your doinges   620 do not agre withe your wordes, but goo your waies daughter withe your father, and take withe you your brother Orestes.

AGAMEMNON Why do you wepe and lament so daughter?

IPHIGENEIA Alas, how shoulde I suffer this troble, seinge that all mortall men ar vexed bothe in the beginninge, the middeste, and the endinge of their miserie.

AGAMEMNON What is the cause, that all you are so sorowfull?

CLYTEMNESTRA I will shewe you, if you will promise me to tell me one thinge, whiche I will require.

630   AGAMEMNON Yes trulie I will graunte you your requeste, for I did thinke to have asked it of you.

CLYTEMNESTRA I heare saie that you goo aboute to sleye your owne childe.

     [*Exit attendant with Orestes.*]

AGAMEMNON What, you have spoken thos thinges, whiche you oughte neither to saye, nor yet to thinke.

CLYTEMNESTRA Answer me I praye you to this question, as you promised.

AGAMEMNON It is not lawfull for me to answer you to thos thinges, whiche you ought not to knowe.

640   CLYTEMNESTRA I have not enquired of any thinge that dothe not becomme me: but take you hede rather, leste you make suche an answer as you ought not.

AGAMEMNON Who hathe done you any injurye, or who hathe given you cause to saie so?

CLYTEMNESTRA Aske you this question of me? as thoughe your crafte coulde not be perceived.

AGAMEMNON Alas, I am trobled more and more, for all my secrete councell is nowe openlie declared.

CLYTEMNESTRA In dede I have harde of all that, whiche you have 650   prepared for your daughter: yea and you your selfe have partelie confessed it in holdinge your peace.

AGAMEMNON I am constrained to holde my peace, bicause I have tolde you so manifest a lye that I can not denie it.

CLYTEMNESTRA Herken nowe I praye you therfore: for I muste nedes tell you of your faute. Do you not remember, that you maried me withe out the good will of all my frindes, takinge me awaye withe stronge hande, after that you had slaine my other husbande Tantalus, whiche cruell dedes my brother Castor and Pollux wolde have revenged, excepte Tindarus my father had 660   delivered you out of that parell: so that by his meanes, you did obtaine me to be your wife, who after I was maried never shewed

my selfe disobedient unto you in any thinge. And then I happened
to have thre sones at one birthe, and afterwarde one daughter,
and will you nowe sleye hir, knowinge no juste cause whie? For if
any man shoulde aske of you the cause of the deathe of your
daughter, you wolde answer for Helens sake, whiche can be no
lawfull cause, for it is not mete, that we sholde sleye our owne
childe for a naughtie womans sake: neither destroie thos that by
nature we oughte to love, for their cause only whiche are hated
of all men. Besides this, if you kille my daughter, what lamentacion   670
muste I nedes make, Whan I shall goo home, and wante the
companie of her? consideringe that she was slaine bi the handes
of her owne father: Wherfore if you will not be moved withe pitie,
take hede leste you compelle me to speke thos thinges, that do
not become a good wife: yea and you your selfe do thos thinges
that a good man ought not. But tell me nowe I praie you, what
good do you obtaine by the deathe of your daughter? do you loke
for a fortunate returne? trulye you can not by this meanes get that,
for that journye can not ende happely whiche is begonne withe
mischefe. Besides this suerlie you shall stirre up the goddes to   680
anger againste you, for they do even hate them, that are manquellers.
Agayne you can not enjoye the companie of your other children
whan you come home, for they will even feare and abhorre you,
seinge that willinglie you do destroie your daughter, and you shall
not only fall into this mischefe, but also you shall purchase your
selfe the name of a cruell tyrante. For you weare chosen the
captaine over the grecians to execute justice to all men, and not
to do bothe me and also your children suche an injurie: For it is
not mete that your children shuld be ponisshed for that whiche
pertaineth not to you, neyther ought I to loose my daughter for   690
Helenas cause who hathe never shewed her selfe faithefull to hir
husbande.

CHORUS It is mete, O Agamemnon, that you shulde folowe your
   wives councell. For it is not lawfull that a father shulde destroy
   his childe.

IPHIGENEIA Nowe O father I knelinge uppon my knees and makinge
   moste humble sute, do mooste ernestely desier you to have pitie
   uppon me your daughter, and not to sleye me so cruelly. For you
   knowe it is geven to all mortall men to be desirous of life. Ageine

700   remember that I am your daughter, and howe you semed ever to
        love me beste of all your children, in so moche that you weare
        wonte ever to desier, that you might see me maried to one worthie
        of my degree, and I did ever wisshe agayne, that I might live to
        see you an olde man, that you might have moche joye bothe of
        me, and also of your other children. And will you nowe consent
        to my dethe? forgettinge bothe that whiche you weare wonte to
        saye, and also what paine you and my mother toke in bringinge
        me up, knowing no cause in me worthie of deathe? for what have
        I to do withe Helena? But nowe father seinge you are nothinge
710   moved withe my lamentation, I will call hether my yonge brother
        Orestes, for I knowe he will be sorye to see his sister slayne, and
        againe you can not choose, but you muste nedes have pitie either
        of him, or els of me, consideringe what a lawfull requeste we do
        desier, for you knowe that all men are desirous of lyfe, and ther
        is no wise man, but he will choose rather to live in miserie than
        to die.

AGAMEMNON I knowe in what thinges I ought to shewe pitie, and
        wherin I ought not, and I love my children as it becommethe a
        father, for I do not this of my selfe, nor yet for my brothers sake,
720   but rather by compulsion of the hooste: for the goddes have
        answered that they can not passe the see without your dethe, and
        they are so desirous to go thither, that they care not what troble
        and miserie they suffer: so that they may see it. Wherfore it lieth
        not in my power to withstande them: for I am not able to make
        any resistance againste them. I am therfore compelled daughter
        to deliver you to them.   [*Exit* AGAMEMNON.]

CLYTEMNESTRA Alas, daughter into what miserie are bothe you and
        I driven, seinge that your owne father will concente to your deathe.

IPHIGENEIA Alas mother this is the laste daie, that ever I shall see
730   you. O Unhappi Troye whiche haste norisshed and brought up
        that wicked man Paris: O Unfortunate Venus whiche diddest
        promise to give Hellena to him, for you have bene the cause of
        my destruction, thoughe in dede I throughe my deathe shall
        purchase the grecians a glorious victorie. Alas mother in what an
        unluckye time was I borne, that myne owne father whiche hathe
        concented unto my deathe, dothe nowe forsake me in this miserie.
        I wolde to god that the grecians had never taken in hande this

jornie. But me thinkes mother, I see a grete companie of men comminge hether, what are they I praye you?

CLYTEMNESTRA Trulye yonder is Achilles.   740

IPHIGENEIA Let me then I praie you go hens that I may hide my face: for I am ashamed.

CLYTEMNESTRA What cause have you so to do?

IPHIGENEIA Trulie bicause it was saied that I shulde have bene his wife.

CLYTEMNESTRA Daughter, you muste laie awaie all shamefastenes nowe, for you may use no nicenes: but rather prove by what meanes you maye beste save your life.

  [*Enter* ACHILLES.]

CHORUS Alas Clitemnestra howe unhappi arte thou for truly ther is grete talkinge of the in the whoole citie.   750

CLYTEMNESTRA Wherof I pray you?

CHORUS Of your daughter how she shalbe slaine.

CLYTEMNESTRA You have brought me verie evell nwes, but tell me I praye you doth no bodie speake againste it?

ACHILLES Yes I my selfe have bene in dawnger of my life, bicause I toke your daughters parte.

CLYTEMNESTRA Who I pray you dare hurte you?

ACHILLES Truly the whoole hooste.

CLYTEMNESTRA Do not your owne contrie men of Mirmido helpe you?   760

ACHILLES No truly, for even they also did speke againste me saienge, that I was in love withe her, and therfore I did preferre myne owne pleasure, above the commodite of my countrie.

CLYTEMNESTRA What answer then made you unto them?

ACHILLES I saied that I ought not to suffer her to be slaine whiche was reported by hir owne father that she shoulde have bene my wife.

CLYTEMNESTRA You saied well in dede: for Agamemnon sente for her from grece, faininge that it was for that purpose.

ACHILLES But thoughe I coulde not prevaile againste suche a multi-   770
tude of people, yet I will do as moche as shall lie in my power for you.

CLYTEMNESTRA Alas then you alone shalbe compelled to strive againste many.

ACHILLES Do you not see a greate companye of harneste men?

CLYTEMNESTRA I praye god they be your frindes.

ACHILLES Yes trulye that they be.

CLYTEMNESTRA Than I hope my daughter shall not die.

ACHILLES No that she shall not, if I can helpe hir.

780 CLYTEMNESTRA But will ther come any bodie hether to sleye hir?

ACHILLES Yea truly Ulisses will be heare anone withe a great companie of men to take her awaie.

CLYTEMNESTRA Is he commanded to do so, or dothe he it but of his owne heade?

ACHILLES No truly he is not commanded.

CLYTEMNESTRA Alas then he hathe taken uppon him a wicked dede, seinge he will defile him selfe withe the daunger and deathe of my daughter.

ACHILLES Truly but I will not suffer him.

790 CLYTEMNESTRA But if he goo aboute to take my daughter awaye withe stronge power what shall I do then?

ACHILLES You ware beste to kepe her by you, for the matter shalbe driven to that pointe.

IPHIGENEIA Herken O mother I praye you unto my wordes, for I perceive you are angrie withe your husband, whiche you may not do. For you can not obtaine your purpose by that meanes: And you ought rather to have thanked Achilles, bicause he so gentelly hathe promised you his helpe, whiche maye happen to bringe him into a greate mischefe. I wolde counsell you therfore to suffer this

800 troble paciently, for I muste nedes die, and will suffer it willingelye. Consider I praie you mother, for what a lawfull cause I shalbe slaine. Dothe not bothe the destruction of Troie, and also the welthe of grece, whiche is the mooste frutefull countrie of the worlde hange upon my deathe? And if this wicked enterprise of the Trojans be not revenged, than truly the grecians shall not kepe neither their children, nor yet their wives in peace: And I shall not onlie remedie all thes thinges withe my deathe: but also get a glorious renowne to the grecians for ever. Againe remember how I was not borne for your sake onlie, but rather for the commodite

810 of my countrie, thinke you therfore that it is mete, that suche a companie of men beinge gathered together to revenge the great injurie, whiche all grece hathe suffered shoulde be let of their

journye for my cause. Suerlie mother we can not speke againste this, for do you not thinke it to be better that I shulde die, then so many noble men to be let of their journye for one womans sake? for one noble man is better than a thousande women. Besides this seinge my deathe is determined amongste the goddes, trulie no mortall man oughte to witstande it. Wherfore I will offer my selfe willingly to deathe, for my countrie: for by this meanes I shall not only leave a perpetuall memorie of my deathe, but I shall cause also the grecians to rule over the barbarians, whiche dothe as it weare properly belonge to them. For the grecians bi nature are free, like as the barbarians are borne to bondage.

820

CHORUS Suerlie you are happie O Iphigeneya, that you can suffer so pacientlye all this troble.

ACHILLES Trulie I wolde counte my selfe happi if I mighte obteine the O Iphigeneya to be my wife, and I thinke the O grece to be verie fortunate bicause thou haste norisshed soche a one: for you have spoken verie well, in that you will not strive againste the determinacion of the goddes. Wherfore I beinge not onlie moved withe pitie, for that I see you brought into suche a necessite, but also stirred up more withe love towardes you, desiringe to have you to my wife, will promise you faithefullye to withstande the grecians, as moche as shall lye in my power, that they shall not sleye you.

830

IPHIGENEIA Suerlie I have spoken even as I thoughte in dede: Wherfore I shall desire you O Achilles, not to put your selfe in daunger for my cause: but suffer me rather to save all grece withe my deathe.

ACHILLES Trulie I wonder gretelie at the bouldenes of your minde. And bicause you seme to be so willinge to die, I can not speake againste you: yet nevertheles I will promise to helpe you still, leste you shulde happen to chaunge your minde. [*Exit* ACHILLES.]

840

IPHIGENEIA Wherfore mother, do you holde your peace lamentinge so withe in your selfe?

CLYTEMNESTRA Alas, I wretched creature have greate cause to mourne.

IPHIGENEIA Be of good comforte mother I praie you, and folowe my councell, and do not teare your clothes so.

CLYTEMNESTRA Howe can I do otherwise, seinge I shall loose you? 850

IPHIGENEIA I praie you mother, studie not to save my life, for I shall get you moche honor by my deathe.

CLYTEMNESTRA What shall not I lament your deathe?

IPHIGENEIA No truly you oughte not, seinge that I shall bothe be sacraficed to the goddes Dyana and also save grece.

CLYTEMNESTRA Well I will folowe your cownsell daughter, seinge you have spoken so well: but tell me, what shall I saye to your sisters from you?

IPHIGENEIA Desier them I praie you, not to mourne for my deathe.

CLYTEMNESTRA And what shall I saye unto the other virgins from you?

IPHIGENEIA Bid them all farewell in my name, and I praye you for my sake bringe up my litell brother Orestes, till he come to mans age.

[*Enter attendant carrying Orestes.*]

CLYTEMNESTRA Take your leave of him, for this is the laste daie, that ever you shall see him.

IPHIGENEIA Farewell my welbeloved brother, for I am even as it weare compelled to love you, bicause you ware so glad to helpe me.   [*Exit attendant carrying Orestes.*]

CLYTEMNESTRA Is ther any other thinge, that I may do for you at grece?

IPHIGENEIA No truly, but I praie you not to hate my father for this dede: for he is compelled to do it for the welthe and honor of grece.

CLYTEMNESTRA If he hath done this willinglye then trulye he hathe committed a dede farre unworthie of suche a noble man as he is.

[*Enter Soldiers.*]

IPHIGENEIA Who is this, that will carie me hence so sone?

CLYTEMNESTRA I will goo withe you O daughter.

IPHIGENEIA Take hede I praye you leste you happen to do that whiche shall not become you: Wherfore O Mother I praye you folowe my councell and tarie heare still, for I muste nedes goo to be sacrafiscd unto the goddes Diana.

CLYTEMNESTRA And will you go awaye, O daughter, levinge me your mother heare?

IPHIGENEIA Yeae suerlye mother, I muste goo from you unto suche a place, from whence I shall never come ageine, althoughe I have not deserved it.

CLYTEMNESTRA I pray you daughter tarie, and do not forsake me nowe.   890

IPHIGENEIA Suerlye I will goo hence Mother, for if I did tarie, I shulde move you to more lamentation. Wherfore I shall desier all you women to singe some songe of my deathe, and to prophecie good lucke unto the grecians: for withe my deathe I shall purchase unto them a glorious victorie; bringe me therfore unto the aultor of the temple of the goddes Diana, that withe my blode I maye pacifie the wrathe of the goddes againste you.

CHORUS O Quene Clitemnestra of moste honor, after what fassion shall we lament, seinge we may not shewe any token of sadnes at the sacrafice.   900

IPHIGENEIA I wolde not have you to mourne for my cause, for I will not refuse to die.

CHORUS In dede by this meanes you shall get your selfe a perpetuall renowne for ever.

IPHIGENEIA Alas thou sone, whiche arte comforte to mans life, O thou light whiche doeste make joyfull all creatures, I shalbe compelled by and by to forsake you all and to chaunge my life.

[*Exeunt soldiers with* IPHIGENEIA.]

CHORUS Beholde yonder goethe the virgine to be sacraficed withe a grete companye of souldiers after hir, whos bewtifull face and faire bodi anone shalbe defiled withe hir owne blode. Yet happie arte   910 thou, O Iphigeneya, that withe thy deathe, thou shalte purchase unto the grecians a quiet passage, whiche I pray god may not only happen fortunatelie unto them, but also that they may returne againe prosperousely withe a glorious victorie.

[*Enter* NUNCIUS.]

NUNCIUS Come hether, O Clitemnestra for I muste speke withe you.

CLYTEMNESTRA Tell me I praie you what woulde you withe me, that you call so hastely, is ther any more mischefe in hande that I muste heare of?

NUNCIUS I muste tell you of a wonder, whiche hathe happened at the sacrafisinge of your daughter.   920

CLYTEMNESTRA Shew me I pray you quickely what it is?

NUNCIUS As we wente unto the place wher the sacrafice shulde be, and passed thorowe the plesant fildes, wher the whole hooste waited for your daughter: Agamemnon seinge hir brought unto her deathe, began to lament and wepe. But she perceyvinge what mone hir father made saied unto him thes wordes, O father, I am come hether to offer my bodie willinglie for the wellthe of my countrie: Wherfore seinge that I shall be sacraficed for the commodite of all grece, I do desier you, that none of the grecians may slaie me previlie: for I will make no resistance ageinste you. And whan she had spoken thes wordes, all they whiche weare present, weare wonderfullye astonied at the stoutenes of her minde: So after this, Achilles withe the reste of the whole hooste began to desier the goddes Diana, that she wolde accepte the sacrafice of the virgins blode, and that she wolde graunte them a prosperous succes of their jorney. And whan they had made an ende: the preste takinge the sworde in his hande, began to loke for a place convenient, wher he might sle your daughter; sodenly there chaunced a grete wonder, for althoughe all the people harde the voice of the stroke, yet she vanisshed sodenlye awaye, And whan all they mervelinge at it, began to give a greate skritche, then ther appeared unto them a white harte lienge before the aultor, strudgelinge for life. And Calchas beinge then present, and seinge what had happened, did wonderfully rejoyse, and tolde the capitaines, that this harte was sente of the goddes, bicause she wolde not have hir aulter defiled withe the blode of your daughter. Moreover he saied that this was a token of good lucke, and that their journie shoulde chaunce prosperousely unto them. Wherfore he willed that they shulde tarye no lenger here. And whan this was so finisshed, Agamemnon willed me to shewe all thes thinges unto you, bicause that I my selfe was present ther: Wherfore I shall desier you, to thinke no unkindnes in the kinge your husbande: for suerlie the secrete power of the goddes will save them whom they love: for this daie your daughter hathe bene bothe alive and deade.　　　　　　　　　　　　　　　　[*Exit* NUNCIUS.]

CHORUS Suerly O Clitemnestra you oughte to rejoise of this nwes, that your daughter is taken up into heaven.

CLYTEMNESTRA But I am in doughte whether I shulde beleve that thou, O daughter, arte amongste the goddes, or els, that they have fained it to comforte me.

CHORUS Beholde yonder commeth Agamemnon, who can tell the truthe of all this matter.

[*Enter* AGAMEMNON.]

AGAMEMNON Trulye wife, we are happie for our daughters sake, for suerlie she is placed in heven: But nowe I thinke it beste that you goo home, seinge that we shall take our journye so shortely unto Troy: Wherfore nowe fare you well. And of this matter I will commune more at my returne, and in the meane season I praie god sende you well to do, and your hartes desier.

CHORUS O happie Agamemnon, the goddes graunte the a fortunate journie unto Troye, and a mooste prosperous returne againe.   970

[*Exeunt omnes.*]

Finis.

The Tragedie of Antonie

TRANSLATED BY

MARY, COUNTESS OF PEMBROKE

The Argument

After the overthrowe of Brutus *and* Cassius, *the libertie of* Rome *being now utterly opressed, and the Empire setled in the hands of* Octavius Caesar *and* Marcus Antonius, (*who for knitting a straiter bonde of amitie betweene them, had taken to wife* Octavia *the sister of* Caesar) Antonius *undertooke a journey against the Parthians, with intent to regaine on them the honor won by them from the Romanes, at the discomfiture and slaughter of* Crassus. *But comming in his journey into Siria the places renewed in his remembrance the long intermitted love of* Cleopatra, Queene *of Aegipte: who before time had both in Cilicia and at Alexandria, entertained him with all the exquisite delightes and sumptuous pleasures, which a great Prince and voluptuous lover could to the uttermost desire. Whereupon omitting his enterprice, he made his returne to Alexandria, againe falling to his former loves, without any regarde of his vertuous wife* Octavia, *by whom nevertheles he had excellent children. This occasion* Octavius *toke of taking armes against him: & preparing a mighty fleet, encountred him at Actium, who also had assembled to that place a great number of Gallies of his own, beside 60 which* Cleopatra *brought with her from Aegipt. But at the very beginning of the battel* Cleopatra *with all her Gallies betooke her to flight, which* Antony *seeing could not but follow: by his departure leaving to* Octavius *the greatest victory which in any Sea battell hath beene hard off. Which he not negligent to pursue, followes them the next spring and besiedgeth them within Alexandria, where* Antony *finding al that he trusted to faile him, beginneth to growe jealouse and to suspect* Cleopatra. *She thereupon enclosed her selfe with two of her women in a monument she had before caused to be built, thence sends him worde she was dead: which he beleeving for truth, gave himselfe with his Sworde a deadly wound: but died not until a messenger came from* Cleopatra *to have him brought to her to the tombe. Which she not daring to open least she should bee made a prisoner to the Romaines, & carried in* Caesars *triumph, cast downe a cord from an high window, by the which (her women helping her) she trussed up* Antonius *halfe dead, & so got him into the monument. The stage supposed Alexandria: the chorus first Egiptians, & after Romane souldiors: The history to be read at large in* Plutarch *in the life of* Antonius.

The Actors

ANTONIUS.

CLEOPATRA.

ERAS *and*
CHARMION $\Big\}$ *Cleopatras women*

PHILOSTRATUS *a Philosopher.*

LUCILIUS.

DIOMEDE *Secretarie to Cleopatra.*

OCTAVIUS CAESAR.

AGRIPPA.

EUPHRON, *teacher of Cleopatras children.*

CHILDREN *of* CLEOPATRA,

DIRCETUS *the Messenger.*

The Tragedie of Antonie

Act I.

ANTONIUS [*sola.*]

ANTONIUS Since cruell Heav'ns against me obstinate,
  Since all mishappes of the round engin doo
  Conspire my harme: since men, since powers divine
  Aire, earth, and Sea are all injurious:
  And that my Queene her selfe, in whome I liv'd,
  The Idoll of my harte, doth me pursue;
  It's meete I dye. For her have I forgone
  My Country, *Caesar* unto warre provok'd
  (For just revenge of Sisters wrong, my wife,
  Who mov'de my Queene (ay me!) to jealousie)   10
  For love of her, in her allurements caught,
  Abandon'd life, I honor have despisde,
  Disdain'd my freends, and of the statelye Rome
  Despoilde the Empire of her best attire,
  Contemn'd that power that made me so much fear'd,
  A slave become unto her feeble face.
  O cruell, traitres, woman most unkinde,
  Thou dost, forsworne, my love and life betraie:
  And giv'st me up to ragefull enemie,
  Which soone (o foole!) will plague thy perjurye.   20

    Yeelded *Pelusium* on this countries shore,
  Yeelded thou hast my Shippes and men of warre,
  That nought remaines (so destitute am I)
  But these same armes which on my back I weare.
  Thou should'st have had them too, and me unarm'de
  Yeelded to *Caesar* naked of defence. ·
  Which while I beare let *Caesar* never thinke
  Triumph of me shall his proud chariot grace
  Not thinke with me his glory to adorne,

30   On me alive to use his victorie.
            Thou only *Cleopatra* triumph hast,
        Thou only hast my fredome servile made,
        Thou only hast me vanquisht: not by force
        (For forste I cannot be) but by sweete baites
        Of thy eyes graces, which did gaine so fast
        Upon my libertie, that nought remain'd.
        None els henceforth, but thou my dearest Queene,
        Shall glorie in commaunding *Antonie*.
            Have *Caesar* fortune and the Gods his freends,
40   To him have love and fatall sisters given
        The Scepter of the earth: he never shall
        Subject my life to his obedience.
        But when that death, my glad refuge, shall have
        Bounded the course of my unstedfast life,
        And frosen corps under a marble colde
        Within tombes bosome widdowe of my soule:
        Then at his will let him it subject make:
        Then what he will let *Caesar* doo with me:
        Make me limme after limme be rent: make me
50   My buriall take in sides of *Thracian* wolfe.
            Poore *Antonie*! alas what was the day,
        The daies of losse that gained thee thy love!
        Wretch *Antonie*! since *Maegaera* pale
        With Snakie haires enchain'd thy miserie.
        The fire thee burnt was never *Cupids* fire
        (For Cupid beares not such a mortall brand)
        It was some furies torch, *Orestes* torche,
        Which somtimes burnt his mother-murdering soule
        (When wandring madde, rage boiling in his bloud,
60   He fled his fault which folow'd as he fled)
        Kindled within his bones by shadow pale
        Of mother slaine return'd from Stygian lake.
            Antony, poore *Antony*! since that daie
        Thy olde good hap did faire from thee retire.
        Thy vertue dead: thy glory made alive
        So ofte by martiall deeds is gone in smoke:
        Since then the Baies so well thy forehead knewe

To Venus mirtles yeelded have their place:
Trumpets to pipes: field tents to courtly bowers:
Launces and Pikes to daunces and to feastes.   70
Since then, o wretch! instead of bloudy warres
Thou shouldst have made upon the Parthian Kings
For Romain honor filde by *Crassus* foile,
Thou threw'st thy Curiace off, and fearfull healme,
With coward courage unto *Aegipts* Queene
In haste to runne, about her necke to hang
Languishing in her armes thy Idoll made:
In summe given up to *Cleopatras* eies.
Thou breakest at length from thence, as one encharm'd
Breakes from th'enchaunter that him strongly helde.   80
For thy first reason (spoyling of their force
The poisned cuppes of thy faire Sorceres)
Recur'd thy sperit: and then on every side
Thou mad'st again the earth with Souldiours swarme.
All Asia hidde: Euphrates bankes do tremble
To see at once so many Romanes there
Breath horror, rage, and with a threatning eye
In mighty squadrons crosse his swelling streames.
Nought seene but horse, and fiery sparkling armes:
Nought heard but hideous noise of muttring troups.   90
The *Parth*, the *Mede*, abandoning their goods
Hide them for feare in hilles of *Hircanie*,
Redoubting thee. Then willing to besiege
The great *Phraate* head of *Media*,
Thou campedst at her walles with vaine assault,
Thy engins fit (mishap!) not thither brought,
    So long thou stai'st, so long thou dost thee rest,
So long thy love with such things nourished
Reframes, reformes it selfe and stealingly
Retakes his force and rebecomes more great.   100
For of thy Queene the lookes, the grace, the words,
Sweetnes, alurements, amorous delights,
Entred againe thy soule, and day and night,
In watch, in sleepe, her Image follow'd thee:
Not dreaming but of her, repenting still

That thou for warre hadst such a goddes left.
    Thou car'st no more for *Parth*, nor *Parthian* bow,
Sallies, assaults, encounters, shocks, alarmes,
For ditches, rampiers, wards, entrenched grounds:
Thy only care is sight of *Nilus* streames,
Sight of that face whose gilefull semblant doth
(Wandring in thee) infect thy tainted hart.
Her absence thee besottes: each hower, each hower
Of staie, to thee impatient seemes an age.
Enough of conquest, praise thou deem'st enough,
If soone enough the bristled fields thou see
Of fruitfull *Aegipt*, and the stranger floud
Thy Queenes faire eyes (another *Pharos*) lights.
    Returned loe, dishonoured, despisde,
In wanton love a woman thee misleades
Sunke in foule sinke: meanewhile respecting nought
Thy wife *Octavia* and her tender babes,
Of whome the long contempt against thee whets
The sword of *Caesar* now thy Lord become.
    Lost thy great Empire, all those goodly townes
Reverenc'd thy name as rebells now thee leave:
Rise against thee, and to the ensignes flocke
Of conqu'ring *Caesar*, who enwalles thee round
Cag'd in thy hold, scarse maister of thy selfe,
Late maister of so many Nations.
    Yet, yet, which is of griefe extreamest griefe,
Which is yet of mischiefe highest mischiefe,
It's *Cleopatra* alas! alas, it's she,
It's she augments the torment of thy paine,
Betraies thy love, thy life alas! betraies,
Caesar to please, whose grace she seekes to gaine:
With thought her crowne to save and fortune make
Onely thy foe which common ought have beene.
    If her I alwaies lov'd, and the first flame
Of her heart-killing love shall burne me last:
Justly complaine I she disloyall is,
Nor constant is, even as I constant am,
To comfort my mishap, despising me

No more, then when the heavens favour'd me.
But ah! by nature women wav'ring are,
Each moment changing and rechanging mindes.
Unwise, who blinde in them, thinkes loyaltie
Ever to finde in beauties companie.   [*Exit* ANTONIUS.]

CHORUS   The boyling tempest still
                  makes not Sea waters fome: 150
                  nor still the Northern blast
                  disquiets quiet streames:
                  Nor who his chest to fill
                  sayles to the morning beames,
                  on waves winde tosseth fast,
                  still kepes his ship from home.
              Nor *Jove* still downe doth cast
                  inflam'd with bloudie ire
                  on man, on tree, on hill,
                  his darts of thundring fire.   160
                  nor still the heat doth last
                  on face of parched plaine
                  nor wrinkled colde doth still
                  on frozen furrowes raigne.
              But still as long as we
                  in this low world remaine,
                  mishapps our daily mates
                  our lifes doe intertaine:
                  and woes which beare no dates
                  still pearch upon our heads;   170
                  none go but straight will be
                  some greater in their steads.
              Nature made us not free
                  When first she made us live:
                  When we began to be,
                  To be began our woe:
                  Which growing evermore
                  As dying life doth growe,
                  Do more and more us greeve,
                  And tire us more and more.   180

No stay in fading states,
　　For more to height they retch,
　　Their fellow miseries
　　The more to height do stretch.
　　They cling even to the crowne,
　　And threatning furious wise
　　From tirannizing pates
　　Do often pull it downe.
In vaine on waves untride
　　To shun them go we should
　　To *Scythes* and *Massagetes*
　　Who neere the Pole reside:
　　In vaine to boiling sandes
　　Which *Phoebus* battry beates,
　　For with us still they would
　　Cut seas and compasse landes.
The darknes no more sure
　　To joyne with heavy night:
　　The light which guildes the days
　　To follow *Titan* pure:
　　No more the shadow light
　　The body to ensue:
　　Than wretchednes alwaies
　　Us wretches to pursue.
O blest who never breath'd,
　　Or whome with pittie mov'de,
　　Death from his cradle reav'de,
　　And swadled in his grave:
　　And blessed also he
　　(As curse may blessing have)
　　Who low and living free
　　No princes charge hath prov'de.
By stealing sacred fire
　　Prometheus then unwise,
　　provoking Gods to ire,
　　the heape of ills did sturre,
　　and sicknes pale and colde
　　our ende which onward spurre,

190

200

210

      to plague our hands too bolde
      to filch the wealth of skies.   220
In heavens hate since then
    of ill with ill enchain'd
    we race of mortall men
    ful fraught our brests have borne
    and thousand thousand woes
    our heav'nly soules now thorne,
    which free before from those
    no earthly passion pain'd.
Warre and warrs bitter cheare
    now long time with us staie,   230
    and feare of hated foe
    still still encreaseth sore:
    our harmes worse dayly grow:
    lesse yesterday they were
    then now, and will be more
    to morrow then to day.

Act II.

[*Enter*] PHILOSTRATUS.

PHILOSTRATUS What horrible furie, what cruell rage,
  O *Aegipt* so extremely thee torments?
  Hast thou the Gods so angred by thy fault?
  Hast thou against them some such crime conceiv'd,
  That their engrained hand lift up in threats
  They should desire in thy heart bloud to bathe?
  And that their burning wrath which noght can quench
  Should pittiles on us still lighten downe?
    We are not hew'n out of the monst'rous masse
  Of *Giantes* those, which heavens wrack conspir'd: 10
  Ixions race, false prater of his loves:
  Nor yet of him who fained lightnings found:
  Nor cruell *Tantalus*, nor bloudy *Atreus*,
  Whose cursed banquet for *Thyestes* plague
  Made the beholding Sunne for horrour turne

His backe, and backward from his course returne:
And hastning his wing-footed horses race
Plunge him in sea for shame to hide his face:
While sulleine night upon the wondring wor'd
For mid-daies light her starrie mantle cast.

    But what we be, what ever wickednesse
By us is done, Alas! with what more plagues,
More eager torments could the Gods declare
To heaven and earth that us they hatefull holde?
With souldiors, strangers, horrible in armes
Our land is hidde, our people drown'd in teares.
But terror here and horror, nought is seene:
And present death prising our life each hower.
Hard at our ports and at our porches waites
Our conquering foe: harts faile us, hopes are dead:
Our Queene laments: and this great Emperour
Somtime (would now they did) whom worlds did fear
Abandoned, betraid, now mindes no more
But from his evils by hast'ned death to passe.

    Come you poore people tirde with ceasles plaints.
With teares and sighes make mournfull sacrifice
On *Isis* altars: not our selves to save,
But soften *Caesar* and him piteous make
To us, his praie: that so his lenitie
May change our death into captivitie.

    Strange are the evils the fates on us have brought;
O but alas! how far more strange the cause!
Love, love (alas, who ever would have thought?)
Hath lost this Realme inflamed with his fire.
Love, playing love, which men say kindles not
But in soft hearts, hath ashes made our townes.
And his sweet shafts, with whose shot none are kill'd,
Which ulcer not, with deaths our lands have fill'd.

    Such was the bloudie, murdring, hellish love
Possest thy hart, faire false guest *Priams* sonne,
Firing a brand which after made to burne
The *Trojan* towers by *Graecians* ruinate.
By this love, *Priam, Hector, Troilus,*

Memnon, Deiphoebus, Glaucus, thousands mo
Whome redd *Scamanders* armor clogged streames
Roll'd into Seas, before their dates are dead.
So plaguie he, so many tempests raiseth,
So murdring he, so many Citties raseth,
When insolent, blinde, lawles, orderles,
With mad delights our sence he entertaines.   60

    All knowing Gods our wracks did us fortell
By signes in earth, by signes in starry Sphaeres,
Which should have mov'd us, had not destinie
With too strong hand warped our miserie.
The *Comets* flaming through the scat'red clouds
With fiery beames, most like unbroaded haires:
The fearfull dragon whistling at the bankes:
And holy *Apis* ceasles bellowing
(As never erst) and shedding endles teares:
Bloud raining down from heav'n in unknow'n showers: 70
Our Gods darke faces overcast with woe,
And dead mens Ghosts appearing in the night.
Yea, even this night while all the Cittie stood
Opprest with terror, horror, servile feare,
Deepe silence over all: the sounds were heard
Of divers songs, and diverse instruments,
Within the voide of aire: and howling noise,
Such as madde *Bacchus* priests in *Bacchus* feasts
On *Nisa* make: and (seem'd) the company,
Our Cittie lost, went to the enemie.   80

    So we forsaken both of Gods and men,
So are we in the mercy of our foes:
And we henceforth obedient must become
To lawes of them who have us overcome.

                        [*Exit* PHILOSTRATUS.]

CHORUS   Lament we our mishaps,
                Drowne we with teares our woe:
                For Lamentable happes
                Lamented easie growe:
                and much lesse torment bring

90

then when they first did spring.
We want that wofull song,
   wherwith wood-musiques Queen
   doth ease her woes, among
   fresh springtimes bushes greene,
   on pleasant branch alone
   renewing auntient mone.
We want that monefull sound,
   that pratling *Progne* makes
   on fields of *Thracian* ground,
   or streames of *Thracian* lakes:
   to empt her brest of paine
   for *Itys* by her slaine.
Though *Halcyons* do still,
   bewailing *Ceyx* lot,
   the Seas with plainings fill
   which his dead limmes have got,
   not ever other grave
   then tombe of waves to have:
And though the bird in death
   that most *Meander* loves
   so sweetly sighes his breath
   when death his fury proves,
   as almost softs his heart,
   and almost blunts his dart:
Yet all the plaints of those,
   nor all their tearfull larmes,
   cannot content our woes,
   nor serve to waile the harmes,
   in soule which we, poore we,
   to feele enforced be.
Nor they of *Phoebus* bredd
   in teares can doo so well,
   they for their brother shedd,
   who into *Padus* fell,
   rash guide of chariot cleere
   surveiour of the yeare.
Nor she whom heav'nly powers

100

110

120

to weping rocke did turne,
whose teares distill in showers,
and shew she yet doth mourne,   130
wherewith his toppe to Skies
mount *Sipylus* doth rise.

Nor weping drops which flowe
from barke of wounded tree,
that *Mirrhas* shame doth showe
with ours compar'd may be,
to quench her loving fire
who durst embrace her sire.

Nor all the howlings made
on *Cybels* sacred hill   140
By Eunukes of her trade,
who *Atys*, *Atys* still
with doubled cries resound,
which *Eccho* makes rebound.

Our plaints no limits stay,
nor more then do our woes:
both infinitely straie
and neither measure knowes.
In measure let them plaine:
Who measur'd griefes sustaine.   150

[*Enter*] CLEOPATRA, ERAS, CHARMION [*and*] DIOMEDE.

CLEOPATRA That I have thee betraide, deare *Antonie*,
My life, my soule, my sunne? I had such thought?
That I have thee betraide my Lord, my King?
That I would breake my vowed faith to thee?
Leave thee? deceive thee? yeelde thee to the rage
Of mightie foe? I ever had that hart?
Rather sharpe lightning lighten on my head:
Rather may I to deepest mischiefe fall:
Rather the opened earth devoure me:
Rather fierce *Tigers* feed them on my flesh: 160
Rather, o rather let our *Nilus* send,
To swallow me quicke, some weeping *Crocodile*.
And didst thou then suppose my royall heart

Had hatcht, thee to ensnare, a faithles love?
And changing minde, as Fortune changed cheare,
I would weake thee, to winne the stronger, loose.
O wretch! o caitive! o too cruell happe!
And did not I sufficient losse sustaine
Loosing my Realme, loosing my libertie,
170 My tender of-spring, and the joyfull light
Of beamy Sunne, and yet, yet loosing more
Thee *Antony* my care, if I loose not
What yet remain'd? thy love alas! thy love,
More deare then Scepter, children, freedome, light.

So readie I to row in *Charons* barge,
Shall leese the joy of dying in thy love:
So the sole comfort of my miserie
To have one tombe with thee is me bereft.
So I in shady plaines shall plaine alone,
180 Not (as I hop'd) companion of thy mone,
O height of griefe!

ERAS   Why with continuall cries
Your griefull harmes doo you exasperate?
Torment your selfe with murthering complaints;
Straine your weake brest so oft, so vehemently?
Water with teares this faire alablaster?
With sorrowes sting so many beauties wound?
Come of so many Kings, want you the hart
Bravely, stoutly, this tempest to resist?

CLEOPATRA My ev'lls are wholy unsupportable,
190 No humain force can them withstand, but death.

ERAS To him that strives nought is impossible.

CLEOPATRA In striving lyes no hope of my mishapps.

ERAS All things do yeelde to force of lovely face.

CLEOPATRA My face too lovely caus'd my wretched case.
My face hath so entrap'd, to cast us downe,
That for his conquest *Caesar* may it thanke,
Causing that *Antonie* one army lost,
The other wholy did to *Caesar* yeld.
For not induring (so his amorouse sprite
200 Was with my beautie fir'de) my shamefull flight,

Soone as he saw from ranke wherein he stoode
In hottest fight, my Gallies making saile:
Forgetfull of his charg (as if his soule
Unto his Ladies soule had beene enchain'd)
He left his men, who so couragiously
Did leave their lives to gaine him victorie,
And carelesse both of fame and armies losse
My oared Gallies follow'd with his ships,
Companion of my flight, by this base parte
Blasting his former flourishing renowne.   210

ERAS Are you therefore cause of his overthrow?
CLEOPATRA I am sole cause: I did it, only I.
ERAS Feare of a woman troubled so his sprite?
CLEOPATRA Fire of his love was by my feare enflam'd.
ERAS And should he then to warre have led a Queene?
CLEOPATRA Alas! this was not his offence, but mine.
   Antony (ay me! who else so brave a chiefe!)
   Would not I should have taken Seas with him:
   But would have left me fearefull woman farre
   From common hazard of the doubtfull warre.   220

      O that I had beleev'd! now, now of *Rome*
   All the great Empire at our beck should bende.
   All should obey, the vagabonding *Scythes,*
   The feared *Germaines,* back-shooting *Parthians,*
   Wandring *Numidians, Brittons* farre remov'd,
   And tawny nations scorched with the Sunne.
   But I car'd not: so was my soule possest,
   (To my great harme) with burning jealousie:
   Fearing least in my absence *Antony*
   Should leaving me retake *Octavia.*   230

CHARMION Such was the rigour of your desteny.
CLEOPATRA Such was my errour and obstinacie.
CHARMION But since Gods would not, could you do withall?
CLEOPATRA Alwaies from Gods good haps, not harms, do fall.
CHARMION And have they not all power on mens affaires?
CLEOPATRA They never bow so low as worldly cares,
   But leave to mortall men to be dispos'd
   Freely on earth what ever mortall is.

If we therein sometimes some faults commit,
240   We may them not to their high majesties,
But to our selves impute; whose passions
Plunge us each day in all afflictions.
Wherwith when we our soules do thorned feele,
Flatt'ring our selves we say they dest'nies are:
That gods would have it so, and that our care
Could not empeach but that it must be so.

CHARMION   Things here below are in the heav'ns begot,
Before they be in this our worlde borne:
And never can our weaknesse turne awry
250   The stailessee course of powerfull destenie.
Nought here, force, reason, humaine providence,
Holie devotion, noble bloud prevailes:
And Jove himselfe whose hand doth heavens rule,
Who both to gods and men as King commands,
Who earth (our firme support) with plenty stores,
Moves aire and sea with twinckling of his eie,
Who all can doe, yet never can undoe
What once hath beene by their hard lawes decreed.

When *Troyan* walles, great *Neptunes* workmanship,
260   Environ'd were with *Greekes*, and Fortunes whele
Doubtfull ten yeares now to the campe did turne,
And now againe towards the towne return'd,
How many times did force and fury swell
In *Hectors* veines egging him to the spoile
Of conquer'd foes, which at his blowes did fly,
As fearefull sheepe at feared wolves approch:
To save (in vaine: for why? it would not be)
Poore walles of *Troy* from adversaries rage,
Who dyed them in bloud, and cast to ground
270   Heap'd them with bloudie burning carcases.

No, Madame, thinke, that if the ancient crowne
Of your progenitors that *Nilus* rul'd,
Force take from you; the Gods have will'd it so,
To whome oft times Princes are odious.
They have to every thing an end ordain'd;
All worldly greatnes by them bounded is:

Some sooner, later some, as they thinke best:
None their decree is able to infringe.
But, which is more, to us disastred men
Which subject are in all things to their will,   280
Their will is hid: nor while we live, we know
How, or how long we must in life remaine.
Yet must we not for that feede on dispaire,
And make us wretched ere we wretched be:
But alwaies hope the best, even to the last,
That from our selves the mischiefe may not grow.
   Then, Madame, helpe your selfe, leave of in time
Antonies wracke, lest it your wracke procure:
Retire you from him, save from wrathfull rage
Of angry *Caesar* both your Realme and you.   290
You see him lost, so as your amitie
Unto his evills can yeeld no more reliefe.
You see him ruin'd, so as your support
No more henceforth can him with comfort raise.
With-draw you from the storme: persist not still
To loose your selfe: this royall diademe
Regaine of *Caesar*.

CLEOPATRA   Sooner shining light
Shall leave the day, and darknes leave the night:
Sooner moist currents of tempestuous seas
Shall wave in heaven, and the nightly trooppes   300
Of starres shall shine within the foming waves,
Then I thee, *Antony*, leave in deepe distres.
I am with thee, be it thy worthy soule
Lodge in thy brest, or from that lodging parte
Crossing the joyles lake to take her place
In place prepared for men Demy-gods.
   Live, if thee please, if life be lothsome die:
Dead and alive, *Antony*, thou shalt see
Thy princesse follow thee, follow, and lament
Thy wrack, no lesse her owne then was thy weale.   310

CHARMION What helps his wrack this ever-lasting love?
CLEOPATRA Help, or help not, such must, such ought I prove.
CHARMION Ill done to loose your selfe, and to no end.

CLEOPATRA How ill thinke you to follow such a frend?

CHARMION But this your love nought mitigates his paine.

CLEOPATRA Without this love I should be inhumaine.

CHARMION Inhumaine he, who his owne death pursues.

CLEOPATRA Not inhumaine who miseries eschues.

CHARMION Live for your sonnes.

CLEOPATRA   Nay for their father die.

CHARMION Hardharted mother!

320 CLEOPATRA   Wife, kindhearted, I.

CHARMION Then will you them deprive of royall right?

CLEOPATRA Do I deprive them? no, it's dest'nies might.

CHARMION Do you not them deprive of heritage,
    That give them up to adversaries hands,
    A man forsaken fearing to forsake,
    Whome such huge numbers hold invironned?
    T'abandon one gainst whome the frowning world
    Banded with *Caesar* makes conspiring warre?

CLEOPATRA The lesse ought I to leave him lest of all.

330 *A frend in most distresse should most assist.*
    If that when *Antonie* great and glorious
    His legions led to drinke *Euphrates* streames,
    So many Kings in traine redoubting him;
    In triumph rais'd as high as highest heav'n;
    Lord-like disposing as him pleased best,
    The wealth of *Greece*, the wealth of *Asia*:
    In that faire fortune had I him exchaung'd
    For *Caesar*, then, men would have counted me
    Faithles, unconstant, light: but now the storme,

340   And blustring tempest driving on his face,
    Readie to drowne, *Alas*! what would they say?
    What would himselfe in *Plutos* mansion say?
    If I, whome alwaies more then life he lov'de,
    If I, who am his heart, who was his hope,
    Leave him, forsake him (and perhaps in vaine)
    Weakly to please who him hath overthrowne?
    Not light, unconstant, faithlesse should I be,
    But vile, forsworne, of treachrous cruelty.

CHARMION Crueltie to shunne you selfe-cruell are:

CLEOPATRA Selfe-cruell him from cruelty to spare.   350

CHARMION Our first affection to ourselfe is due.

CLEOPATRA He is my selfe.

CHARMION   Next it extends unto
 Our children, frends, and to our country soile.
 And you for some respect of wively love,
 (Albee scarce wively) loose your native land,
 Your children, frends, and (which is more) your life.
 With so strong charmes doth love bewitch our witts:
 So fast in us this fire once kindled flames.
 Yet if his harme by yours redresse might have,—

CLEOPATRA With mine it may be clos'de in darksome grave.   360

CHARMION And that, as *Alcest* to her selfe unkind,
 You might exempt him from the lawes of death.
 But he is sure to die: and now his sword
 Already moisted is in his warme bloud,
 Helples for any succour you can bring
 Against deaths sting, which he must shortly feele.
  Then let your love be like the love of olde
 Which *Carian* Queene did nourish in hir heart
 Of hir Mausolus: builde for him a tombe
 Whose statelinesse a wonder new may make.   370
 Let him, let him have sumptuous funeralls:
 Let grave thereon the horror of his fights:
 Let earth be buri'd with unburied heaps.
 Frame the *Pharsaly*, and discolour'd streams
 Of deepe *Enipeus*: frame the grassie plaine,
 Which lodg'd his campe at siege of *Mutina*.
 Make all his combats, and couragious acts:
 And yearely plaies to his praise institute:
 Honor his memory: with doubled care
 Breed and bring up the children of you both   380
 In *Caesars* grace: who as a noble Prince
 Will leave them Lords of this most glorious realme.

CLEOPATRA What shame were that! ah Gods! what infemie!
 With *Antony* in his good haps to share,
 And overlive him dead: deeming enough
 To shed some teares upon a widdow tombe!

The after-livers justly might report
That I him only for his Empire lov'd,
And high estate: and that in hard estate
390   I for another did him lewdly leave.
Like to those birds wafted with wandring wings
From foraine lands in spring-time here arrive:
And live with us so long as Somers heate,
And their foode lasts, then seeke another soile.
And as we see with ceaslesse fluttering
Flocking of seelly flies a brownish cloud
To vintag'd wine yet working in the tonne:
Not parting thence while they sweete liquor taste:
After, as smoke, all vanish in the aire,
400   And of the swarme not one so much appeare.

ERAS By this sharpe death what profit can you winne?

CLEOPATRA I neither gaine nor profit seeke therein.

ERAS What praise shall you of after-ages get?

CLEOPATRA Nor praise, nor Glory in my cares are set.

ERAS What other end ought you respect, then this?

CLEOPATRA My only end my onely duty is.

ERAS Your duty must upon some good be founded!

CLEOPATRA On vertue it, the onely good, is grounded.

ERAS What is that *vertue*?

CLEOPATRA   That which us beseemes.

410 ERAS Outrage our selves? who that beseeming deemes?

CLEOPATRA Finish I will my sorrowes dieng thus.

ERAS Minish you will your glories doing thus.

CLEOPATRA Good frends I pray you seeke not to revoke
My fix'd intent of folowing *Antony*.
I will die. I will die: must not his life,
His life and death by mine be followed?
    Meane while, deare sisters, live: and while you live,
Do often honor to our loved Tombes.
Straw them with flowers: and sometimes happely
420   The tender thought of *Antony* your Lord
And me poore soule to teares shall you invite,
And our true loves your dolefull voice commend.

CHARMION And thinke you Madame, we from you will part?

Thinke you alone to feele deaths ougly darte?
Thinke you to leave us? and that the same sunne
Shall see at once you dead, and us alive?
Weele die with you: and *Clotho* pittilesse
Shall us with you in hellish boate imbarque.

CLEOPATRA Ah live, I praie you: this disastred woe
   Which racks my heart, alone to me belongs: 430
   My lot longs not to you: servants to be
   No shame, no harme to you, as is to me.
     Live sisters, live, and seing his suspect
   Hath causlesse me in sea of sorrowes drown'd,
   And that I cannot live, if so I would,
   Nor yet would leave this life, if so I could,
   Without his love: procure me, *Diomed*,
   That gainst poore me he be no more incensd.
   Wrest out of his conceit that harmefull doubt,
   That since his wracke he hath of me conceiv'd   440
   Though wrong conceiv'd: witnes you reverent Gods,
   Barking *Anubis, Apis* bellowing.
   Tell him, my soule burning, impatient,
   Forlorne with love of him, for certaine seale
   Of her true loialtie my corpse hath left,
   T'encrease of dead the number numberlesse.
     Go then, and if as yet he me bewaile,
   If yet for me his heart one sigh forth breathe
   Blest shall I be: and far with more content
   Depart this world, where so I me torment.   450
   Meane season us let this sad tombe enclose,
   Attending here till death conclude our woes.

DIOMEDE I will obey your will.

CLEOPATRA   So the desert
   The Gods repay of thy true faithfull heart.

        [*Exeunt* CLEOPATRA, ERAS *and* CHARMION.]

DIOMEDE And is't not pittie, Gods, ah Gods of heav'n!
   To see from love such hatefull frutes to spring?
   And is't not pittie that this firebrand so
   Laies waste the trophes of *Phillippi* fieldes?
   Where are those sweet allurements, those sweet lookes,

460   Which gods themselves right hart sick wuld have made?
         What doth that beautie, rarest guift of heav'n,
         Wonder of earth? Alas! what do those eies?
         And that sweete voice all *Asia* understoode,
         And sunburnt *Africke* wide in deserts spred?
         Is their force dead? have they no further power?
         Can not by them *Octavius* be surpriz'd?
         Alas! if *Jove* in middst of all his ire,
         With thunderbolt in hand some land to plague,
         Had cast his eies on my Queene, out of hand
470   His plaguing bolte had falne out of his hand:
         Fire out of his wrath into vaine smoke should turne,
         And other fire within his brest should burne.
            Nought lives so faire. Nature by such a worke
         Her selfe, should seeme, in workmanship hath past.
         She is all heav'nly: never any man
         But seeing hir was ravish'd with her sight.
         The Allablaster covering of her face,
         The corall coullor hir two lips engraines,
         Her beamy eies, two Sunnes of this our world,
480   Of hir faire haire the fine and flaming golde,
         Her brave streight stature, and her winning partes
         Are nothing else but fiers, fetters, dartes.
            Yet this is nothing [to] th'enchaunting skilles
         Of her celestiall Spirite, hir training speach,
         Her grace, hir majesty, and forcing voice,
         Whether she it with fingers speach consorte,
         Or hearing sceptred kings embassadors
         Answere to each in his owne language make.
            Yet now at neede it aides her not at all
490   With all these beauties, so her sorrow stinges.
         Darkned with woe her only study is
         To weepe, to sigh, to seeke for lonelines.
         Careles of all, hir haire disordred hangs:
         Hir charming eies whence murthring looks did flie,
         Now rivers grown, whose wellspring anguish is,
         Do trickling wash the marble of hir face.
         Hir faire discover'd brest with sobbing swolne

Selfe cruell she still martirith with blowes.
   Alas! It's our ill hap, for if hir teares
She would convert into her loving charmes,   500
To make a conquest of the conqueror,
(As well she might, would she hir force imploie)
She should us safetie from these ills procure,
Hir crowne to hir, and to hir race assure.
Unhappy he, in whome selfe-succour lies,
Yet selfe-forsaken wanting succour dies.   [*Exit* DIOMEDE.]

CHORUS   O sweete fertile land, wherein
                 Phoebus did with breth inspire
                 man who men did first begin,
                 formed first of *Nilus* mire,   510
                 whence of *Artes* the eldest kindes,
                 earths most heavenly ornament,
                 were as from their fountaine sent
                 to enlight our misty mindes.
                 whose grose sprite from endles time
                 as in darkned prison pente,
                 never did to knowledge clime.
              Wher the *Nile*, our father good,
                 father-like doth never misse
                 yearely us to bring such food,   520
                 as to life required is:
                 visiting each yeare this plaine,
                 and with fat slime cov'ring it,
                 which his seaven mouthes do spit,
                 as the season comes againe,
                 making therby greatest growe
                 busie reapers joyfull paine,
                 when his flouds do highest flow.
              Wandring Prince of rivers thou,
                 honor of the *Aethiops* lande,   530
                 of a Lord and maister now
                 thou a slave in awe must stand.
                 now of *Tiber* which is spred
                 lesse in force, and lesse in fame

reverence thou must the name,
whome all other rivers dread,
for his children swolne in pride,
who by conquest seeke to treade
round this earth on every side.

540   Now thou must begin to send
tribute of thy watry store,
as sea pathes thy steps shall bend,
yearely presents more and more.
thy fat skumme, our fruitfull corne,
pill'd from hence with thevish hands
all uncloth'd shal leave our lands
into forraine country borne,
which puft up with such a pray
shall thereby the praise adorne
550   of that scepter *Rome* doth sway.

Nought thee helps thy hornes to hide
far from hence in unknown grounds,
that thy waters wander wide,
yerely breaking banks, and bounds.
and that thy Skie-coullor'd brooks
through a hundred peoples passe,
drawing plots for trees and grasse
with a thousand turnes and crookes,
whome all weary of their way
560   thy throats which in widenesse passe
powre into their mother Sea.

Nought so happie haplesse life
in this world as freedome findes:
nought wherin more sparkes are rife
to inflame couragious mindes.
but if force must us inforce
needes a yoke to undergo,
under foraine yoke to go,
still it proves a bondage worse,
570   and doubled subjection
see we shall, and feele, and know
subject to a stranger growne.

From hence forward for a King,
   whose first being from this place
   should his brest by nature bring
   care of country to imbrace,
We at surly face must quake
   of some *Romaine* madly bent:
   who our terrour to augment
   his *Proconsuls* axe will shake,   580
   driving with our Kings from hence
   our establish'd government,
   justice sword, and lawes defence.
Nothing worldly of such might
   but more mighty *Destiny*,
   by swift *Times* unbridled flight,
   makes in end his end to see.
   Every thing *Time* overthrowes,
   nought to end doth steadfast staie.
   his great sithe mowes all away   590
   as the stalke of tender rose.
   onely immortalitie
   of the heavens doth it oppose
   gainst his powrefull *Deitie*.
One day there will come a day
   which shall quaile thy fortunes flower
   and thee ruinde low shall laie
   in some barbarous Princes power,
   when the pittie-wanting fire
   shall, O *Rome*, thy beauties burne,   600
   and to humble ashes turne
   thy proud wealth and rich attire,
   those guilt roofes which turretwise,
   justly making envy mourne,
   threaten now to pearce Skies.
As thy forces fill each land
   harvest making here and there,
   reaping all with ravening hand
   they find growing any where:
   from each land so to thy fall   610

multitudes repaire shall make,
from the common spoile to take
what to each mans share may fall.
fingred all thou shalt behold:
no iote left for tokens sake
that thou wert so great of olde.
Like unto the ancient *Troie*
whence deriv'd thy founders be,
conqu'ring foe shall thee enjoie,
620   and a burning praie in thee.
for within this turning ball
this we see, and see each daie:
all things fixed ends do staie,
ends to first beginnings fall.
& that nought, how strong or strange
chaungeles doth endure alwaie,
but endureth fatall change.

Act III.

[*Enter*] M[ARCUS] ANTONIUS [*and*] LUCILIUS.

ANTONIUS *Lucill* sole comfort of my bitter case,
The only trust, the only hope I have,
In last despaire: Ah is not this the daie
That death should me of life and love bereave?
What waite I for that have no refuge left,
But am sole remnant of my fortune left?
All leave me, flie me: none, noe not of them
Which of my greatnes greatest good receiv'd,
Stands with my fall: they seeme as now asham'd
10   That heretofore they did me ought regard:
They draw them backe, shewing they folow'd me,
Not to partake my harms, but coozen me.
LUCILIUS *In this our world nothing is stedfast found,*
In vaine he hopes, who here his hopes doth ground.
ANTONIUS Yet nought afflicts me, nothing killes me so,
As that I so my *Cleopatra* see

Practise with *Caesar*, and to him transport
My flame, her love, more deare then life to me.

LUCILIUS Beleeve it not: Too high a heart she beares,
Too princely thoughts.

ANTONIUS   Too wise a head she weares   20
Too much enflam'd with greatnes, evermore
Gaping for our great Empires government.

LUCILIUS So long time you her constant love have tri'de.

ANTONIUS But still with me good fortune did abide.

LUCILIUS Her changed love what token makes you know?

ANTONIUS *Pelusium* lost, and *Actian* overthrow,
Both by her fraud: my well appointed fleet,
And trusty Souldiors in my quarrell arm'd,
Whome she, false she, in stede of my defence,
Came to perswade to yelde them to my foe: 30
Such honor *Thyre* done, such welcome given,
Their long close talkes I neither knew, nor would,
And trecherous wrong *Alexas* hath me donne,
Witnes too well her perjur'd love to me.
But you O Gods (if any faith regarde)
With sharpe revenge her faithlesse change reward.

LUCILIUS The dole she made upon our overthrow,
Her realme given up for refuge to our men,
Her poore attire when she devoutly kept
The solemne day of her nativitie,   40
Againe the cost and prodigall expence
Shew'd when she did your birth day celebrate,
Do plaine enough her heart unfained prove,
Equally toucht, you loving, as you love.

ANTONIUS Well, be her love to me or false, or true,
Once in my soule a cureles wound I feele.
I love: nay burne in fire of her love:
Each day, each night hir Image haunts my minde.
Her selfe my dreames: and still I tired am,
And still I am with burning pincers nipt.   50
Extreame my harme: yet sweeter to my sence
Then boiling Torch of jealous torments fire:
This griefe, nay rage, in me such sturre doth keepe,

And thornes me still, both when I wake and sleepe.

   Take *Caesar* conquest, take my goods, take he
Th'onor to be Lord of the earth alone,
My sonnes, my life bent headlong to mishapps:
No force, so not my *Cleopatra* take.
So foolish I, I cannot her forget,
Though better were I banisht her my thought.
Like to the sicke whose throte the feavers fire
Hath vehemently with thirstie drought enflam'd,
Drinkes still, albee the drinke he still desires
Be nothing else but fewell to his flame.
He cannot rule himselfe: his health's respect
Yealdeth to his distempered stomacks heate.

LUCILIUS Leave of this love, that thus renewes your woe.

ANTONIUS I do my best, but ah! can not do so.

LUCILIUS Thinke how you have so brave a captaine bene,
And now are by this vaine affection falne.

ANTONIUS The ceasles thought of my felicitie
Plunges me more in this adversitie.
For nothing so a man in ill torments,
As who to him his good state represents.
This makes my rack, my anguish, and my woe
Equall unto the hellish passions growe,
When I to mind my happie puisance call
Which erst I had by warlike conquest wonne,
And that good fortune which me never left,
Which hard disastre now hath me bereft.

   With terror tremble all the world I made
At my sole word, as Rushes in the streames
At waters will: I conquer'd Italie,
I conquer'd *Rome*, that nations so redoubt,
I bare (meane while besieging *Mutina*)
Two consuls armies for my ruine brought;
Bath'd in their bloud, by their deaths witnessing
My force and skill in matters Martiall.

   To wreake thy unkle, unkind *Caesar*, I
With bloud of enemies the bankes embru'd
Of stain'd *Enipeus*, hindring his course

Stopped with heapes of piled carcases:
When *Cassius* and *Brutus* ill betide
Marcht against us, by us twise put to flight,
But by my sole conduct: for all the time
Caesar hart-sicke with feare and feaver lay.
Who knowes it not? and how by every one
Fame of the fact was giv'n to me alone.

 There sprang the love, the never changing love,
Wherin my heart hath since to yours bene bound: 100
There was it, my *Lucill*, you *Brutus* sav'de,
And for your *Brutus Antony* you found.
Better my hap in gaining such a frend,
Then in subduing such an enimie.
Now former vertue dead doth me forsake,
Fortune engulfes me in extreame distresse:
She turnes from me her smiling countenance,
Casting on me mishapp upon mishapp.
Left and betraide of thousand thousand frends,
Once of my sute, but you *Lucill* are left,   110
Remaining to me stedfast as a tower
In holy love, in spite of fortunes blastes.
But if of any God my voice be heard,
And be not vainely scatt'red in the heav'ns,
Such goodnes shall not glorilesse be loste.
But comming ages still thereof shall boste.

LUCILIUS Men in their frendship ever should be one,
And never ought with fickle Fortune shake,
Which still removes, nor will, nor knowes the way,
Her rowling bowle in one sure state to staie.   120
Wherfore we ought as borrow'd things receive
The goods light she lends us to pay againe:
Not hold them sure, nor on them build our hopes
As on such goods as cannot faile, and fall:
But thinke againe, nothing is dureable,
Vertue except, our never failing host:
So bearing saile when favoring windes do blow,
As frowning tempests may us least dismaie
When they on us do fall: not over-glad

130   With good estate, nor over-griev'd with bad,
                    Resist mishap.
        ANTONIUS   Alas! it is too strong.
                    Mishappes oft times are by some comfort borne:
                    But these, ay me! whose weights oppresse my hart,
                    Too heavie lie, no hope can them relieve.
                        There rests no more, but that with cruell blade
                    For lingring death a hastie waie be made.
        LUCILIUS *Caesar*, as heire unto his fathers state,
                    So will his Fathers goodnes imitate,
                    To you ward: whome he know's allied in bloud,
140   Allied in mariage, ruling equally
                    Th'Empire with him, and with him making warre
                    Have purg'd the earth of *Caesars* murtherers.
                    You into portions parted have the world
                    Even like coheirs their heritages parte:
                    And now with one accord so many yeares
                    In quiet peace both have your charges rul'd.
        ANTONIUS Bloud and alliance nothing do prevaile
                    To coole the thirst of hote ambitious brests:
                    The sonne his Father hardly can endure,
150   Brother his brother, in one common Realme.
                    So fervent this desire to commaund:
                    Such jealousie it kindleth in our hearts,
                    Sooner will men permit another should
                    Love her they love, then weare the crowne they weare.
                    All lawes it breakes, turnes all things upside downe:
                    Amitie, kindred, nought so holy is
                    But it defiles. A monarchie to gaine
                    None cares which way, so he may it obtaine.
        LUCILIUS Suppose he Monarch be and that this world
160   No more acknowledg sundry Emperours,
                    That *Rome* him only feare, and that he joyne
                    The east with west, and both at once do rule:
                    Why should he not permitt you peaceablie
                    Discharg'd of charge and Empires dignitie,
                    Private to live reading *Philosophy*,
                    In learned *Greece*, *Spaine*, *Asia*, any land?

ANTONIUS Never will he his Empire thinke assur'de
　　While in this world *Marke Antony* shall live.
　　Sleepeles Suspicion, Pale distrust, cold feare
　　Alwaies to princes companie do beare　　　　　　170
　　Bred of reports: reports which night and day
　　Perpetuall guests from court go not away.
LUCILIUS He hath not slaine your brother *Lucius,*
　　Nor shortned hath the age of *Lepidus,*
　　Albeit both into his hands were falne,
　　And he with wrath against them both enflam'd.
　　Yet one, as Lord in quiet rest doth beare,
　　The greatest sway in great *Iberia*:
　　The other with his gentle Prince retaines
　　Of highest Priest the sacred dignitie.　　　　　　180
ANTONIUS He feares not them, their feeble force he knowes.
LUCILIUS He feares no vanquisht overfill'd with woes.
ANTONIUS Fortune may chaunge againe.
LUCILIUS　　　　　　　　　　　　A down-cast foe
　　Can hardly rise, which once is brought so low.
ANTONIUS All that I can is donne: for last assay
　　(When all means fail'd) I to entreaty fell,
　　(Ah coward creature!) whence againe repulst
　　Of combate I unto him proffer made:
　　Though he in prime, and I by feeble age
　　Mightily weakned both in force and skill.　　　　　190
　　Yet could not he his coward heart advaunce
　　Basely affraide to trie so praisefull chaunce.
　　This makes me plaine, makes me my selfe accuse,
　　Fortune in this her spitefull force doth use
　　'Gainst my gray hayres: in this unhappy I
　　Repine at heav'ns in my happes pittiles.
　　A man, a woman both in might and minde,
　　In *Mars his* schole who never lesson learn'd,
　　Should me repulse, chase, overthrow, destroy,
　　Me of such fame, bring to so low an ebbe?　　　　200
　　Alcides bloud, who from my infancy
　　With happy prowesse crowned have my praise,
　　Witnesse thou *Gaule* unus'd to servile yoke,

   Thou valiant *Spaine*, you fields of *Thessalie*,
   With millions of mourning cries bewail'd,
   Twise watred now with bloud of *Italie*.
LUCILIUS Witnes may *Afrique*, and of conquer'd world
   All fower quarters witnesses may be.
   For in what part of earth inhabited,
210   Hungry of praise have you not ensignes spred?
ANTONIUS Thou know'st rich *Aegipt* (*Aegipt* of my deedes
   Faire and foule subject) *Aegypt* ah! thou know'st
   How I behav'd me fighting for thy kinge,
   When I regainde him his rebellious Realme:
   Against his foes in battaile shewing force,
   And after fight in victory remorse.
    Yet if to bring my glory to the ground,
   Fortune had made me overthrowne by one
   Of greater force, of better skill then I:
220   One of those Captaines feared so of olde,
   Camill, *Marcellus*, worthy *Scipio*,
   This late great *Caesar*, honor of our state,
   Or that great *Pompei* aged growne in armes;
   That after harvest of a world of men
   Made in a hundred battailes, fights, assaults,
   My body thorow pearst with push of pike
   Had vomited my bloud, in bloud my life,
   In midd'st of millions, felowes in my fall:
   The lesse her wrong, the lesse should be my woe:
230   Nor she should paine, nor I complaine me so.
    No, no, wheras I should have died in armes,
   And vanquisht oft new armies should have arm'd,
   New battailes given, and rather lost with me
   All this whole world submitted unto me:
   A man who never saw enlaced pikes
   With bristled points against his stomake bent,
   Who feares the field, and hides him cowardly
   Dead at the very noise the souldiors make,
   His vertue, fraud, deceit, malicious guile,
240   His armes the arts that false *Ulisses* us'de,
   (Knowne at Modena, where the *Consuls* both

Death-wounded were, and wounded by his men
To get their armie, war with it to make
Against his faith, against his country soile.
Of *Lepidus*, which to his succours came,
To honor whome he was by dutie bound,
The Empire he usurpt: corrupting first
With baites and bribes the most part of his men)
Yet me hath overcome, and made his pray,
And state of *Rome* with me hath overcome.   250

    Strange! one disordred act at *Actium*
The earth subdu'de, my glory hath obscur'd.
For since, as one whome heavens wrath attaints,
With furie caught, and more then furious
Vex'd with my evills, I never more had care
My armies lost, or lost name to repaire:
I did no more resist.

LUCILIUS   All warres affaires,
But battailes most, dayly have their successe
Now good, now ill: and though that fortune have
Great force and power in every worldly thing,   260
Rule all, do all, have all things fast enchaind
Unto the circle of hir turning wheele:
Yet seemes it more then any practise else
She doth frequent *Bellonas* bloudy trade:
And that hir favour, wavering as the wind,
Hir greatest power therein doth oftnest shewe.
Whence growes, we dailie see, who in their youth
Gatt honor ther, do loose it in their age,
Vanquisht by some lesse warlike then themselves:
Whome yet a meaner man shall overthrowe.   270
Hir use is not to lend us still her hande,
But sometimes headlong backe againe to throwe,
When by hir favor she hath us extolld
Unto the topp of highest happines.

ANTONIUS Well ought I curse within my grieved soule,
Lamenting daie and night, this sencelesse love,
Whereby my faire entising foe entrap'd
My hedelesse *Reason*, could no more escape.

It was not fortunes ever chaunging face:
280 *It was not Destnies chaungles violence*
Forg'd my mishap. Alas! who doth not know
They make, nor marre nor anything can doe.
Fortune, which men so feare, adore, detest,
Is but a chaunce whose cause unknow'n doth rest,
Although oft times the cause is well perceiv'd,
But not th'effect the same that was conceiv'd.
Pleasure, nought else, the plague of this our life,
Our life which still a thousand plagues pursue,
Alone hath me this strange disastre spunne,
290 Falne from a souldior to a chamberer,
Careles of vertue, careles of all praise.
Nay, as the fatted swine in filthy mire
With glutted heart I wallowed in delights,
All thoughts of honor troden under foote.
So I me lost: for finding this sweet cupp
Pleasing my tast, unwise I drunke my fill,
And through the sweetnes of that poisons power
By steps I drave my former wits astraie.
I made my frends, offended, me forsake,
300 I holpe my foes against my selfe to rise.
I robd my subjects, and for followers
I saw my selfe beset with flatterers,
Mine idle armes faire wrought with spiders worke,
My scattred men without their ensignes strai'd:
Caesar meane while who never would have dar'de
To cope with me, me sodainely despis'de,
Tooke hart to fight, and hop'de for victorie
On one so gone, who glorie had forgone.

LUCILIUS Enchaunting pleasure, *Venus* sweete delights
310 Weaken our bodies, over-cloud our sprights,
Trouble our reason, from our hearts out chase
All holie vertues lodging in their place:
Like as the cunning fisher takes the fishe
By traitor baite whereby the hooke is hid:
So *Pleasure* serves to vice in steede of foode
To baite our soules thereon too liquorishe.

This poison deadly is alike to all,
But on great kings doth greatest outrage worke,
Taking the roiall scepters from their hands,
Thence forward to be by some stranger borne: 320
While that their people charg'd with heavie loades
Their flatt'rers pill, and suck their mary drie,
Not rul'd but left to great men as a pray,
While this fonde Prince himselfe in pleasures drowns
Who hears nought, sees nought, doth nought of a king
Seming himselfe against himselfe conspirde.
Then equall Justice wandreth banished,
And in her seat sitts greedie Tyrannie.
Confus'd disorder troubleth all estates,
Crimes without feare and outrages are done.   330
Then mutinous *Rebellion* shewes her face,
Now hid with this, and now with that pretence,
Provoking enimies, which on each side
Enter at ease, and make them Lords of all.
The hurtfull workes of pleasure here behold.

ANTONIUS The wolfe is not so hurtfull to the folde,
Frost to the grapes, to ripened frutes the raine:
As pleasure is to princes full of paine.

LUCILIUS There nedes no proofe, but by th'*Assirian* kinge,
On whom that Monster woefull wrack did bring.   340

ANTONIUS There nedes no proofe, but by unhappie I,
Who lost my empire, honor, life thereby.

LUCILIUS Yet hath this ill so much the greater force,
As scarcely any do against it stand:
No not the Demy-gods the olde world knew,
Who all subdu'de, could *Pleasures* power subdue.
   Great *Hercules*, *Hercules* once that was
Wonder of earth and heaven, matchles in might,
Who *Anteus*, *Lycus*, *Geryon* overcame,
Who drew from hell the triple-headed dogg,   350
Who *Hydra* kill'd, vanquishd *Achelous*,
Who heavens weight on his strong shoulders bare:
Did he not under *Pleasures* burthen bow?
Did he not Captive to this passion yelde,

When by his Captive, so he was inflam'd,
As now your selfe in *Cleopatra* burne?
Slept in hir lapp, hir bosome kist and kiste,
With base unseemely service bought her love,
Spinning at distaffe, and with sinewy hand
360   Winding on spindles threde, in maides attire?
His conqu'ring clubbe at rest on wal did hang:
His bow unstringd he bent not as he us'de:
Upon his shafts the weaving spiders spunne:
And his hard cloake the fretting mothes did pierce.
The monsters free and fearles all the time
Throughout the world the people did torment,
And more and more encreasing daie by daie
Scorn'd his weake heart become a mistresse play.

ANTONIUS   In onely this like *Hercules* am I,
370   In this I prove me of his lignage right:
In this himselfe, his deedes I shew in this:
In this, nought else, my ancestor he is.
   But goe we: die I must, and with brave end
Conclusion make of all foregoing harmes:
Die, die I must: I must a noble death,
A glorious death unto my succour call:
I must deface the shame of time abus'd,
I must adorne the wanton loves I us'de,
With some couragious act: that my last day
380   By mine owne hand my spots may wash away.
   Come deare *Lucill*: alas! why weepe you thus!
This mortall lot is common to us all.
We must all die, each doth in homage owe
Unto that God that shar'd the Realmes belowe.
Ah sigh no more: alas! appeace your woes,
For by your greife my griefe more eager growes.

                              [*Exeunt* ANTONIUS *and* LUCILIUS.]

CHORUS   Alas, with what tormenting fire
              Us martireth this blind desire
                 To stay our life from flieng!
390   How ceasleslie our minds doth rack,

How heavie lies upon our back
  This dastard feare of dieng!
Death rather healthfull succour gives,
Death rather all mishapps relieves
  That life upon us throweth:
And ever to us doth unclose
The dore whereby from curelesse woes
  Our weary soule out goeth.
What Goddesse else more milde then she
To burie all our paine can be,   400
  What remedie more pleasing?
Our pained hearts when dolor stings,
And nothing rest, or respite brings,
  What help have we more easing?
Hope which to us doth comfort give,
And doth our fainting harts revive,
  Hath not such force in anguish:
For promising a vaine reliefe
She oft us failes in midst of griefe,
  And helples lets us languish.   410
But Death who call on her at neede
Doth never with vaine semblant feed,
  But when them sorrow paineth,
So riddes their soules of all distresse
Whose heavie weight did them oppresse,
  That not one griefe remaineth.
Who feareles and with courage bolde
Can *Acherons* black face behold,
  Which muddie water beareth:
And crossing over in the way   420
Is not amaz'd at Perruque gray
  Olde rusty *Charon* weareth?
Who voide of dread can looke upon
The dreadfull shades that roame alone,
  On bankes where sound no voices:
Whome with hir fire-brands and her Snakes
No whit afraide *Alecto* makes,
  Nor triple-barking noises:

Who freely can himselfe dispose
Of that last hower which all must close,
   And leave this life at pleasure:
This noble freedome more esteemes,
And in his heart more precious deemes,
   Then crowne and kinglie treasure.
The waves which *Boreas* blasts turmoile
And cause with foaming furie boile,
   Make not his heart to tremble:
Nor brutish broile, when with strong head
A rebell people madly ledde
   Against their Lords assemble:
Nor fearefull face of Tirant wood,
Who breaths but threats, & drinks but bloud,
   No, nor the hand which thunder,
The hand of *Jove* which thunder beares,
And ribbs of rocks in sunder teares,
   Teares mountains sides in sunder:
Nor bloudy *Marses* butchering bands,
Whose lightnings desert laie the lands
   Whome dustie cloudes do cover:
From of whose armour sun-beames flie,
And under them make quaking lie
   The plaines wheron they hover:
Nor yet the cruell murth'ring blade
Warme in the moistie bowels made
   Of people pell-mell dieng
In some great Cittie put to sack,
By savage Tirant brought to wrack,
   At his colde mercie lieng.
How abject him, how base thinke I,
Who wanting courage can not dye
   When need him thereto calleth?
From whome the dagger drawne to kill
The cureles griefes that vexe him still
   For feare and faintnes falleth?
O *Antony* with thy deare mate
Both in misfortunes fortunate!

430

440

450

460

    Whose thoughts to death aspiring
Shall you protect from victors rage,
Who on each side doth you encage,
    To triumph much desiring.   470
That *Caesar* may you not offend
Nought else but death can you defend,
    Which his weake force derideth.
And all in this round earth contain'd,
Pow'rles on them whome once enchain'd
    Avernus prison hideth:
Where great *Psammetiques* ghost doth rest,
Not with infernall paine possest,
    But in sweete fields detained:
And olde *Amasis* soule likewise,   480
And all our famous *Ptolomies*
    That whilome on us raigned.

Act IV.

[*Enter*] CAESAR [*and*] AGRIPPA.
CAESAR You ever-living Gods which all things holde
    Within the power of your celestiall hands,
    By whome heate, colde, the thunder, and the wind,
    The properties of enterchaunging months
    Their course and being have; which do set downe
    Of Empires by your destinied decree
    The force, age, time, and subject to no chaunge
    Chaunge all, reserving nothing in one state:
    You have advaunst, as high as thundring heav'n
    The *Romaines* greatnes by *Bellonas* might: 10
    Maistring the world with fearefull violence,
    Making the world widdow of libertie.
    Yet at this day this proud exalted *Rome*
    Despoil'd, captiv'd, at one mans will doth bend:
    Her Empire mine, her life is in my hand,
    As Monarch I both world and *Rome* commaund;
    Do all, can all; foorth my commandment cast

Like thundring fire from one to other Pole
Equall to Jove: bestowing by my word
20 Happs and mishappes, as Fortunes King and Lord.
 No towne there is, but up my Image settes,
But sacrifice to me doth dayly make:
Whether where *Phoebus* joyne his morning steedes,
Or where the night them weary entertaines,
Or where the heat the *Garamante* doth scorch,
Or where the colde from *Boreas* breath is blowne:
All *Caesar* do both awe and honor beare,
And crowned Kings his verie name doth feare.
 Antony knowes it well, for whome not one
30 Of all the Princes all this earth do rule,
Armes against me: for all redoubt the power
Which heav'nly powers on earth have made me beare.
 Antony, he poore man with fire inflam'de
A womans beauties kindled in his heart,
Rose against me, who longer could not beare
My sisters wrong he did so ill intreat:
Seing her left while that his leud delights
Her husband with his *Cleopatra* tooke
In *Alexandria*, where both nights and daies
40 Their time they pass'd in nought but loves and plaies.
 All *Asias* forces into one he drewe,
And forth he set upon the azur'd waves
A thousand and a thousand Shipps, which fill'd
With Souldiors, pikes, with targets, arrowes, darts,
Made *Neptune* quake, and all the watry troupes
Of *Glauques*, and *Tritons* lodg'd at *Actium*,
But mightie Gods, who still the force withstand
Of him, who causeles doth another wrong,
In lesse then moments space redus'd to nought
50 All that proud power by Sea or land he brought.
AGRIPPA Presumptuous pride of high and hawtie sprite,
Voluptuous care of fond and foolish love,
Have justly wrought his wrack: who thought he helde
(By overweening) Fortune in his hand.
Of us he made no count, but as to play,

So feareles came our forces to assay.
   So sometimes fell to Sonnes of mother earth,
Which crawl'd to heav'n warre on the Gods to make,
Olymp on *Pelion*, *Ossa* on *Olymp*,
Pindus on *Ossa* loading by degrees: 60
That at hand-strokes with mightie clubs they might
On mossie rocks the Gods make tumble downe:
When mightie *Jove* with burning anger chaf'd,
Disbraind with him *Gyges* and *Briareus*,
Blunting his darts upon their brused bones.
For no one thing the Gods can lesse abide
In deedes of men, then Arrogance and pride.
And still the proud, which too much takes in hand,
Shall fowlest fall, where best he thinkes to stand.

CAESAR Right as some Pallace, or some stately tower,   70
Which over-lookes the neighbour buildings round
In scorning wise, and to the starres up growes,
Which in short time his owne weight overthrowes.
   What monstrous pride, nay what impietie
Incenst him onward to the Gods disgrace?
When his two children, *Cleopatras* bratts,
To *Phoebe* and her brother he compar'd,
Latonas race, causing them to be call'd
The Sunne and Moone? Is not this follie right
And is not this the Gods to make his foes?   80
And is not this himselfe to worke his woes?

AGRIPPA In like proud sort he causd his hed to leese
The Jewish king *Antigonus*, to have
His Realme for balme, that *Cleopatra* lov'd,
As though on him he had some treason prov'd.

CAESAR *Lidia* to her, and *Siria* he gave,
Cyprus of golde, *Arabia* rich of smelles:
And to his children more *Cilicia*,
Parth's, Medes, Armenia, Phoenicia:
The kings of kings proclaming them to be,   90
By his owne word, as by a sound decree.

AGRIPPA What? Robbing his owne country of her due?
Triumph'd he not in *Alexandria*,

       Of *Artabasus* the *Armenian* King,

       Who yeelded on his perjur'd word to him?

CAESAR Nay, never *Rome* more injuries receiv'd,

       Since thou, o *Romulus*, by flight of birds

       With happy hand the *Romain* walles did'st build,

       Then *Antonyes* fond loves to it hath done.

100   Nor ever warre more holie, nor more just,

       Nor undertaken with more hard constraint,

       Then is this warre: which were it not, our state

       Within small time all dignitie should loose:

       Though I lament (thou Sunne my witnes art,

       And thou great *Jove*) that it so deadly proves:

       That *Romaine* bloud should in such plentie flowe,

       Watring the fields and pastures where we go.

       What *Carthage* in olde hatred obstinate,

       What *Gaule* still barking at our rising state,

110   What rebell *Samnite*, what fierce *Pyrrhus* power,

       What cruell *Mithridate*, what *Parth* hath wrought

       Such woe to *Rome*? whose common wealth he had,

       (Had he bene victor) into *Egypt* brought.

AGRIPPA Surely the Gods, which have this cittie built

       Steadfast to stand as long as time endures,

       Which keepe the Capitoll, of us take care,

       And care will take of those shall after come,

       Have made you victor, that you might redresse

       Their honor growne by passed mischieves lesse.

120 CAESAR The seelie man when all the Greekish Sea

       His fleete had hid, in hope me sure to drowne,

       Me battaile gave: where fortune in my stede,

       Repulsing him his forces disaraied.

       Himselfe tooke flight, soone as his love he saw

       All wanne through feare with full sailes flie away.

       His men, though lost, whome none did now direct,

       With courage fought, fast grappled shipp with shipp,

       Charging, resisting, as their oares would serve,

       With darts, with swords, with pikes, with fiery flames.

130   So that the darkned night her starrie vaile

       Upon the bloudy sea had over-spred,

Whilst yet they held: and hardly, hardly then
They fell to flieng on the wavie plaine,
All full of soldiors overwhelm'd with waves.
The aire throughout with cries & grones did sound:
The sea did blush with bloud: the neighbour shores
Groned, so they with shipwracks pestred were,
And floting bodies left for pleasing foode
To birds, and beasts, and fishes of the sea.
You know it well *Agrippa*.

AGRIPPA   Mete it was   140
The *Romain* Empire so should ruled be,
As heav'n is rul'd: which turning over us,
All under things by his example turnes.
Now as of heav'n one onely Lord we know:
One onely Lord should rule this earth below.
When one selfe pow're is common made to two
Their duties they nor suffer will, nor doe.
In quarell still, in doubt, in hate, in feare;
Meanewhile the people all the smart do beare.

CAESAR Then to the end none, while my daies endure,   150
Seeking to raise himselfe may succours find,
We must with bloud marke this our victory,
For just example to all memorie
Murther we must, until not one we leave,
Which may hereafter us of rest bereave.

AGRIPPA Marke it with murthers? Who of that can like?

CAESAR Murthers must use, who doth assurance seeke.

AGRIPPA Assurance call you enemies to make?

CAESAR I make no such, but such away I take.

AGRIPPA Nothing so much as rigour doth displease.   160

CAESAR Nothing so much doth make me live at ease.

AGRIPPA What ease to him that feared is of all?

CAESAR Feared to be, and see his foes to fall.

AGRIPPA Commonly feare doth brede and nourish hate.

CAESAR Hate without pow'r comes commonly too late.

AGRIPPA A feared Prince hath oft his death desir'd.

CAESAR A Prince not fear'd hath oft his wrong conspir'd.

AGRIPPA No guard so sure, no forte so strong doth prove,

No such defence, as is the peoples love.

170 CAESAR Nought more unsure, more weak, more like the winde,
Then *Peoples* favour still to change enclinde.

AGRIPPA Good Gods! what love to gratious prince men beare!

CAESAR What honor to the Prince that is severe!

AGRIPPA Nought more divine then is *Benignitie.*

CAESAR Nought likes the *Gods* as doth *Severity.*

AGRIPPA *Gods* all forgive.

CAESAR   On faults they paines do lay.

AGRIPPA And give their goods.

CAESAR   Oft times they take away.

AGRIPPA They wreake them not, o *Caesar*, at each time
That by our sinnes they are to wrath provok'd.

180 Neither must you (beleeve, I humblie praie)
Your victorie with crueltie defile.
The Gods it gave, it must not be abus'd,
But to the good of all men mildely us'd,
And they be thank'd that having giv'n you grace
To raigne alone, and rule this earthly masse,
They may hence-forward hold it still in rest,
All scattered power united in one brest.

CAESAR But what is he that breathles comes so fast,
Approching us, and going in such hast?

190 AGRIPPA He seemes affraid: and under his arme I
(But much I erre) a bloudy sword espie.

CAESAR I long to understand what it may be.

AGRIPPA He hither comes: it's best we stay and see.
    [*Enter* DIRCETUS.]

DIRCETUS What good God now my voice will reenforce,
That tell I may to rocks, and hilles, and woods,
To waves of sea, which dash upon the shore,
To earth, to heaven, the woefull newes I bring?

AGRIPPA What sodaine chance thee towards us hath broght?

DIRCETUS A lamentable chance. O wrath of heav'ns!
O Gods too pittiles!

200 CAESAR   What monstrous hap
Wilt thou recount?

DIRCETUS   Alas, too hard mishap!

When I but dreame of what mine eies beheld,
My hart doth freeze, my limmes do quivering quake,
I senceles stand, my brest with tempest tost
Killes in my throte my words, ere fully borne.
Dead, dead he is: be sure of what I say,
This murthering sword hath made the man away.

CAESAR Alas my heart doth cleave, pittie me rackes,
My brest doth pant to heare this dolefull tale.
Is *Antony* then dead? to death, alas!   210
I am the cause despaire him so compelld.
But soldior, of his death the manner showe,
And how he did this living light forgoe.

DIRCETUS When *Antony* no hope remaining saw
How warre he might, or how agreement make,
Saw him betraid by all his men of warre
In every fight as well by sea, as land;
That not content to yeeld them to their foes
They also came against himselfe to fight:
Alone in court he gan himselfe torment,   220
Accuse the Queene, himselfe of hir lament,
Call'd hir untrue and traitresse, as who sought
To yeeld him up she could no more defend:
That in the harmes which for hir sake he bare,
As in his blisfull state, she might not share.

  But she againe, who much his fury fear'd,
Gat to the tombes, darke horror's dwelling place:
Made lock the doores, and pull the hearses downe.
Then fell she wretched, with hir selfe to fight.
A thousand plaints, a thousand sobbes she cast   230
From hir weake brest which to the bones was torne.
Of women hir the most unhappy call'd,
Who by hir love, hir woefull love, had lost
Hir realme, hir life, and more, the love of him
Who while he was, was all hir woes support.
But that she faultles was she did invoke
For witnes heav'n, and aire, and earth, and sea.
Then sent him word, she was no more alive,
But lay inclosed dead within her tombe.

240   This he beleev'd; and fell to sigh and grone,
     And crost his armes, then thus began to mone.
  CAESAR Poore hopeles man!
  DIRCETUS   What dost thou more attend
     Ah *Antony*! why dost thou death deferre,
     Since *Fortune* thy professed enimie,
     Hath made to die, who only made thee live?
     Soone as with sighes hee had these words up clos'd,
     His armor he unlaste and cast it off,
     Then all disarm'd he thus againe did say:
     My Queene, my heart, the griefe that now I feele,
250   Is not that I your eies, my Sunne, do loose,
     For soone againe one tombe shall us conjoyne:
     I grieve, whome men so valorous did deeme,
     Should now, then you, of lesser valor seeme.
      So said, forthwith he *Eros* to him call'd,
     Eros his man; summond him on his faith
     To kill him at his nede. He tooke the sword,
     And at that instant stab'd therwith his breast,
     And ending life fell dead before his feete.
     O *Eros* thankes (quoth *Antony*) for this
260   Most noble acte, who pow'rles me to kill,
     On thee hast done, what I on mee should do.
      Of speaking thus he scarsce had made an end,
     And taken up the bloudy sword from ground,
     But he his bodie piers'd; and of red bloud
     A gushing fountaine all the chamber fill'd.
     He staggred at the blow, his face grew pale,
     And on a couche all feeble downe he fell,
     Swounding with anguish: deadly cold him tooke,
     As if his soule had then his lodging left.
270   But he reviv'd, and marking all our eies
     Bathed in teares, and how our breasts we beate
     For pittie, anguish, and for bitter griefe,
     To see him plong'd in extreame wretchednes,
     He prai'd us all to haste his lingring death:
     But no man willing, each himselfe withdrew.
     Then fell he new to cry and vexe himselfe,

Untill a man from *Cleopatra* came,
Who said from hir he had commaundement
To bring him to hir to the monument.

    The poore soule at these words even rapt with joy   280
Knowing she liv'd, prai'd us him to convey
Unto his Lady. Then upon our armes
We bare him to the Tombe, but entred not.
For she who feared captive to be made,
And that she should to *Rome* in triumph goe,
Kept close the gate, but from a window high
Cast downe a corde, wherein he was impackt.
Then by hir womens help the corps she rais'd,
And by strong armes into hir window drew.

    So pittifull a sight was never seene.   290
Little and little *Antony* was pull'd,
Now breathing death: his beard was all unkempt,
His face and brest al bathed in his bloud.
So hideous yet, and dieng as he was,
His eies half-clos'd uppon the Queene he cast:
Held up his hands, and holpe himselfe to raise,
But still with weaknes back his bodie fell.
The miserable ladie with moist eies,
With haire which careles on hir forhead hong,
With brest which blowes had bloudily benumb'd,   300
With stooping head, and body down-ward bent,
Enlast hir in the corde, and with all force
This life-dead man couragiously uprais'd.
The bloud with paine into hir face did flowe,
Hir sinewes stiff, her selfe did breathles grow.

    The people which beneath in flocks beheld,
Assisted her with gesture, speach, desire:
Cride and incourag'd her, and in their soules
Did sweate, and labor, no whit lesse then she,
Who never tir'd in labor, held so long   310
Helpt by her women, and hir constant heart,
That *Antony* was drawne into the tombe,
And there (I thinke) of dead augments the summe.

    The cittie all to teares and sighes is turn'd,

To plaints and outcries horrible to heare:
Men, women, children, hoary-headed age
Do all pell mell in house and streete lament,
Scratching their faces, tearing of their haire,
Wringing their hands, and martyring their brests:
320   Extreame their dole: and greater misery
In sacked townes can hardlie ever be.
Not if the fire had scal'de the highest towers:
That all things were of force and murther full;
That in the streets the bloud in rivers stream'd.
The sonne his sire saw in his bosome slaine,
The sire his sonne: the husband reft of breath
In his wives armes, who furious runnes to death.
    Now my brest wounded with their piteouse plaints
I left their towne, and tooke with me this sworde,
330   Which I tooke up at what time *Antony*
Was from his chamber caried to the tombe:
And brought it you, to make his death more plaine,
And that thereby my words may credite gaine.

CAESAR Ah Gods what cruell hap! poore *Antony*,
Alas hast thou this sword so long time borne
Against thy foe, that in the end it should
Of thee his Lord the cursed murth'rer be?
O *Death* how I bewaile thee! we (alas!)
So many warres have ended, brothers, frends,
340   Companions, coozens, equalls in estate:
And must it now to kill thee be my fate?

AGRIPPA Why trouble you your selfe with bootles griefe?
For *Antony* why spend you teares in vaine?
Why darken you with dole your victory?
Me seemes your selfe your glory do envie.
Enter the towne, give thanks unto the Gods.

CAESAR I cannot but his tearefull chaunce lament,
Although not I, but his owne pride the cause,
And unchast love of this *Aegiptian*.

350 AGRIPPA But best we sought into the tombe to get,
Lest she consume in this amazed case
So much rich treasure, with which happely

Despaire in death may make hir feede the fire:
Suffring the flames hir Jewells to deface,
You to defraud, hir funerall to grace.
Sende then to hir, and let some meane be us'd
With some devise so hold her still alive,
Some faire large promises: and let them marke
Whither they may by some fine cunning slight
Enter the tombes.

CAESAR   Let *Proculeius* goe,   360
And feede with hope hir soule disconsolate.
Assure hir soe, that we may wholy get
Into our hands hir treasure and her selfe.
For this of all things most I do desire
To keepe her safe until our going hence:
That by hir presence beautified may be
The glorious triumph *Rome* prepares for me.

                    [*Exeunt* CAESAR, AGRIPPA *and* DIRCETUS.]
        [*Enter* CHORUS OF ROMAINE SOULDIORS.]

CHORUS OF ROMAINE SOULDIORS Shall ever civile bate
                    gnaw and devour our state?
                    shall never we this blade,   370
                    our bloud hath bloudy made,
                    lay downe? these armes downe lay
                    as robes we weare alway?
                    but as from age to age
                    so passe from rage to rage?
                Our hands shall we not rest
                    to bath in our owne brest?
                    and shall thick in each land
                    our wretched trophees stand,
                    to tell posteritie,   380
                    what madd Impietie
                    our stonie stomacks led
                    against the place us bred?
                Then still must heaven view
                    the plagues that us pursue,

and everywher descrie
heaps of us scattred lie,
making the stranger plaines
fat with our bleeding reines,
390   proud that on them their grave
so many legions have.
And with our fleshes still
Neptune his fishes fill
and dronke with bloud from blue
the sea take blushing hue:
as juice of *Tyrian* shell,
when clarified well
to wolle of finest fields
a purple glosse it yeeldes.
400   But since the rule of *Rome*,
to one mans hand is come,
who governes without mate
hir now united state,
late jointly rulde by three
envieng mutuallie,
whose triple yoke much woe
on *Latines* necks did throwe:
I hope the cause of jarre,
and of this bloudie warre,
410   and deadly discord gone
by what wc last have done:
our banks shall cherish now
the branchie pale-hew'd bow
of *Olive*, *Pallas* praise,
in stede of barraine baies.
And that his temple dore,
which bloudy *Mars* before
held open, now at last
olde *Janus* shall make fast:
420   and rust the sword consume,
and, spoild of waving plume,
the useles morion shall
on crooke hang by the wall.

At least if warre returne
　　it shall not here sojourne,
　　to kill us with those armes
　　were forg'd for others harmes:
　　but have their points addrest,
　　against the *Germaines* brest,
　　the *Parthians* fayned flight,　　　　　　430
　　the *Biscaines* martiall might.
Olde Memory doth there
　　painted on forehead weare
　　our Fathers praise: thence torne
　　our triumphs baies have worne:
　　therby our matchles *Rome*
　　whilome of Shepeheards come
　　rais'd to this greatnes stands,
　　the Queene of forraine lands.
Which now even seemes to face　　　　　　440
　　the heav'ns, her glories place:
　　nought resting under skies
　　that dares affront her eies.
　　So that she needes but feare
　　the weapons *Jove* doth beare,
　　who angry at one blowe
　　may her quite overthrowe.　　　　　[*Exeunt.*]

Act V.

[*Enter*] CLEOPATRA, EUPHRON, CHILDREN OF
　　CLEOPATRA, CHARMION [*and*] ERAS.
CLEOPATRA O cruell fortune! o accursed lot!
　O plaguy love! o most detested brand!
　O wretched joyes! o beauties miserable!
　O deadly state! o deadly roialtie!
　O hatefull life! o Queene most lamentable!
　O *Antony* by my faulte buriable!
　O hellish worke of heav'n! alas! the wrath
　Of all the Gods at once on us is falne.

Unhappie Queene! o would I in this world
10 The wandring light of day had never seene?
Alas! of mine the plague and poison I
The crowne have lost my ancestors me left,
This Realme I have to strangers subject made,
And robd my children of their heritage.

   Yet this is nought (alas!) unto the price
Of you deare husband, whome my snares intrap'd:
Of you, whome I have plagu'd, whom I have made
With bloudy hand a guest of mouldie tombe:
Of you, whome I destroied, of you, deare Lord,
20 Whome I of Empire, honor, life have spoil'd.

   O hurtfull woman! and can I yet live,
Yet longer live in this Ghost-haunted tombe?
Can I yet breathe! can yet in such annoy,
Yet can my soule within this body dwell?
O Sisters you that spin the thredes of death!
O *Styx*! o *Plegethon*! you brookes of hell!
O Impes of *Night*!

EUPHRON   Live for your childrens sake:
Let not your death of kingdome them deprive.
Alas what shall they do? who will have care?
30 Who will preserve this royall race of yours?
Who pittie take? even now me seemes I see
These little soules to servile bondage falne,
And borne in triumph.

CLEOPATRA   Ah most miserable!

EUPHRON Their tender armes with cursed cord fast bound
At their weake backs.

CLEOPATRA   Ah Gods what pitty more!

EUPHRON Their seely necks to ground with weaknes bend.

CLEOPATRA Never on us, good Gods, such mischiefe send.

EUPHRON And pointed at with fingers as they go.

CLEOPATRA Rather a thousand deaths.

EUPHRON   Lastly his knife
40 Some cruell cative in their bloud embrue.

CLEOPATRA Ah my heart breaks. By shady banks of hell,
By fields whereon the lonely Ghosts do treade,

By my soule, and the soule of *Antony*
I you besech, *Euphron*, of them have care.
Be their good Father, let your wisedome lett
That they fall not into this Tyrants hands.
Rather conduct them where their freezed locks
Black *Aethiops* to neighbour Sunne do shew;
On wavie *Ocean* at the waters will;
On barraine cliffes of snowie *Caucasus*;   50
To Tigers swift, to Lions, and to Beares;
And rather, rather unto every coaste,
To ev'ry land and sea: for nought I feare
As rage of him, whose thirst no bloud can quench.

    Adieu deare children, children deare adieu:
Good *Isis* you to place of safety guide,
Farre from our foes, where you your lives may leade
In free estate devoid of servile dread.

    Remember not, my children, you were borne
Of such a Princely race: remember not   60
So many brave Kings which have *Egipt* rul'de
In right descent your ancestors have beene:
That this great *Antony* your father was,
Hercules bloud, and more then he in praise.
For your high courage such remembrance will,
Seing your fall with burning rages fill.

    Who knowes if that your hands false *Destinie*
The Scepters promis'd of imperious *Rome*,
In stede of them shall crooked shepehookes beare,
Needles or forkes, or guide the carte, or plough?   70
Ah learne t'endure: your birth and high estate
Forget, my babes, and bend to force of fate.

    Farwell, my babes, farwell my heart is clos'd,
With pittie and paine, my selfe with death enclos'd,
My breath doth faile. Farwell for evermore,
Your Sire and me you shall see never more.
Farwell sweet care, farwell.

CHILDREN   Madame Adieu.

CLEOPATRA Ah this voice killes me. Ah good Gods! I swound.
    I can no more, I die.

ERAS   Madame, alas!

80   And will you yeld to woe? Ah speake to us.

EUPHRON   Come Children.

CHILDREN   We come.

EUPHRON   Follow we our chance.

    The Gods shall guide us.

                        [*Exeunt* EUPHRON *and* THE CHILDREN.]

CHARMION   O too cruell lot!

    O too hard chaunce! Sister what shall we do,

    What shall we do, alas! if murthring darte

    Of death arrive while that in slumbring swound

    Halfe dead she lie with anguish overgone?

ERAS   Her face is frozen.

CHARMION   Madame for Gods love

    Leave us not thus: bid us yet first farwell.

    Alas! wepe over *Antony*: Let not

90   His bodie be without due rites entomb'd.

CLEOPATRA   Ah, ah.

CHARMION   Madame.

CLEOPATRA   Ay me!

CHARMION   How fainte she is!

CLEOPATRA   My Sisters, holde me up. How wretched I,

    How cursed am: and was there ever one

    By Fortunes hate into more dolours throwne?

        Ah, weeping *Niobe*, although thy heart

    Beholds it selfe enwrap'd in causefull woe

    For thy dead children, that a sencelesse rocke

    With griefe become, on *Sipylus* thou stand'st

    In endles teares: yet didst thou never feele

100   The weights of griefe that on my heart do lie.

    Thy Children thou, mine I poore soule have lost,

    And lost their Father, more then them I waile,

    Lost this faire realme; yet me the heavens wrath

    Into a stone not yet transformed hath.

        Phaetons sisters, daughters of the Sunne,

    Which waile your brother falne into the streames

    Of stately *Po*: the Gods upon the bankes

    Your bodies to banke-loving Alders turn'd.

For me, I sigh, I ceasles wepe, and waile,
And heaven pittiles laughes at my woe,   110
Revives, renewes it still: and in the ende
(Oh cruelty!) doth death for comfort lend.
   Die *Cleopatra* then, no longer stay
From *Antony*, who thee at *Styx* attends:
Go joyne thy Ghost with his, and sob no more
Without his love within these tombes enclos'd.

ERAS Alas! yet let us wepe, lest sodaine death
From him our teares, and those last duties take
Unto his tombe we owe.

CHARMION   Ah let us wepe
While moisture lasts, then die before his feete.   120

CLEOPATRA Who furnish will mine eies with streaming teares
My boiling anguish worthily to waile,
Waile thee *Antony*, *Antony* my heart?
Alas, how much I weeping liquor want!
Yet have mine eies quite drawne their Condits drie
By long beweeping my disastred harmes.
Now reason is that from my side they sucke
First vitall moisture, then the vitall bloud.
Then let the bloud from my sad eies outflowe,
And smoking yet with thine in mixture grow.   130
Moist it, and heat it newe, and never stop,
All watring thee, while yet remaines one drop.

CHARMION *Antony* take our teares: this is the last
Of all the duties we to thee can yelde,
Before we die.

ERAS   These sacred obsequies
Take *Antony*, and take them in good parte.

CLEOPATRA O Goddesse thou whom *Cyprus* doth adore,
Venus of *Paphos*, bent to worke us harme
For olde *Iulus* broode, if thou take care
Of *Caesar*, why of us tak'st thou no care?   140
Antony did descend, as well as he,
From thine owne Sonne by long enchained line:
And might have rul'd by one and selfe same fate,
True *Trojan* bloud, the stately *Romain* state.

Antony, poore *Antony*, my deare soule,
Now but a blocke, the bootie of a tombe,
Thy life thy heat is lost, thy coullour gone,
And hideous palenes on thy face hath seaz'd.
Thy eies, two Sunnes, the lodging place of love,

150   Which yet for tents to warlike *Mars* did serve,
Lock'd up in lidds (as faire daies cherefull light
Which darkeness flies) do winking hide in night.
   Antony by our true loves I thee beseeche,
And by our hearts sweete sparks have set on fire,
Our holy mariage, and the tender ruthe
Of our deare babes, knot of our amitie:
My dolefull voice they eare let entertaine,
And take me with thee to the hellish plaine,
Thy wife, thy frend: heare *Antony*, o heare

160   My sobbing sighes, if here thou be, or there.
   Lived thus long, the winged race of yeares
Ended I have as *Destinie* decreed,
Flourish'd and raign'd, and taken just revenge
Of him who me both hated and despisde.
Happie, alas too happie: if of *Rome*
Only the fleete had hither never come.
And now of me an Image great shall goe
Under the earth to bury there my woe.
What say I? where am I? o *Cleopatra*,

170   Poore *Cleopatra*, griefe thy reason reaves.
No, no, most happie in this happles case,
To die with thee, and dieng thee embrace:
My bodie joynde with thine, my mouth with thine,
My mouth, whose moisture burning sighes have dried
To be in one selfe tombe, and one selfe chest,
And wrapt with thee in one selfe sheete to rest.
   The sharpest torment in my heart I feele
Is that I stay from thee, my heart, this while.
Die will I straight now, now streight will I die,

180   And streight with thee a wandring shade will be,
Under the *Cypres* trees thou haunt'st alone,
Where brookes of hell do falling seeme to mone.

But yet I stay, and yet thee overlive,
That ere I die due rites I may thee give.
   A thousand sobbes I from my brest will teare,
With thousand plaints thy funeralls adorne:
My haire shall serve for thy oblations,
My boiling teares for thy effusions,
Mine eies thy fire: for out of them the flame
(Which burnt thy heart on me enamour'd) came.   190
   Weepe my companions, weepe, and from your eies
Raine downe on him of teares a brinish streame.
Mine can no more, consumed by the coales
Which from my brest, as from a furnace rise.
Martir your breasts with multiplied blowes,
With violent hands teare of your hanging haire,
Outrage your face: alas! why should we seeke
(Since now we die) our beauties more to keepe?
   I spent in teares, not able more to spende,
But kisse him now, what rests me more to doe?   200
Then let me kisse you, you faire eies, my light,
Front seat of honor, face most fierce, most faire!
O neck, o armes, o hands, o breast where death
(O mischiefe) comes to choake up vitall breath.
A thousand kisses, thousand thousand more
Let you my mouth for honors farewell give:
That in this office weake my limmes may growe,
Fainting on you, and forth my soule may flow.

The Tragedie of Mariam

BY

ELIZABETH CARY

TO DIANAES

EARTHLIE DEPUTESSE,

and my worthy Sister, Mistris Elizabeth Carye.

When cheerful *Phoebus* his full course hath run,
His sisters fainter beames our harts doth cheere:
So your faire Brother is to mee the Sunne,
And you his Sister as my Moone appeere.

You are my next belov'd, my second Friend,
For when my *Phoebus* absence makes it Night,
Whilst to th'*Antipodes* his beames do bend,
From you my *Phoebe*, shines my second Light.

Hee like to *SOL*, cleare-sighted, constant, free,
You *LUNA*-like, unspotted, chast, divine: 10
Hee shone on *Sicily*, you destin'd bee,
T'illumine the now obscurde *Palestine*.
My first was consecrated to *Apollo*,
My second to *DIANA* now shall follow.

E. C.

The names of the Speakers.

HEROD, *King of Judea.*
DORIS, *his first Wife.*
MARIAM, *his second Wife.*
SALOME, *Herods Sister.*
ANTIPATER, *his sonne by Doris.*
ALEXANDRA, *Mariams mother.*
SILLEUS, *Prince of Arabia.*
CONSTABARUS, *husband to Salome.*
PHAERORAS, *Herods Brother.*
GRAPHINA, *his Love.*
BABUS FIRST SONNE.
BABUS SECOND SONNE.
ANNANELL, *the high Priest.*
SOHEMUS, *a Counsellor to Herod.*
NUNTIO.
BU[TLER], *another Messenger.*
CHORUS, *a Companie of Jewes.*
[SILLEUS' MAN.]
[SOLDIERS.]

The Argument

Herod the sonne of *Antipater* (an *Idumean*,) having crept by the favor of the *Romanes*, into the Jewish Monarchie, married *Mariam* the daughter of *Hircanus*, the rightfull *King and Priest*, and for her (besides her high blood, being of singular beautie) hee reputiated *Doris*, his former Wife, by whome hee had Children.

This *Mariam* had a Brother called *Aristobolus*, and next him and *Hircanus* his Graund-father, *Herod* in his Wives right had the best title. Therefore to remoove them, he charged the first with treason: and put him to death; and drowned the second under colour of sport. *Alexandra*, Daughter to the one, and Mother to the other, accused   10 him for their deaths before *Anthony*.

So when hee was forc'te to goe answere this Accusation at *Rome*, he left the custodie of his wife to *Josephus* his Uncle, that had married his Sister *Salome*, and out of a violent affection (unwilling any should enjoy her after him) hee gave strict and private commaundement, that if hee were slaine, shee should be put to death. But he returned with much honour, yet found his Wife extreamely discontented, to whom *Josophus* had (meaning it for the best, to prove *Herod* loved her) revealed his charge.

So by *Salomes* accusation hee put *Josephus* to death, but was reconciled   20 to *Mariam*, who still bare the death of her Friends exceeding hardly.

In this meane time *Herod* was againe necessarily to revisite *Rome*, for *Caesar* having overthrowne *Anthony* his great friend, was likely to make an alteration of his Fortune.

In his absence, newes came to *Jerusalem* that *Caesar* had put him to death, their willingnes it should be so, together with the likelyhood, gave this Rumor so good credit, as *Sohemus* that had suceeded *Josephus* charge, succeeded him likewise in revealing it. So at *Herods* returne which was speedy and unexpected, he found *Mariam* so farre from joye, that she shewed apparant signes of sorrow. Hee still desiring to   30 winne her to a better humour, she being very unable to conceale her passion, fell to upbraiding him with her Brothers death. As they were thus debating, came in a fellow with a Cuppe of Wine, who hired by *Salome*, saide first, it was a Love potion, which *Mariam* desired to deliver to the King: but afterwards he affirmed that it was a poyson, and that *Sohemus* had tolde her somewhat, which procured the vehement hate in her.

The King hearing this, more moved with Jealousie of *Sohemus*, then with this intent of poyson, sent her away, and presently after by the instigation of *Salome*, she was beheaded. Which rashnes was afterward punished in him, with an intollerable and almost Frantike passion for her death.

Act I. Scene I

MARIAM *sola*.

MARIAM How oft have I with publike voyce runne on?
   To censure *Romes* last *Hero* for deceit:
   Because he wept when *Pompeis* life was gone,
   Yet when he liv'd, hee thought his Name too great.
   But now Í doe recant, and *Roman* Lord
   Excuse too rash a judgement in a woman:
   My Sexe pleads pardon, pardon then afford,
   Mistaking is with us, but too too common.
   Now doe I finde by selfe Experience taught,
   One Object yeelds both griefe and joy:
   You wept indeed, when on his worth you thought,
   But joyd that slaughter did your Foe destroy.
   So at his death your Eyes true droppes did raine,
   Whom dead, you did not wish alive againe.
   When *Herod* liv'd, that now is done to death,
   Oft have I wisht that I from him were free:
   Oft have I wisht that he might lose his breath,
   Oft have I wisht his Carkas dead to see.
   Then Rage and Scorne had put my love to flight,
   That Love which once on him was firmely set:
   Hate hid his true affection from my sight,
   And kept my heart from paying him his debt.
   And blame me not, for *Herods* Jealousie
   Had power even constancie it selfe to change:
   For hee by barring me from libertie,
   To shunne my ranging, taught me first to range.

But yet too chast a Scholler was my hart,
To learne to love another then my Lord:
To leave his Love, my lessons former part,
I quickly learn'd, the other I abhord.   30
But now his death to memorie doth call,
The tender love, that he to *Mariam* bare:
And mine to him, this makes those rivers fall,
Which by an other thought unmoistned are.
For *Aristobolus* the lovlyest youth
That ever did in Angels shape appeare:
The cruell *Herod* was not mov'd to ruth,
Then why grieves *Mariam Herods* death to heare?
Why joy I not the tongue no more shall speake,
That yeelded forth my brothers latest dome: 40
Both youth and beautie might thy furie breake,
And both in him did ill befit a Tombe.
And worthy Grandsire ill did he requite,
His high Assent alone by thee procur'd,
Except he murdred thee to free the spright
Which still he thought on earth too long immur'd.
How happie was it that *Sohemus* mind
Was mov'd to pittie my distrest estate?
Might *Herods* life a trustie servant finde,
My death to his had bene unseparate.   50
These thoughts have power, his death to make me beare,
Nay more, to wish the newes may firmely hold:
Yet cannot this repulse some falling teare,
That will against my will some griefe unfold.
And more I owe him for his love to me,
The deepest love that ever yet was seene:
Yet had I rather much a milke-maide bee,
Then be the Monarke of *Judeas* Queene.
It was for nought but love, he wisht his end
Might to my death, but the vaunt-currier prove: 60
But I had rather still be foe then friend,
To him that saves for hate, and kills for love.

Hard-hearted *Mariam*, at thy discontent,
What flouds of teares have drencht his manly face?
How canst thou then so faintly now lament,
Thy truest lovers death, a deaths disgrace:
I now mine eyes you do begin to right
The wrongs of your admirer. And my Lord,
Long since you should have put your smiles to flight,
70   Ill doth a widowed eye with joy accord.
Why now me thinkes the love I bare him then,
When virgin freedome left me unrestraind:
Doth to my heart begin to creepe agen,
My passion now is far from being faind.
But teares flie backe, and hide you in your bankes,
You must not be to *Alexandra* seene:
For if my mone be spide, but little thankes
Shall *Mariam* have, from that incensed Queene.

Act I. Scene 2

[*Enter*] ALEXANDRA.

ALEXANDRA What meanes these teares? my *Mariam* doth mistake,
The newes we heard did tell the *Tyrants* end:
What weepst thou for thy brothers murthers sake,
Will ever wight a teare for *Herod* spend?
My curse pursue his breathles trunke and spirit,
Base *Edomite* the damned *Esaus* heire:
Must he ere *Jacobs* child the crowne inherit?
Must he vile wretch be set in *Davids* chaire?
No *Davids* soule within the bosome plac'te,
10   Of our forefather *Abram* was asham'd:
To see his seat with such a toade disgrac'te,
That seat that hath by *Judas* race bene famed.
Thou fatall enemie to royall blood,
Did not the murther of my boy suffice,
To stop thy cruell mouth that gaping stood?
But must thou dim the milde *Hercanus* eyes?

My gratious father, whose too readie hand
Did lift this *Idumean* from the dust:
And he ungratefull catiffe did withstand,
The man that did in him most friendly trust.   20
What kingdomes right could cruell *Herod* claime,
Was he not *Esaus* Issue, heyre of hell?
Then what succession can he have but shame?
Did not his Ancestor his birth-right sell?
O yes, he doth from *Edoms* name derive,
His cruell nature which with blood is fed:
That made him me of Sire and sonne deprive,
He ever thirsts for blood, and blood is red.
Weepst thou because his love to thee was bent?
And readst thou love in crimson caracters?   30
Slew he thy friends to worke thy hearts content?
No: hate may Justly call that action hers.
He gave the sacred Priesthood for thy sake,
To *Aristobolus*. Yet doomde him dead:
Before his backe the *Ephod* warme could make,
And ere the *Myter* setled on his head:
Oh had he given my boy no lesse then right,
The double oyle should to his forehead bring:
A double honour, shining doubly bright,
His birth annoynted him both Priest and King.   40
And say my father, and my sonne he slewe,
To royalize by right your Prince borne breath:
Was love the cause, can *Mariam* deeme it true,
That *Herod* gave commandment for her death?
I know by fits, he shewd some signes of love,
And yet not love, but raging lunacie:
And this his hate to thee may justly prove,
That sure he hates *Hercanus* familie.
Who knowes if he unconstant wavering Lord,
His love to *Doris* had renew'd againe?   50
And that he might his bed to her afford,
Perchance he wisht that *Mariam* might be slaine.

MARIAM *Doris*, Alas her time of love was past,
    Those coales were rakte in embers long agoe:
    If *Mariams* love and she was now disgrast,
    Nor did I glorie in her overthrowe.
    He not a whit his first borne sonne esteem'd,
    Because as well as his he was not mine:
    My children onely for his owne he deem'd,
60   These boyes that did descend from royall line.
    These did he stile his heyres to *Davids* throne,
    My *Alexander* if he live, shall sit
    In the Majesticke seat of *Salamon*,
    To will it so, did *Herod* thinke it fit.

ALEXANDRA Why? who can claime from *Alexanders* brood
    That Gold adorned Lyon-guarded Chaire?
    Was *Alexander* not of *Davids* blood?
    And was not *Mariam Alexanders* heire?
    What more then right could *Herod* then bestow,
70   And who will thinke except for more then right,
    He did not raise them, for they were not low,
    But borne to weare the Crowne in his despight:
    Then send those teares away that are not sent
    To thee by reason, but by passions power:
    Thine eyes to cheere, thy cheekes to smiles be bent,
    And entertaine with joy this happy houre.
    Felicitie, if when shee comes, she findes
    A mourning habite, and a cheerlesse looke,
    Will thinke she is not welcome to thy minde,
80   And so perchance her lodging will not brooke.
    Oh keepe her whilest thou hast her, if she goe
    She will not easily returne againe:
    Full many a yeere have I indur'd in woe,
    Yet still have sude her presence to obtaine:
    And did not I to her as presents send
    A Table, that best Art did beautifie
    Of two, to whom Heaven did best feature lend,
    To woe her love by winning *Anthony*:

For when a Princes favour we doe crave,
We first their Mynions loves do seeke to winne: 90
So I, that sought Felicitie to have,
Did with her Mynion *Anthony* beginne,
With double slight I sought to captivate
The warlike lover, but I did not right:
For if my gift had borne but halfe the rate,
The *Roman* had beene over-taken quite.
But now he fared like a hungry guest,
That to some plenteous festivall is gone,
Now this, now that, hee deems to eate were best,
Such choice doth make him let them all alone.   100
The boyes large forehead first did fayrest seeme,
Then glaunst his eye upon my *Mariams* cheeke:
And that without comparison did deeme,
What was in eyther but he most did seeke.
And thus distracted, eythers beauties might
Within the others excellence was drown'd:
Too much delight did bare him from delight,
For eithers love, the others did confound.
Where if thy portraiture had onely gone,
His life from *Herod*, *Anthony* had taken: 110
He would have loved thee, and thee alone,
And left the browne *Egyptian* cleane forsaken.
And *Cleopatra* then to seeke had bene,
So firme a lover of her wayned face:
Then great *Anthonius* fall we had not seene,
By her that fled to have him holde the chase.
Then *Mariam* in a *Romans* Chariot set,
In place of *Cleopatra* might have showne:
A mart of Beauties in her visage met,
And part in this, that they were all her owne.   120
MARIAM   Not to be Emprise of aspiring *Rome*,
Would *Mariam* like to *Cleopatra* live:
With purest body will I presse my Toome,
And wish no favours *Anthony* could give.

ALEXANDRA Let us retire us, that we may resolve
How now to deale in this reversed state:
Great are th'affaires that we must now revolve,
And great affaires must not be taken late.

Act I. Scene 3

[*Enter*] SALOME.

SALOME More plotting yet? Why? now you have the thing
For which so oft you spent your supliant breath:
And *Mariam* hopes to have another King,
Her eyes doe sparkle joy for *Herods* death.

ALEXANDRA If she desir'd another King to have,
She might before she came in *Herods* bed
Have had her wish. More Kings then one did crave,
For leave to set a Crowne upon her head.
I thinke with more then reason she laments,
That she is freed from such a sad annoy:
Who ist will weepe to part from discontent,
And if she joy, she did not causelesse joy.

SALOME You durst not thus have given your tongue the raine,
If noble *Herod* still remain in life:
Your daughters betters farre I dare maintaine,
Might have rejoyc'd to be my brothers wife.

MARIAM My betters farre, base woman t'is untrue,
You scarce have ever my superiors seene:
For *Mariams* servants were as good as you,
Before she came to be *Judeas* Queene.

SALOME Now stirs the tongue that is so quickly mov'd,
But more then once your collor have I borne:
Your fumish words are sooner sayd then prov'd,
And *Salomes* reply is onely scorne.

MARIAM Scorne those that are for thy companions held,
Though I thy brothers face had never seene,
My birth, thy baser birth so farre exceld,
I had to both of you the Princesse bene.

Thou party Jew, and party Edomite,
Thou Mongrell: issu'd from rejected race,   30
Thy Ancestors against the Heavens did fight,
And thou like them wilt heavenly birth disgrace.

SALOME Still twit you me with nothing but my birth,
What ods betwixt your ancestors and mine?
Both borne of *Adam*, both were made of Earth,
And both did come from holy *Abrahams* line.

MARIAM I favour thee when nothing else I say,
With thy blacke acts ile not pollute my breath:
Else to thy charge I might full justly lay
A shamefull life, besides a husbands death.   40

SALOME Tis true indeed, I did the plots reveale,
That past betwixt your favorites and you:
I ment not I, a traytor to conceale.
Thus *Salome* your Mynion *Joseph* slue.

MARIAM Heaven, dost thou meane this Infamy to smother?
Let slandred *Mariam* ope thy closed eare:
Selfe-guilt hath ever bene suspitions mother,
And therefore I this speech with patience beare.
No, had not *Salomes* unstedfast heart,
In *Josephus* stead her *Constabarus* plast,   50
To free her selfe, she had not usde the art,
To slander haplesse *Mariam* for unchast.

ALEXANDRA Come *Mariam*, let us goe: it is no boote
To let the head contend against the foote.

> [*Exeunt* MARIAM *and* ALEXANDRA.]

Act I. Scene 4

SALOME Lives *Salome*, to get so base a stile
As foote, to the proud *Mariam*: *Herods* spirit
In happy time for her endured exile,
For did he live she should not misse her merit:

But he is dead: and though he were my Brother,
His death such store of Cinders cannot cast
My Coales of love to quench: for though they smother
The flames a while, yet will they out at last.
Oh blest *Arabia*, in best climate plast,
I by the Fruit will censure of the Tree:
Tis not in vaine, thy happy name thou hast,
If all *Arabians* like *Silleus* bee:
Had not my Fate bene too too contrary,
When I on *Constabarus* first did gaze,
Silleus had beene object to mine eye:
Whose lookes and personage must all eyes amaze.
But now ill Fated *Salome*, thy tongue
To *Constabarus* by it selfe is tide:
And now except I doe the Ebrew wrong
I cannot be the faire *Arabian* Bride:
What childish lets are these? Why stand I now
On honourable points? Tis long agoe
Since shame was written on my tainted brow:
And certaine tis, that shame is honours foe.
Had I upon my reputation stood,
Had I affected an unspotted life,
Josephus vaines had still bene stuft with blood,
And I to him had liv'd a sober wife.
Then had I never cast an eye of love,
On *Constabarus* now detested face,
Then had I kept my thoughts without remove:
And blusht at motion of the least disgrace:
But shame is gone, and honour wipt away,
And Impudencie on my forehead sits:
She bids me worke my will without delay,
And for my will I will imploy my wits.
He loves, I love; what then can be the cause,
Keepes me for being the *Arabians* wife?
It is the principles of *Moses* lawes,
For *Constabarus* still remaines in life,

If he to me did beare as Earnest hate,
As I to him, for him there were an ease,
A separating bill might free his fate:
From such a yoke that did so much displease.
Why should such priviledge to man be given?
Or given to them, why bard from women then?
Are men then we in greater grace with Heaven?
Or cannot women hate as well as men?
Ile be the custome-breaker: and beginne
To shew my Sexe the way to freedomes doore,   50
And with an offring will I purge my sinne,
The lawe was made for none but who are poore.
If *Herod* had liv'd, I might to him accuse
My present Lord. But for the futures sake
Then would I tell the King he did refuse
The sonnes of *Baba* in his power to take.
But now I must divorse him from my bed,
That my *Silleus* may possesse his roome:
Had I not begd his life he had bene dead,
I curse my tongue the hindrer of his doome,   60
But then my wandring heart to him was fast,
Nor did I dreame of chaunge: *Silleus* said,
He would be here, and see he comes at last,
Had I not nam'd him longer had he staid.

Act I. Scene 5

[*Enter*] SILLEUS.

SILLEUS Well found faire *Salome Judaeas* pride,
  Hath thy innated wisedome found the way
  To make *Silleus* deeme him deified,
  By gaining thee a more then precious pray?
SALOME I have devisde the best I can devise,
  A more imperfect meanes was never found:
  But what cares *Salome*, it doth suffice

If our indevours with their end be crown'd.
In this our land we have an ancient use,
Permitted first by our law-givers head:
Who hates his wife, though for no just abuse,
May with a bill divorce her from his bed.
But in this custome women are not free,
Yet I for once will wrest it, blame not thou
The ill I doe, since what I do'es for thee,
Though others blame, *Silleus* should allow.

SILLEUS Thinkes *Salome*, *Silleus* hath a tongue
To censure her faire actions: let my blood
Bedash my proper brow, for such a wrong,
The being yours, can make even vices good:
Arabia joy, prepare thy earth with greene,
Thou never happie wert indeed till now:
Now shall thy ground be trod by beauties Queene,
Her foote is destin'd to depresse thy brow.
Thou shalt faire *Salome* commaund as much
As if the royall ornament were thine:
The weaknes of *Arabias* King is such,
The kingdome is not his so much as mine.
My mouth is our *Obodas* oracle,
Who thinkes not ought but what *Silleus* will?
And thou rare creature. *Asias* miracle,
Shalt be to me as It: *Obodas* still.

SALOME Tis not for glory I thy love accept,
Judea yeelds me honours worthy store:
Had not affection in my bosome crept,
My native country should my life deplore.
Were not *Silleus* he with whome I goe,
I would not change my *Palastine* for *Rome*:
Much lesse would I a glorious state to shew,
Goe far to purchase an *Arabian* toome.

SILLEUS Far be it from *Silleus* so to thinke,
I know it is thy gratitude requites
The love that is in me, and shall not shrinke
Till death doe sever me from earths delights.

SALOME But whist; me thinkes the wolfe is in our talke,

    Be gone *Silleus*, who doth here arrive?

    Tis *Constabarus* that doth hither walke,

    Ile find a quarrell, him from me to drive.

SILLEUS Farewell, but were it not for thy commaund,

    In his despight *Silleus* here would stand.   [*Exit* SILLEUS.]   50

Act I. Scene 6

    [*Enter*] CONSTABARUS.

CONSTABARUS Oh *Salome*, how much you wrong your name,

    Your race, your country, and your husband most?

    A straungers private conference is shame,

    I blush for you, that have your blushing lost.

    Oft have I found, and found you to my griefe,

    Consorted with this base *Arabian* heere:

    Heaven knowes that you have bin my comfort chiefe,

    Then doe not now my greater plague appeare.

    Now by the stately Carved edifice

    That on Mount *Sion* makes so faire a show,   10

    And by the Altar fit for sacrifice,

    I love thee more then thou thy selfe doest know.

    Oft with a silent sorrow have I heard

    How ill *Judeas* mouth doth censure thee:

    And did I not thine honour much regard,

    Thou shouldst not be exhorted thus for mee.

    Didst thou but know the worth of honest fame,

    How much a vertuous woman is esteem'd,

    Thou wouldest like hell eschew deserved shame,

    And seeke to be both chast and chastly deem'd.   20

    Our wisest Prince did say, and true he said,

    A vertuous woman crownes her husbands head.

SALOME Did I for this, upreare thy lowe estate?

    Did I for this requitall begge thy life,

    That thou hadst forfeited haples fate?

    To be to such a thankles wretch the wife.

This hand of mine hath lifted up thy head,
Which many a day agoe had falne full lowe,
Because the sonnes of *Baba* are not dead,
30   To me thou doest both life and fortune owe.

CONSTABARUS You have my patience often exercisde,
Use make my choller keepe within the bankes:
Yet boast no more, but be by me advisde.
A benefit upbraided, forfeits thankes:
I prethy *Salome* dismisse this mood,
Thou doest not know how ill it fits thy place:
My words were all intended for thy good,
To raise thine honour and to stop disgrace.

SALOME To stop disgrace? take thou no care for mee,
40   Nay do thy worst, thy worst I set not by:
No shame of mine is like to light on thee,
Thy love and admonitions I defie.
Thou shalt no hower longer call me wife,
Thy jealousie procures my hate so deepe:
That I from thee doe meane to free my life,
By a divorcing bill before I sleepe.

CONSTABARUS Are Hebrew women now transform'd to men?
Why do you not as well our battels fight,
And weare our armour? suffer this, and then
50   Let all the world be topsie turved quite.
Let fishes graze, beastes swim, and birds descend,
Let fire burne downewards whilst the earth aspires:
Let Winters heat and Summers cold offend,
Let Thistels growe on Vines, and Grapes on Briers,
Set us to Spinne or Sowe, or at the best
Make us Wood-hewers, Water-bearing wights:
For sacred service let us take no rest,
Use us as *Joshua* did the *Gibonites*.

SALOME Hold on your talke, till it be time to end,
60   For me I am resolv'd it shall be so:
Though I be first that to this course do bend,
I shall not be the last full well I know.

CONSTABARUS Why then be witnesse Heav'n, the Judge of sinnes,
　　　Be witnesse Spirits that eschew the darke:
　　　Be witnesse Angels, witnesse Cherubins,
　　　Whose semblance sits upon the holy Arke:
　　　Be witnesse earth, be witnesse *Palestine*,
　　　Be witnesse *Davids* Citie, if my heart
　　　Did ever merit such an act of thine:
　　　Or if the fault be mine that makes us part,　　　　　　70
　　　Since mildest *Moses* friend unto the Lord,
　　　Did worke his wonders in the land of *Ham*,
　　　And slew the first-borne Babes without a sword,
　　　In signe whereof we eate the holy Lambe:
　　　Till now that foureteene hundred yeeres are past,
　　　Since first the Law with us hath beene in force:
　　　You are the first, and will I hope, be last,
　　　That ever sought her husband to divorce.

SALOME I meane not to be led by president,
　　　My will shall be to me in stead of Law.　　　　　　80

CONSTABARUS I feare me much you will too late repent,
　　　That you have ever liv'd so void of awe:
　　　This is *Silleus* love that makes you thus
　　　Reverse all order: you must next be his.
　　　But if my thoughts aright the cause discusse,
　　　In winning you, he gaines no lasting blisse,
　　　I was *Silleus*, and not long agoe
　　　Josephus then was *Constabarus* now:
　　　When you became my friend you prov'd his foe,
　　　As now for him you breake to me your vow.　　　　　90

SALOME If once I lov'd you, greater is your debt:
　　　For certaine tis that you deserved it not.
　　　And undeserved love we soone forget,
　　　And therefore that to me can be no blot.
　　　But now fare ill my once beloved Lord,
　　　Yet never more belov'd then now abhord.　　　[*Exit* SALOME.]

CONSTABARUS Yet *Constabarus* biddeth thee farewell.
　　　Farewell light creature. Heaven forgive thy sinne:
　　　My prophecying spirit doth foretell
　　　Thy wavering thoughts doe yet but new beginne.　　　100

Yet I have better scap'd then *Joseph* did,
But if our *Herods* death had bene delayd,
The valiant youths that I so long have hid,
Had bene by her, and I for them betrayd.
Therefore in happy houre did *Caesar* give
The fatall blow to wanton *Anthony*:
For had he lived, our *Herod* then should live,
But great *Anthonius* death made *Herod* dye.
Had he enjoyed his breath, not I alone
Had beene in danger of a deadly fall:
But *Mariam* had the way of perill gone,
Though by the Tyrant most belov'd of all.
The sweet fac'd *Mariam* as free from guilt
As Heaven from spots, yet had her Lord come backe
Her purest blood had bene unjustly spilt.
And *Salome* it was would worke her wracke.
Though all *Judea* yeeld her innocent,
She often hath bene neere to punishment.

[*Exit* CONSTABARUS.]

CHORUS Those mindes that wholy dote upon delight,
       Except they onely joy in inward good:
       Still hope at last to hop upon the right,
       And so from Sand they leape in loathsome mud.
         Fond wretches, seeking what they cannot finde,
         For no content attends a wavering minde.

       If wealth they doe desire, and wealth attaine,
       Then wondrous faine would they to honor lep:
       If meane degree they doe in honor gaine,
       They would but wish a little higher step.
         Thus step to step, and wealth to wealth they ad,
         Yet cannot all their plenty make them glad.

       Yet oft we see that some in humble state,
       Are cheerfull, pleasant, happy, and content:
       When those indeed that are of higher state,

With vaine additions do their thoughts torment.
  Th'one would to his minde his fortune binde,
  T'hother to his fortune frames his minde.

To wish varietie is signe of griefe,
For if you like your state as now it is,
Why should an alteration bring reliefe?
Nay change would then be fear'd as losse of blis.   140
  That man is onely happy in his Fate,
  That is delighted in a setled state.

Still *Mariam* wisht she from her Lord were free,
For expectation of varietie:
Yet now she sees her wishes prosperous bee,
She grieves, because her Lord so soone did die.
  Who can those vast imaginations feede,
  Where in a propertie, contempt doth breede?

Were *Herod* now perchance to live againe,
She would againe as much be grieved at that: 150
All that she may, she ever doth disdaine,
Her wishes guide her to she knowes not what.
  And sad must be their lookes, their honor sower,
  That care for nothing being in their power.

Act II. Scene 1

[*Enter*] PHAERORAS *and* GRAPHINA.

PHAERORAS Tis true *Graphina*, now the time drawes nye
  Wherin the holy Priest with hallowed right,
  The happy long desired knot shall tie,
  Pheroras and *Graphina* to unite:
How oft have I with lifted hands implor'd
This blessed houre, till now implord in vaine,
Which hath my wished libertie restor'd,
And made my subject selfe my owne againe.

Thy love faire Mayd upon mine eye doth sit,
Whose nature hot doth dry the moysture all,
Which were in nature, and in reason fit
For my monachall Brothers death to fall:
Had *Herod* liv'd, he would have pluckt my hand
From faire *Graphinas* Palme perforce: and tide
The same in hatefull and despised band,
For I had had a Baby to my Bride:
Scarce can her Infant tongue with easie voice
Her name distinguish to anothers eare:
Yet had he liv'd, his power, and not my choise
Had made me solembly the contract sweare.
Have I not cause in such a change to joy?
What? though she be my Neece, a Princesse borne:
Neere bloods without respect: high birth a toy.
Since Love can teach blood and kindreds scorne.
What booted it that he did raise my head,
To be his Realmes Copartner, Kingdomes mate,
Withall, he kept *Graphina* from my bed,
More wisht by me then thrice *Judeas* state.
Oh, could not he be skilfull Judge in love,
That doted so upon his *Mariams* face?
He, for his passion, *Doris* did remove.
I needed not a lawfull Wife displace,
It could not be but he had power to judge,
But he that never grudg'd a Kingdomes share,
This well knowne happinesse to me did grudge:
And ment to be therein without compare.
Else had I bene his equall in loves hoast,
For though the Diadem on *Mariams* head
Corrupt the vulgar judgements, I will boast
Graphinas brow's as white, her cheekes as red.
Why speaks thou not faire creature? move thy tongue,
For Silence is a signe of discontent:
It were to both our loves too great a wrong
If now this hower do find thee sadly bent.

GRAPHINA Mistake me not my Lord, too oft have I
    Desir'd this time to come with winged feete,
    To be inwrapt with griefe when tis too nie,
    You know my wishes ever yours did meete:
    If I be silent, tis no more but feare
    That I should say too little when I speake: 50
    But since you will my imperfections beare,
    In spight of doubt I will my silence breake:
    Yet might amazement tie my moving tongue,
    But that I know before *Pheroras* minde,
    I have admired your affection long:
    And cannot yet therein a reason finde.
    Your hand hath lifted me from lowest state,
    To highest eminencie wondrous grace,
    And me your hand-maid have you made your mate,
    Though all but you alone doe count me base.   60
    You have preserved me pure at my request,
    Though you so weake a vassaile might constraine
    To yeeld to your high will, then last not best
    In my respect a Princesse you disdaine,
    Then need not all these favours studie crave,
    To be requited by a simple maide:
    And studie still you know must silence have,
    Then be my cause for silence justly waide,
    But studie cannot boote nor I requite,
    Except your lowly hand-maides steadfast love   70
    And fast obedience may your mind delight,
    I will not promise more then I can prove.
PHAERORAS That studie needs not let *Graphinas* smile,
    And I desire no greater recompence:
    I cannot vaunt me in a glorious stile,
    Nor shew my love in far-fetcht eloquence:
    But this beleeve me, never *Herods* heart
    Hath held his Prince-borne beautie famed wife
    In neerer place then thou faire virgin art,
    To him that holds the glory of his life.   80

Should *Herods* body leave the Sepulcher,
And entertaine the sever'd ghost againe:
He should not be my nuptiall hinderer,
Except he hindred it with dying paine.
Come faire *Graphina*, let us goe in state,
This wish-indeered time to celebrate.

[*Exeunt* PHAERORAS *and* GRAPHINA.]

Act II. Scene 2

[*Enter*] CONSTABARUS *and* BABUS SONNES.

BABUS FIRST SONNE Now valiant friend you have our lives
    redeem'd,
Which lives as sav'd by you, to you are due:
Command and you shall see your selfe esteem'd,
Our lives and liberties belong to you.
This twice six yeares with hazard of your life,
You have conceal'd us from the tyrants sword:
Though cruell *Herods* sister were your wife,
You durst in scorne of feare this grace afford.
In recompence we know not what to say,
10   A poore reward were thankes for such a merit,
Our truest friendship at your feete we lay,
The best requitall to a noble spirit.

CONSTABARUS Oh how you wrong our friendship valiant youth,
With friends there is not such a word as det:
Where amitie is tide with bond of truth,
All benefits are there in common set.
Then is the golden age with them renew'd,
All names of properties are banisht quite:
Division, and distinction, are eschew'd:
20   Each hath to what belongs to others right.
And tis not sure so full a benefit,
Freely to give, as freely to require:
A bountious act hath glory following it,
They cause the glory that the act desire.

All friendship should the patterne imitate,
Of *Jesses* Sonne and valiant *Jonathan*:
For neither Soveraignes nor fathers hate,
A friendship fixt on vertue sever can.
Too much of this, tis written in the heart,
And need no amplifying with the tongue: 30
Now may you from your living tombe depart,
Where *Herods* life hath kept you over long.
Too great an injury to a noble minde,
To be quicke buried, you had purchast fame,
Some yeares a goe, but that you were confinde.
While thousand meaner did advance their name.
Your best of life the prime of all your yeares,
Your time of action is from you bereft.
Twelve winters have you overpast in feares:
Yet if you use it well, enough is left.   40
And who can doubt but you will use it well?
The sonnes of *Babus* have it by descent:
In all their thoughts each action to excell,
Boldly to act, and wisely to invent.

BABUS SECOND SONNE Had it not like the hatefull cuckoe beene,
Whose riper age his infant nurse doth kill:
So long we had not kept our selves unseene,
But *Constabarus* safety crost our will:
For had the Tyrant fixt his cruell eye,
On our concealed faces wrath had swaide   50
His Justice so, that he had forst us die.
And dearer price then life we should have paid,
For you our truest friend had falne with us:
And we much like a house on pillers set,
Had cleane deprest our prop, and therefore thus
Our readie will with our concealement met.
But now that you faire Lord are daungerlesse,
The Sonnes of *Baba* shall their rigor show:
And prove it was not basenes did oppresse
Our hearts so long, but honour kept them low.   60

BABUS FIRST SONNE Yet do I feare this tale of *Herods* death,
    At last will prove a very tale indeed:
    It gives me strongly in my minde, his breath
    Will be preserv'd to make a number bleed:
    I wish not therefore to be set at large,
    Yet perill to my selfe I do not feare:
    Let us for some daies longer be your charge,
    Till we of *Herods* state the truth do heare.

CONSTABARUS What art thou turn'd a coward noble youth,
70   That thou beginst to doubt, undoubted truth?

BABUS FIRST SONNE Were it my brothers tongue that cast this
    doubt,
    I from his hart would have the question out:
    With this keene fauchion, but tis you my Lord
    Against whose head I must not lift a sword:
    I am so tide in gratitude.

CONSTABARUS   Believe
    You have no cause to take it ill,
    If any word of mine your heart did grieve
    The word discented from the speakers will,
    I know it was not feare the doubt begun,
80   But rather valour and your care of me,
    A coward could not be your fathers sonne,
    Yet know I doubts unnecessarie be:
    For who can thinke that in *Anthonius* fall,
    Herod his bosome friend should scape unbrusde:
    Then *Caesar* we might thee an idiot call,
    If thou by him should'st be so farre abusde.

BABUS SECOND SONNE Lord *Constabarus* let me tell you this,
    Upon submission *Caesar* will forgive:
    And therefore though the tyrant did amisse,
90   It may fall out that he will let him live.
    Not many yeares agone it is since I
    Directed thither by my fathers care,
    In famous *Rome* for twice twelve monthes did lie,
    My life from *Hebrewes* crueltie to spare,

There though I were but yet of boyish age,
I bent mine eye to marke, mine eares to heare.
Where I did see *Octavious* then a page,
When first he did to *Julions* sight appeare:
Me thought I saw such mildnes in his face,
And such a sweetnes in his lookes did grow,   100
Withall, commixt with so majesticke grace,
His Phismony his Fortune did foreshow:
For this I am indebted to mine eye,
But then mine eare receiv'd more evidence,
By that I knew his love to clemency,
How he with hottest choller could dispence.

CONSTABARUS But we have more then barely heard the news,
It hath bin twice confirm'd. And though some tongue
Might be so false, with false report t'abuse,
A false report hath never lasted long.   110
But be it so that *Herod* have his life,
Concealement would not then a whit availe:
For certaine t'is, that she that was my wife,
Would not to set her accusation faile.
And therefore now as good the venture give,
And free our selves from blot of cowardise:
As show a pittifull desire to live,
For, who can pittie but they must despise?

BABUS FIRST SONNE I yeeld, but to necessitie I yeeld,
I dare upon this doubt ingage mine arme: 120
That *Herod* shall againe this kingdome weeld,
And prove his death to be a false alarme.

BABUS SECOND SONNE I doubt it too: God grant it be an error,
Tis best without a cause to be in terror:
And rather had I, though my soule be mine,
My soule should lie, then prove a true divine.

CONSTABARUS Come, come, let feare goe seeke a dastards nest,
Undanted courage lies in a noble brest.   [*Exeunt.*]

Act II. Scene 3

[*Enter*] DORIS *and* ANTIPATER.

DORIS You royall buildings bow your loftie side,
And scope to her that is by right your Queen:
Let your humilitie upbraid the pride
Of those in whom no due respect is seene:
Nine times have we with Trumpets haughtie sound,
And banishing sow'r Leaven from our taste:
Observ'd the feast that takes the fruit from ground.
Since I faire Citie did behold thee last,
So long it is since *Mariams* purer cheeke
10 Did rob from mine the glory. And so long
Since I returnd my native Towne to seeke:
And with me nothing but the sence of wrong.
And thee my Boy, whose birth though great it were,
Yet have thy after fortunes prov'd but poore:
When thou wert borne how little did I feare
Thou shouldst be thrust from forth thy Fathers doore.
Art thou not *Herods* right begotten Sonne?
Was not the haples *Doris*, *Herods* wife?
Yes: ere he had the Hebrew kingdome wonne,
20 I was companion to his private life.
Was I not faire enough to be a Queene?
Why ere thou wert to me false Monarch tide,
My lake of beauty might as well be seene,
As after I had liv'd five yeeres thy Bride.
Yet then thine oath came powring like the raine,
Which all affirm'd my face without compare:
And that if thou might'st *Doris* love obtaine,
For all the world besides thou didst not care.
Then was I yong, and rich, and nobly borne,
30 And therefore worthy to be *Herods* mate:
Yet thou ungratefull cast me off with scorne,
When Heavens purpose raisd your meaner fate.

Oft have I begd for vengeance for this fact,
And with dejected knees, aspiring hands
Have prayd the highest power to inact
The fall of her that on my Trophee stands.
Revenge I have according to my will,
Yet where I wisht this vengeance did not light:
I wisht it should high-hearted *Mariam* kill.
But it against my whilome Lord did fight   40
With thee sweet Boy I came, and came to try
If thou before his bastards might be plac'd
In *Herods* royall seat and dignitie.
But *Mariams* infants here arc onely grac'd,
And now for us there doth no hope remaine:
Yet we will not returne till *Herods* end
Be more confirmd, perchance he is not slaine.
So glorious Fortunes may my Boy attend,
For if he live, hee'll thinke it doth suffice,
That he to *Doris* shows such crueltie: 50
For as he did my wretched life dispise,
So doe I know I shall despised die.
Let him but prove as naturall to thee,
As cruell to thy miserable mother:
His crueltie shall not upbraided bee
But in thy fortunes. I his faults will smother.

ANTIPATER Each mouth within the Citie loudly cries
  That *Herods* death is certaine: therefore wee
  Had best some subtill hidden plot devise,
  That *Mariams* children might subverted bee,   60
  By poisons drinke, or else by murtherous Knife,
  So we may be advanc'd, it skils not how:
  They are but Bastards, you were *Herods* wife,
  And foule adultery blotteth *Mariams* brow.

DORIS They are too strong to be by us remov'd,
  Or else revenges foulest spotted face:
  By our detested wrongs might be approv'd,
  But weakenesse must to greater power give place.

But let us now retire to grieve alone,
70   For solitarines best fitteth mone.

                      [*Exeunt* DORIS *and* ANTIPATER.]

Act II. Scene 4

[*Enter*] SILLEUS *and* CONSTABARUS.

SILLEUS Well met *Judean* Lord, the onely wight
    Silleus wisht to see. I am to call
    Thy tongue to strict account.

CONSTABARUS   For what despight
    I ready am to heare, and answere all.
    But if directly at the cause I gesse
    That breeds this challenge, you must pardon me:
    And now some other ground of fight professe,
    For I have vow'd, vowes must unbroken be.

SILLEUS What may be your expectation? let me know.

10 CONSTABARUS Why? ought concerning *Salom*, my sword
    Shall not be welded for a cause so low,
    A blow for her my arme will scorne t'afford.

SILLEUS It is for slandering her unspotted name,
    And I will make thee in thy vowes despight,
    Sucke up the breath that did my Mistris blame,
    And swallow it againe to doe her right.

CONSTABARUS I prethee give some other quarrell ground
    To finde beginning, raile against my name:
    Or strike me first, or let some scarlet wound
20   Inflame my courage, give me words of shame,
    Doe thou our *Moses* sacred Lawes disgrace,
    Deprave our nation, doe me some despight:
    I'm apt enough to fight in any case,
    But yet for *Salome* I will not fight.

SILLEUS Nor I for ought but *Salome*: My sword
    That owes his service to her sacred name:
    Will not an edge for other cause afford,
    In other fight I am not sure of fame.

CONSTABARUS For her, I pitty thee enough already,
 For her, I therefore will not mangle thee: 30
 A woman with a heart so most unsteady,
 Will of her selfe sufficient torture bee.
 I cannot envy for so light a gaine,
 Her minde with such unconstancie doth runne:
 As with a word thou didst her love obtaine,
 So with a word she will from thee be wonne.
 So light as her possessions for most day
 Is her affections lost, to me tis knowne:
 As good goe hold the winde as make her stay,
 Shee never loves, but till she call her owne.   40
 She meerly is a painted sepulcher,
 That is both faire, and vilely foule at once:
 Though on her out-side graces garnish her,
 Her mind is fild with worse then rotten bones.
 And ever readie lifted is her hand,
 To aime destruction at a husbands throat:
 For proofes, *Josephus* and my selfe do stand,
 Though once on both of us, she seem'd to doat.
 Her mouth though serpent-like it never hisses,
 Yet like a Serpent, poysons where it kisses.   50
SILLEUS Well *Hebrew* well, thou bark'st, but wilt not bite.
CONSTABARUS I tell thee still for her I will not fight.
SILLEUS Why then I call thee coward.
CONSTABARUS   From my heart
 I give thee thankes. A cowards hatefull name,
 Cannot to valiant mindes a blot impart,
 And therefore I with joy receive the same.
 Thou know'st I am no coward: thou wert by
 At the *Arabian* battaile th'other day:
 And saw'st my sword with daring valiancy,
 Amongst the faint *Arabians* cut my way.   60
 The blood of foes no more could let it shine,
 And twas inameled with some of thine.

But now have at thee, not for *Salome*
I fight: but to discharge a cowards stile:
Here gins the fight that shall not parted be,
Before a soule or two indure exile.   [*They fight.*]

SILLEUS Thy sword hath made some windowes for my blood,
To shew a horred crimson phisnomie:
To breath for both of us me thinkes twere good,
70   The day will give us time enough to die.

CONSTABARUS With all my hart take breath, thou shalt have time,
And if thou list a twelve month, let us end:
Into thy cheekes there doth a palenes clime,
Thou canst not from my sword thy selfe defend.
What needest thou for *Salome* to fight,
Thou hast her, and may'st keepe her, none strives for her:
I willingly to thee resigne my right,
For in my very soule I do abhorre her.
Thou seest that I am fresh, unwounded yet,
80   Then not for feare I do this offer make:
Thou art with losse of blood, to fight unfit,
For here is one, and there another take.

SILLEUS I will not leave, as long as breath remaines
Within my wounded body: spare your words,
My heart in bloods stead, courage entertaines,
Salomes love no place for feare affords.

CONSTABARUS Oh could thy soule but prophesie like mine,
I would not wonder thou should'st long to die:
For *Salome* if I aright divine
90   Will be then death a greater miserie.

SILLEUS Then list, Ile breath no longer.

CONSTABARUS   Do thy will,
I hateles fight, and charitably kill.   *They fight.*
Pittie thy selfe *Silleus*, let not death
Intru'd before his time into thy hart:
Alas it is too late to feare, his breath
Is from his body now about to part.

How far'st thou brave *Arabian*?

SILLEUS   Very well,
   My legge is hurt, I can no longer fight:
   It onely grieves me, that so soone I fell,
   Before faire *Saloms* wrongs I came to right.   100

CONSTABARUS Thy wounds are lesse then mortall. Never feare,
   Thou shalt a safe and quicke recoverie finde:
   Come, I will thee unto my lodging beare,
   I hate thy body, but I love thy minde.

SILLEUS Thankes noble Jew, I see a courtious foe,
   Sterne enmitie to friendship can no art:
   Had not my heart and tongue engagde me so,
   I would from thee no foe, but friend depart.
   My heart to *Salome* is tide so fast,
   To leave her love for friendship, yet my skill   110
   Shall be imploy'd to make your favour last,
   And I will honour *Constabarus* still.

CONSTABARUS I ope my bosome to thee, and will take
   Thee in, as friend, and grieve for thy complaint:
   But if we doe not expedition make,
   Thy losse of blood I feare will make thee faint.

             [*Exeunt* CONSTABARUS *and* SILLEUS.]

CHORUS To heare a tale with eares prejudicate,
     It spoiles the judgement, and corrupts the sence:
     That humane error given to every state,
     Is greater enemie to innocence.   120
       It makes us foolish, heddy, rash, unjust,
       It makes us never try before we trust.

It will confound the meaning, change the words,
     For it our sence of hearing much deceives:
     Besides no time to Judgement it affords,
     To way the circumstance our eare receives.
       The ground of accidents it never tries,
       But makes us take for truth ten thousand lies.

Our eares and hearts are apt to hold for good,
130   That we our selves doe most desire to bee:
And then we drowne objections in the flood
Of partialitie, tis that we see
    That makes false rumours long with credit past,
    Though they like rumours must conclude at last.

The greatest part of us prejudicate,
With wishing *Herods* death do hold it true:
The being once deluded doth not bate,
The credit to a better likelihood due.
    Those few that wish it not the multitude,
140   Doe carrie headlong, so they doubts conclude.

They not object the weake uncertaine ground,
Whereon they built this tale of *Herods* end:
Whereof the Author scarcely can be found,
And all because their wishes that way bend.
    They thinke not of the perill that ensu'th,
    If this should prove the contrary to truth.

On this same doubt, on this so light a breath,
They pawne their lives, and fortunes. For they all
Behave them as the newes of *Herods* death,
150   They did of most undoubted credit call:
    But if their actions now doe rightly hit,
    Let them commend their fortune, not their wit.

Act III. Scene 1

[*Enter*] PHAERORAS [*and*] SALOME.
PHAERORAS Urge me no more *Graphina* to forsake,
    Not twelve howers since I married her for love:
    And doe you thinke a sisters power can make
    A resolute decree, so soone remove?

SALOME Poore minds they are that honour not affects.

PHAERORAS Who hunts for honour, happines neglects.

SALOME You might have bene both of felicitie,
    And honour too in equall measure seasde.

PHAERORAS It is not you can tell so well as I,
    What tis can make me happie, or displeasde.   10

SALOME To match for neither beautie nor respects
    One meane of birth, but yet of meaner minde,
    A woman full of naturall defects,
    I wonder what your eye in her could finde.

PHAERORAS Mine eye found lovelines, mine eare found wit,
    To please the one, and to enchant the other:
    Grace on her eye, mirth on her tongue doth sit,
    In lookes a child, in wisedomes house a mother.

SALOME But say you thought her faire, as none thinks else,
    Knowes not *Pheroras*, beautie is a blast: 20
    Much like this flower which to day excels,
    But longer then a day it will not last.

PHAERORAS Her wit exceeds her beautie.

SALOME   Wit may show
    The way to ill, as well as good you know.

PHAERORAS But wisedome is the porter of her head,
    And bares all wicked words from issuing thence.

SALOME But of a porter, better were you sped,
    If she against their entrance made defence.

PHAERORAS But wherefore comes the sacred *Ananell*,
    That hitherward his hastie steppes doth bend?   30
      [*Enter* ANNANELL.]
    Great sacrificer y'are arrived well,
    Ill newes from holy mouth I not attend.

Act III. Scene 2

ANNANELL My lippes, my sonne, with peacefull tidings blest,
    Shall utter Honey to your listning eare:
    A word of death comes not from Priestly brest,
    I speake of life: in life there is no feare.

And for the newes I did the Heavens salute,
And fill'd the Temple with my thankfull voice:
For though that mourning may not me pollute,
At pleasing accidents I may rejoyce.

PHAERORAS Is *Herod* then reviv'd from certaine death?

10 SALOME What? can your news restore my brothers breath?

ANNANELL Both so, and so, the King is safe and sound,
And did such grace in royall *Caesar* meet:
That he with larger stile then ever crownd,
Within this houre Jerusalem will greet.
I did but come to tell you, and must backe
I make preparatives for sacrifice:
I knew his death, your hearts like mine did racke,
Though to conceale it, prov'd you wise.   [*Exit* ANNANELL.]

SALOME How can my joy sufficiently appeare?

20 PHAERORAS A heavier tale did never pierce mine eare.

SALOME Now *Salome* of happinesse may boast.

PHAERORAS But now *Pheroras* is in danger most.

SALOME I shall enjoy the comfort of my life.

PHAERORAS And I shall loose it, loosing of my wife.

SALOME Joy heart, for *Constabarus* shall be slaine.

PHAERORAS Grieve soule, *Graphina* shall from me be tane.

SALOME Smile cheekes, the faire *Silleus* shall be mine.

PHAERORAS Weepe eyes, for I must with a child combine.

SALOME Well brother, cease your mones, on one condition
30 Ile undertake to winne the Kings consent:
Graphina still shall be in your tuition,
And her with you be nere the lesse content.

PHAERORAS What's the condition? let me quickly know,
That I as quickly your command may act:
Were it to see what Hearbs in *Ophir* grow,
Or that the lofty *Tyrus* might be sackt.

SALOME Tis not so hard a taske: It is no more,
But tell the King that *Constabarus* hid
The sonnes of *Baba*, doomed to death before:
40 And tis no more then *Constabarus* did.

And tell him more that I for *Herods* sake,
Not able to endure our brothers foe:
Did with a bill our separation make,
Though loth from *Constabarus* else to goe.

PHAERORAS Beleeve this tale for told, Ile goe from hence,
In *Herods* eare the Hebrew to deface:
And I that never studied eloquence,
Doe meane with eloquence this tale to grace.

Exit [PHAERORAS].

SALOME This will be *Constabarus* quicke dispatch,
Which from my mouth would lesser credit finde: 50
Yet shall he not decease without a match,
For *Mariam* shall not linger long behinde.
First Jealousie, if that availe not, feare
Shalbe my minister to worke her end:
A common error moves not *Herods* eare,
Which doth so firmly to his *Mariam* bend.
She shall be charged with so horrid crime,
As *Herods* feare shall turne his love to hate:
Ile make some sweare that she desires to clime,
And seekes to poyson him for his estate.   60
I scorne that she should live my birth t'upbraid,
To call me base and hungry Edomite:
With patient show her choller I betrayd,
And watcht the time to be reveng'd by slite.
Now tongue of mine with scandall load her name,
Turne hers to fountaines, *Herods* eyes to flame:
Yet first I will begin *Pheroras* suite,
That he my earnest businesse may effect:
And I of *Mariam* will keepe me mute,
Till first some other doth her name detect.   70

[*Enter* SILLEUS' MAN.]

Who's there, *Silleus* man? How fares your Lord?
That your aspects doe beare the badge of sorrow?

SILLEUS' MAN He hath the marks of *Constabarus* sword,
And for a while desires your sight to borrow.

SALOME My heavy curse the hatefull sword pursue,
My heavier curse on the more hatefull arme
That wounded my *Silleus*. But renew
Your tale againe. Hath he no mortall harme?

SILLEUS' MAN No signe of danger doth in him appeare,
80   Nor are his wounds in place of perill seene:
Hee bids you be assured you need not feare,
He hopes to make you yet *Arabias* Queene.

SALOME Commend my heart to be *Silleus* charge,
Tell him, my brothers suddaine comming now:
Will give my foote no roome to walke at large,
But I will see him yet ere night I vow.

> [*Exeunt* SALOME *and* SILLEUS' MAN.]

Act III. Scene 3

[*Enter*] MARIAM *and* SOHEMUS.

MARIAM *Sohemus*, tell me what the newes may be
That makes your eyes so full, your cheeks so blew?

SOHEMUS I know not how to call them. Ill for me
Tis sure they are: not so I hope for you.
Herod.

MARIAM Oh, what of *Herod*?

SOHEMUS   *Herod* lives.

[MARIAM] How! lives? What in some Cave or forrest hid?

SOHEMUS Nay, backe return'd with honor. *Caesar* gives
Him greater grace then ere *Anthonius* did.

MARIAM Foretell the ruine of my family,
10   Tell me that I shall see our Citie burnd:
Tell me I shall a death disgracefull die,
But tell me not that *Herod* is returnd.

SOHEMUS Be not impatient Madam, be but milde,
His love to you againe will soone be bred.

MARIAM I will not to his love be reconcilde,
With solemne vowes I have forsworne his Bed.

SOHEMUS But you must breake those vowes.

MARIAM Ile rather breake
 The heart of *Mariam*. Cursed is my Fate:
 But speake no more to me, in vaine ye speake   20
 To live with him I so profoundly hate.

SOHEMUS Great Queene, you must to me your pardon give,
 Sohemus cannot now your will obey:
 If your command should me to silence drive,
 It were not to obey, but to betray.
 Reject, and slight my speeches, mocke my faith,
 Scorne my observance, call my counsell nought:
 Though you regard not what *Sohemus* saith,
 Yet will I ever freely speake my thought.
 I feare ere long I shall faire *Mariam* see   30
 In wofull state, and by her selfe undone:
 Yet for your issues sake more temp'rate bee,
 The heart by affabilitie is wonne.

MARIAM And must I to my Prison turne againe?
 Oh, now I see I was an hypocrite:
 I did this morning for his death complaine,
 And yet doe mourne, because he lives ere night.
 When I his death beleev'd, compassion wrought,
 And was the stickler twixt my heart and him:
 But now that Curtaine's drawne from off my thought, 40
 Hate doth appeare againe with visage grim:
 And paints the face of *Herod* in my heart,
 In horred colours with detested looke:
 Then feare would come, but scorne doth play her part,
 And saith that scorne with feare can never brooke.
 I know I could inchaine him with a smile:
 And lead him captive with a gentle word,
 I scorne my looke should ever man beguile,
 Or other speech, then meaning to afford.
 Else *Salome* in vaine might spend her winde,   50
 In vaine might *Herods* mother whet her tongue:
 In vaine had they complotted and combinde,
 For I could overthrow them all ere long.

Oh what a shelter is mine innocence,
To shield me from the pangs of inward griefe:
Gainst all mishaps it is my faire defence,
And to my sorrowes yeelds a large reliefe.
To be commandresse of the triple earth,
And sit in safetie from a fall secure:

60 To have all nations celebrate my birth,
I would not that my spirit were impure.
Let my distressed state unpittied bee,
Mine innocence is hope enough for mee.   *Exit* [MARIAM].

SOHEMUS Poore guiltles Queene. Oh that my wish might place
A little temper now about thy heart:
Unbridled speech is *Mariams* worst disgrace,
And will indanger her without desart.
I am in greater hazard. O're my head,
The fattall axe doth hang unstedily:

70 My disobedience once discovered,
Will shake it downe: *Sohemus* so shall die.
For when the King shall find, we thought his death
Had bene as certaine as we see his life:
And markes withall I slighted so his breath,
As to preserve alive his matchles wife.
Nay more, to give to *Alexanders* hand
The regall dignitie. The soveraigne power,
How I had yeelded up at her command,
The strength of all the citie, *Davids* Tower.

80 What more then common death may I expect,
Since I too well do know his crueltie:
Twere death, a word of *Herods* to neglect,
What then to doe directly contrarie?
Yet life I quite thee with a willing spirit,
And thinke thou could'st not better be imploi'd:
I forfeit thee for her that more doth merit,
Ten such were better dead then she destroi'd.
But fare thee well chast Queene, well may I see
The darknes palpable, and rivers part:

90 The sunne stand still. Nay more retorted bee,
But never woman with so pure a heart.

Thine eyes grave majestie keepes all in awe,
And cuts the winges of every loose desire:
Thy brow is table to the modest lawe,
Yet though we dare not love, we may admire.
And if I die, it shall my soule content,
My breath in *Mariams* service shall be spent. [*Exit* SOHEMUS.]

CHORUS Tis not enough for one that is a wife
To keepe her spotles from an act of ill:
But from suspition she should free her life,   100
And bare her selfe of power as well as will.
  Tis not so glorious for her to be free,
  As by her proper selfe restrain'd to bee.

When she hath spatious ground to walke upon,
Why on the ridge should she desire to goe?
It is no glory to forbeare alone,
Those things that may her honour overthrowe.
  But tis thanke-worthy, if she will not take
  All lawfull liberties for honours sake.

That wife her hand against her fame doth reare,   110
That more then to her Lord alone will give
A private word to any second eare,
And though she may with reputation live.
  Yet though most chast, she doth her glory blot,
  And wounds her honour, though she killes it not.

When to their Husbands they themselves doe bind,
Doe they not wholy give themselves away?
Or give they but their body not their mind,
Reserving that though best, for others pray?
  No sure, their thoughts no more can be their owne,   120
  And therefore should to none but one be knowne.

Then she usurpes upon anothers right,
That seekes to be by publike language grac't:
And though her thoughts reflect with purest light,

Her mind if not peculiar is not chast.
  For in a wife it is no worse to finde,
  A common body, then a common minde.

And every mind though free from thought of ill,
That out of glory seekes a worth to show:
When any's eares but one therewith they fill,
Doth in a sort her purenes overthrow.
  Now *Mariam* had, (but that to this she bent)
  Beene free from feare, as well as innocent.

Act IV. Scene 1

Enter HEROD *and his attendants.*

HEROD Haile happie citie, happie in thy store,
  And happy that thy buildings such we see:
  More happie in the Temple where w'adore,
  But most of all that *Mariam* lives in thee.
    Enter NUNTIO.
  Art thou return'd? how fares my *Mariam*?
NUNTIO She's well my Lord, and will anon be here
  As you commanded.
HEROD   Muffle up thy browe
  Thou daies darke taper. *Mariam* will appeare.
  And where she shines, we need not thy dimme light,
  Oh hast thy steps rare creature, speed thy pace:
  And let thy presence make the day more bright,
  And cheere the heart of *Herod* with thy face.
  It is an age since I from *Mariam* went,
  Me thinkes our parting was in *Davids* daies:
  The houres are so increast by discontent,
  Deepe sorrow, *Josua*like the season staies:
  But when I am with *Mariam*, time runnes on,
  Her sight, can make months, minutes, daies of weekes:
  An hower is then no sooner come then gon.
  When in her face mine eye for wonders seekes.

You world commanding citie, *Europes* grace,
Twice hath my curious eye your streets survai'd,
And I have seene the statue filled place,
That once if not for geese had bene betrai'd.
I all your *Roman* beauties have beheld,
And seene the showes your *Ediles* did prepare,
I saw the sum of what in you exceld,
Yet saw no miracle like *Mariam* rare.
The faire and famous *Livia*, *Caesars* love,
The worlds commaunding Mistresse did I see: 30
Whose beauties both the world and *Rome* approve,
Yet *Mariam*: *Livia* is not like to thee.
Be patient but a little, while mine eyes
Within your compast limits be contain'd:
That object straight shall your desires suffice,
From which you were so long a while restrain'd.
How wisely *Mariam* doth the time delay,
Least suddaine joy my sence should suffocate:
I am prepar'd, thou needst no longer stay:
Whose there, my *Mariam*, more then happie fate?   40
Oh no, it is *Pheroras*, welcome Brother,
Now for a while, I must my passion smother.

Act IV. Scene 2

[*Enter*] PHAERORAS.

PHAERORAS All health and safetie waite upon my Lord,
    And may you long in prosperous fortunes live
    With *Rome* commanding *Caesar* at accord,
    And have all honors that the world can give.
HEROD Oh brother, now thou speakst not from thy hart,
    No, thou hast strooke a blow at *Herods* love:
    That cannot quickly from my memory part,
    Though *Salome* did me to pardon move.

      Valiant *Phasaelus*, now to thee farewell,
10   Thou wert my kinde and honorable brother:
      Oh haples houre, when you selfe striken fell,
      Thou fathers Image, glory of thy mother.
      Had I desir'd a greater sute of thee,
      Then to withhold thee from a harlots bed,
      Thou wouldst have granted it: but now I see
      All are not like that in a wombe are bred.
      Thou wouldst not, hadst thou heard of *Herods* death,
      Have made his buriall time, thy bridall houre:
      Thou wouldst with clamours, not with joyfull breath,
20   Have show'd the newes to be not sweet but soure.

PHAERORAS *Phasaelus* great worth I know did staine
      Pheroras petty valour: but they lie
      (Excepting you your selfe) that dare maintaine,
      That he did honor *Herod* more then I.
      For what I showd, loves power constraind me show,
      And pardon loving faults for *Mariams* sake.

HEROD *Mariam*, where is she?

PHAERORAS   Nay, I do not know,
      But absent use of her faire name I make:
      You have forgiven greater faults then this,
30   For *Constabarus* that against your will
      Preserv'd the sonnes of *Baba*, lives in blisse,
      Though you commanded him the youths to kill.

HEROD Goe, take a present order for his death,
      And let those traytors feele the worst of feares:
      Now *Salome* will whine to begge his breath,
      But Ile be deafe to prayers: and blind to teares.

PHAERORAS He is my Lord from *Salome* divorst,
      Though her affection did to leave him grieve:
      Yet was she by her love to you inforst,
40   To leave the man that would your foes relieve.

HEROD Then haste them to their death. I will requite
      Thee gentle *Mariam*. *Salome* I meane
      The thought of *Mariam* doth so steale my spirit,
      My mouth from speech of her I cannot weane.

                        Exit [PHAERORAS].

Act IV. Scene 3

[*Enter*] MARIAM.

HEROD And heere she comes indeed: happily met
My best, and deerest halfe: what ailes my deare?
Thou doest the difference certainly forget
Twixt Duskey habits, and a time so cleare.

MARIAM My Lord, I suit my garment to my minde,
And there no cheerfull colours can I finde.

HEROD Is this my welcome? have I longd so much
To see my dearest *Mariam* discontent?
What ist that is the cause thy heart to touch?
Oh speake, that I thy sorrow may prevent.   10
Art thou not *Juries* Queene, and *Herods* too?
Be my Commandres, be my Soveraigne guide:
To be by thee directed I will woo,
For in thy pleasure lies my highest pride.
Or if thou thinke *Judaeas* narrow bound,
Too strict a limit for thy great command:
Thou shalt be Empresse of *Arabia* crownd,
For thou shalt rule, and I will winne the Land.
Ile robbe the holy *Davids* Sepulcher
To give thee wealth, if thou for wealth do care: 20
Thou shalt have all, they did with him inter,
And I for thee will make the Temple bare.

MARIAM I neither have of power nor riches want,
I have enough, nor doe I wish for more:
Your offers to my heart no ease can grant,
Except they could my brothers life restore.
No, had you wisht the wretched *Mariam* glad,
Or had your love to her bene truly tide:
Nay, had you not desir'd to make her sad,
My brother nor my Grandsyre had not dide.   30

HEROD Wilt thou beleeve no oathes to cleere thy Lord?
How oft have I with execration sworne:
Thou art by me belov'd, by me ador'd,
Yet are my protestations heard with scorne.

Hercanus plotted to deprive my head
Of this long setled honor that I weare:
And therefore I did justly doome him dead,
To rid the Realme from perill, me from feare.
Yet I for *Mariams* sake doe so repent
40   The death of one: whose blood she did inherit:
I wish I had a Kingdomes treasure spent,
So I had nere expeld *Hercanus* spirit.
As I affected that same noble youth,
In lasting infamie my name inrole:
If I not mournd his death with heartie truth.
Did I not shew to him my earnest love,
When I to him the Priesthood did restore?
And did for him a living Priest remove,
Which never had bene done but once before.
50 MARIAM I know that mov'd by importunitie,
You made him Priest, and shortly after die.
HEROD I will not speake, unles to be beleev'd,
This froward humor will not doe you good:
It hath too much already *Herod* griev'd,
To thinke that you on termes of hate have stood.
Yet smile my dearest *Mariam*, doe but smile,
And I will all unkind conceits exile.
MARIAM I cannot frame disguise, nor never taught
My face a looke dissenting from my thought.
60 HEROD By heav'n you vexe me, build not on my love.
MARIAM I wil not build on so unstable ground.
HEROD Nought is so fixt, but peevishnes may move.
MARIAM Tis better sleightest cause then none were found.
HEROD Be judge your selfe, if ever *Herod* sought
Or would be mov'd a cause of change to finde:
Yet let your looke declare a milder thought,
My heart againe you shall to *Mariam* binde.
How oft did I for you my Mother chide,
Revile my Sister, and my brother rate:
70   And tell them all my *Mariam* they belide,
Distrust me still, if these be signes of hate.

Act IV. Scene 4

[*Enter* BUTLER.]

HEROD What hast thou here?

BUTLER   A drinke procuring love,
    The Queene desir'd me to deliver it.

MARIAM Did I? some hatefull practise this will prove,
    Yet can it be no worse then Heavens permit.

HEROD Confesse the truth thou wicked instrument,
    To her outragious will, tis passion sure:
    Tell true, and thou shalt scape the punishment,
    Which if thou doe conceale thou shalt endure.

BUTLER I know not, but I doubt it be no lesse,
    Long since the hate of you her heart did cease.   10

HEROD Know'st thou the cause thereof?

BUTLER   My Lord I gesse,
    Sohemus told the tale that did displease.

HEROD Oh Heaven! *Sohemus* false! Goe let him die,
    Stay not to suffer him to speake a word: [*Exit* BUTLER.]
    Oh damned villaine, did he falsifie
    The oath he swore ev'n of his owne accord?
    Now doe I know thy falshood, painted Divill
    Thou white Inchantres. Oh thou art so foule,
    That Ysop cannot clense thee worst of evill.
    A beautious body hides a loathsome soule,   20
    Your love *Sohemus* mov'd by his affection,
    Though he have ever heretofore bene true:
    Did blab forsooth, that I did give direction,
    If we were put to death to slaughter you.
    And you in blacke revenge attended now
    To adde a murther to your breach of vow.

MARIAM Is this a dream?

HEROD   Oh Heaven, that t'were no more,
    Ile give my Realme to who can prove it so:
    I would I were like any begger poore,
    So I for false my *Mariam* did not know.   30

Foule pith contain'd in the fairest rinde,
That ever grac'd a Caedar. Oh thine eye
Is pure as heaven, but impure thy minde,
And for impuritie shall *Mariam* die.
Why didst thou love *Sohemus?*

MARIAM   They can tell
That say I lov'd him, *Mariam* saies not so.

HEROD Oh cannot impudence the coales expell,
That for thy love in *Herods* bosome glowe:
It is as plaine as water, and deniall
40   Makes of thy falsehood but a greater triall.
Hast thou beheld thy selfe, and couldst thou staine
So rare perfection: even for love of thee
I doe profoundly hate thee. Wert thou plaine,
Thou shoul'dst the wonder of *Judea* bee.
But oh thou art not. Hell it selfe lies hid
Beneath thy heavenly show. Yet wert thou chast:
Thou might'st exalt, pull downe, command, forbid,
And be above the wheele of fortune plast.
Hadst thou complotted *Herods* massacre,
50   That so thy sonne a Monarch might be stilde,
Not halfe so grievous such an action were,
As once to thinke, that *Mariam* is defilde.
Bright workmanship of nature sulli'd ore,
With pitched darknes now thine end shall bee:
Thou shalt not live faire fiend to cozen more,
With heav'nly semblance, as thou cousnedst mee.
Yet must I love thee in despight of death,
And thou shalt die in the dispight of love:
For neither shall my love prolong thy breath,
60   Nor shall thy losse of breath my love remove.
I might have seene thy falsehood in thy face,
Where coul'dst thou get thy stares that serv'd for eyes?
Except by theft, and theft is foule disgrace:
This had appear'd before were *Herod* wise,

But I'me a sot, a very sot, no better:
My wisedome long agoe a wandring fell,
Thy face incountring it, my wit did fetter,
And made me for delight my freedome sell.
Give me my heart false creature, tis a wrong,
My guiltles heart should now with thine be slaine: 70
Thou hadst no right to locke it up so long,
And with usurpers name I *Mariam* staine.

  Enter BU[TLER.]

HEROD Have you design'd *Sohemus* to his end?
BUTLER I have my Lord.
HEROD   Then call our royall guard
 To doe as much for *Mariam*, they offend
 Leave ill unblam'd, or good without reward.

  [*Enter* SOLDIERS.]

 Here take her to her death. Come backe, come backe,
 What ment I to deprive the world of light:
 To muffle *Jury* in the foulest blacke,
 That ever was an opposite to white.   80
 Why whither would you carrie her?
SOLDIERS   You bad
 We should conduct her to her death my Lord.
HEROD Wie sure I did not, *Herod* was not mad,
 Why should she feele the furie of the sword?
 Oh now the griefe returnes into my heart,
 And pulles me peecemeale: love and hate doe fight:
 And now hath love acquir'd the greater part,
 Yet now hath hate, affection conquer'd quite.
 And therefore beare her hence: and *Hebrew* why
 Seaze you with Lyons pawes the fairest lam   90
 Of all the flocke? she must not, shall not, die,
 Without her I most miserable am.
 And with her more then most, away, away,
 But beare her but to prison not to death:
 And is she gon indeed, stay villaines stay,
 Her lookes alone preserv'd your Soveraignes breath.

Well let her goe, but yet she shall not die,
I cannot thinke she ment to poison me:
But certaine tis she liv'd too wantonly,
100   And therefore shall she never more be free.

    [*Exeunt* HEROD, ATTENDANTS *and* SOLDIERS *with* MARIAM.]

Act IV. Scene 5

BUTLER Foule villaine, can thy pitchie coloured soule
    Permit thine eare to heare her causeles doome?
    And not inforce thy tongue that tale controule,
    That must unjustly bring her to her toome.
    Oh *Salome* thou hast thy selfe repaid,
    For all the benefits that thou hast done:
    Thou art the cause I have the queene betraid,
    Thou hast my hart to darkest false-hood wonne.
    I am condemn'd, heav'n gave me not my tongue
10   To slander innocents, to lie, deceive:
    To be the hatefull instrument to wrong,
    The earth of greatest glory to bereave.
    My sinne ascends and doth to heav'n crie,
    It is the blackest deed that ever was:
    And there doth sit an Angell notarie,
    That doth record it downe in leaves of brasse.
    Oh how my heart doth quake: *Achitophel*,
    Thou founds a meanes thy selfe from shame to free:
    And sure my soule approves thou didst not well,
20   All follow some, and I will follow thee.   [*Exit* BUTLER.]

Act IV. Scene 6

    [*Enter*] CONSTABARUS, BABUS SONNES, *and their guard.*
CONSTABARUS Now here we step our last, the way to death,
    We must not tread this way a second time:
    Yet let us resolutely yeeld our breath,
    Death is the onely ladder, Heav'n to clime.

BABUS FIRST SONNE With willing mind I could my selfe resigne,
  But yet it grieves me with a griefe untold:
  Our death should be accompani'd with thine,
  Our friendship we to thee have dearely sold.

CONSTABARUS Still wilt thou wrong the sacred name of friend?
  Then should'st thou never stile it friendship more: 10
  But base mechanicke traffique that doth lend,
  Yet will be sure they shall the debt restore.
  I could with needlesse complement returne,
  Tis for thy ceremonie I could say:
  Tis I that made the fire your house to burne,
  For but for me she would not you betray.
  Had not the damned woman sought mine end,
  You had not bene the subject of her hate:
  You never did her hatefull minde offend,
  Nor could your deaths have freed our nuptiall fate.   20
  Therefore faire friends, though you were still unborne,
  Some other subtiltie devisde should bee:
  Where by my life, though guiltles should be torne,
  Thus have I prov'd, tis you that die for mee.
  And therefore should I weakely now lament,
  You have but done your duties, friends should die
  Alone their friends disaster to prevent,
  Though not compeld by strong necessitie.
  But now farewell faire citie, never more
  Shall I behold your beautie shining bright: 30
  Farewell of *Jewish* men the worthy store,
  But no farewell to any female wight.
  You wavering crue: my curse to you I leave,
  You had but one to give you any grace:
  And you your selves will *Mariams* life bereave,
  Your common-wealth doth innocencie chase.
  You creatures made to be the humane curse,
  You Tygers, Lyonesses, hungry Beares,
  Teare massacring *Hienas*: nay far worse,
  For they for pray doe shed their fained teares.   40
  But you will weepe, (you creatures crosse to good)
  For your unquenched thirst of humane blood:

You were the Angels cast from heave'n for pride,
And still doe keepe your Angels outward show,
But none of you are inly beautifide,
For still your heav'n depriving pride doth grow.
Did not the sinnes of many require a scourge,
Your place on earth had bene by this withstood:
But since a flood no more the world must purge,
You staid in office of a second flood.
You giddy creatures, sowers of debate,
You'll love to day, and for no other cause,
But for you yesterday did deply hate,
You are the wreake of order, breach of lawes.
You best, are foolish, froward, wanton, vaine,
Your worst adulterous, murderous, cunning, proud:
And *Salome* attends the latter traine,
Or rather she their leader is allowd.
I do the sottishnesse of men bewaile,
That doe with following you inhance your pride:
T'were better that the humane race should faile,
Then be by such a mischiefe multiplide.
Chams servile curse to all your sexe was given,
Because in Paradise you did offend:
Then doe we not resist the will of Heaven,
When on your willes like servants we attend?
You are to nothing constant but to ill,
You are with nought but wickednesse indude:
Your loves are set on nothing but your will,
And thus my censure I of you conclude.
You are the least of goods, the worst of evils,
Your best are worse then men: your worst then divels.

BABUS SECOND SONNE Come let us to our death: are we not blest?
Our death will freedome from these creatures give:
Those trouble quiet sowers of unrest,
And this I vow that had I leave to live,
I would for ever leade a single life,
And never venter on a divellish wife.   [*Exeunt.*]

Act IV. Scene 7

[*Enter*] HEROD *and* SALOME.

HEROD Nay, she shall die. Die quoth you, that she shall:
　　But for the meanes. The meanes! Me thinks tis hard
　　To finde a meanes to murther her withall,
　　Therefore I am resolv'd she shall be spar'd.

SALOME Why? let her be beheaded.

HEROD 　　　　　　　　　　That were well,
　　Thinke you that swords are miracles like you:
　　Her skinne will ev'ry Curtlax edge repell,
　　And then your enterprise you well may rue.
　　What if the fierce Arabian notice take,
　　Of this your wretched weaponlesse estate: 　　　　　　　10
　　They answere when we bid resistance make,
　　That *Mariams* skinne their fanchions did rebate.
　　Beware of this, you make a goodly hand,
　　If you of weapons doe deprive our Land.

SALOME Why drowne her then.

HEROD 　　　　　　　　　Indeed a sweet device,
　　Why? would not ev'ry River turne her course
　　Rather then doe her beautie prejudice?
　　And be reverted to the proper sourse.
　　So not a drop of water should be found
　　In all Judeas quondam firtill ground. 　　　　　　　　20

SALOME Then let the fire devoure her.

HEROD 　　　　　　　　　　　T'will not bee:
　　Flame is from her deriv'd into my heart:
　　Thou nursest flame, flame will not murther thee,
　　My fairest *Mariam*, fullest of desert.

SALOME Then let her live for me.

HEROD 　　　　　　　　　Nay, she shall die:
　　But can you live without her?

SALOME 　　　　　　　　Doubt you that?

HEROD I'me sure I cannot, I beseech you trie:
　　I have experience but I know not what.

SALOME How should I try?

HEROD   Why let my love be slaine,
30   But if we cannot live without her sight
       Youle finde the meanes to make her breathe againe,
       Or else you will bereave my comfort quite.

SALOME Oh I: I warrant you.   [*Exit* SALOME.]

HEROD   What is she gone?
       And gone to bid the world be overthrowne:
       What? is her hearts composure hardest stone?
       To what a passe are cruell women growne?   [*Enter* SALOME.]
       She is return'd already: have you done?
       Ist possible you can command so soone?
       A creatures heart to quench the flaming Sunne,
40   Or from the skie to wipe away the Moone.

SALOME If *Mariam* be the Sunne and Moone, it is:
       For I already have commanded this.

HEROD But have you seene her cheek?

SALOME   A thousand times.

HEROD But did you marke it too?

SALOME   I very well.

HEROD What ist?

SALOME   A Crimson bush, that ever limes
       The soule whose foresight doth not much excell.

HEROD Send word she shall not dye. Her cheek a bush,
       Nay, then I see indeed you markt it not.

SALOME Tis very faire, but yet will never blush,
50   Though foule dishonors do her forehead blot.

HEROD Then let her die, tis very true indeed,
       And for this fault alone shall *Mariam* bleed.

SALOME What fault my Lord?

HEROD   What fault ist? you that aske:
       If you be ignorant I know of none,
       To call her backe from death shall be your taske,
       I'm glad that she for innocent is knowne.
       For on the brow of *Mariam* hangs a Fleece,
       Whose slenderest twine is strong enough to binde
       The hearts of Kings, the pride and shame of *Greece*,
60   *Troy* flaming *Helens* not so fairely shinde.

SALOME Tis true indeed, she layes them out for nets,
       To catch the hearts that doe not shune a baite:
       Tis time to speake: for *Herod* sure forgets
       That *Mariams* very tresses hide deceit.

HEROD Oh doe they so? nay, then you doe but well,
       Insooth I thought it had beene haire:
       Nets call you them? Lord, how they doe excell,
       I never saw a net that show'd so faire.
       But have you heard her speake?

SALOME   You know I have.

HEROD And were you not amaz'd?

SALOME   No, not a whit.   70

HEROD Then t'was not her you heard, her life Ile save,
       For *Mariam* hath a world amazing wit.

SALOME She speaks a beautious language, but within
        Her heart is false as powder: and her tongue
        Doth but allure the auditors to sinne,
        And is the instrument to doe you wrong.

HEROD It may be so: nay, tis so: shee's unchaste,
       Her mouth will ope to ev'ry strangers eare:
       Then let the executioner make haste,
       Lest she inchant him, if her words he heare.   80
       Let him be deafe, lest she do him surprise
       That shall to free her spirit be assignde:
       Yet what boots deafenes if he have his eyes,
       Her murtherer must be both deafe and blinde.
       For if he see, he needs must see the starres
       That shine on eyther side of *Mariams* face:
       Whose sweet aspect will terminate the warres,
       Wherewith he should a soule so precious chase.
       Her eyes can speake, and in their speaking move,
       Oft did my heart with reverence receive   90
       The worlds mandates. Pretty tales of love
       They utter, which can humane bondage weave.
       But shall I let this heavens modell dye?
       Which for a small selfe-portraiture she drew:
       Her eyes like starres, her forehead like the skie,
       She is like Heaven, and must be heavenly true.

SALOME Your thoughts do rave with doating on the Queen,
    Her eyes are ebon hewde, and you'll confesse:
    A sable starre hath beene but seldome seene,
100   Then speake of reason more, of *Mariam* lesse.

HEROD Your selfe are held a goodly creature heere,
    Yet so unlike my *Mariam* in your shape:
    That when to her you have approached neere,
    My selfe hath often tane you for an Ape.
    And yet you prate of beautie: goe your waies,
    You are to her a Sun-burnt Blackamore:
    Your paintings cannot equall *Mariams* praise,
    Her nature is so rich, you are so poore.
    Let her be staide from death, for if she die;
110   We do we know not what to stop her breath:
    A world cannot another *Mariam* buy,
    Why stay you lingring? countermaund her death.

SALOME Then youle no more remember what hath past,
    Sohemus love, and hers shall be forgot:
    Tis well in truth: that fault may be her last,
    And she may mend, though yet she love you not.

HEROD Oh God: tis true. *Sohemus*: earth and heav'n,
    Why did you both conspire to make me curst:
    In cousning me with showes, and proofes unev'n?
120   She show'd the best, and yet did prove the worst.
    Her show was such, as had our singing king
    The holy *David, Mariams* beautie seene:
    The *Hittits* had then felt no deadly sting,
    Nor *Bethsabe* had never bene a Queene.
    Or had his sonne the wisest man of men,
    Whose fond delight did most consist in change:
    Beheld her face, he had bene staid agen,
    No creature having her, can wish to range.
    Had *Asuerus* seene my *Mariams* brow,
130   The humble *Jewe*, she might have walkt alone:
    Her beautious vertue should have staid below,
    Whiles *Mariam* mounted to the Persian throne.

But what availes it all: for in the waight
She is deceitfull, light as vanitie:
Oh she was made for nothing but a bait,
To traine some haples man to miserie.
I am the haples man that have bene trainde,
To endles bondage. I will see her yet:
Me thinkes I should discerne her if she fainde,
Can humane eyes be dazde by womans wit?   140
Once more these eyes of mine with hers shall meet,
Before the headsman doe her life bereave:
Shall I for ever part from thee my sweet?
Without the taking of my latest leave.

SALOME You had as good resolve to save her now,
Ile stay her death, tis well determined:
For sure she never more will breake her vow,
Sohemus and *Josephus* both are dead.

HEROD She shall not live, nor will I see her face,
A long heald wound, a second time doth bleed: 150
With *Joseph* I remember her disgrace,
A shamefull end ensues a shamefull deed.
Oh that I had not cald to minde anew,
The discontent of *Mariams* wavering hart:
Twas you: you foule mouth'd *Ate*, none but you,
That did the thought hereof to me impart.
Hence from my sight, my blacke tormenter hence,
For hadst not thou made *Herod* unsecure:
I had not doubted *Mariams* innocence,
But still had held her in my heart for pure.   160

SALOME Ile leave you to your passion: tis no time
To purge me now, though of a guiltles crime.   *Exit* [SALOME].

HEROD Destruction take thee: thou hast made my hart
As heavie as revenge, I am so dull,
Me thinkes I am not sensible of smart,
Though hiddious horrors at my bosome pull.
My head waies downwards: therefore will I goe
To try if I can sleepe away my woe.   [*Exit* HEROD.]

Act IV. Scene 8

[*Enter*] MARIAM.

MARIAM Am I the *Mariam* that presum'd so much,
    And deem'd my face must needes preserve my breath?
    I, I it was that thought my beautie such,
    As it alone could countermaund my death.
    Now death will teach me: he can pale aswell
    A cheeke of roses, as a cheeke lesse bright:
    And dim an eye whose shine doth most excell,
    Assoone as one that casts a meaner light.
    Had not my selfe against my selfe conspirde,
10   No plot: no adversarie from without
    Could *Herods* love from *Mariam* have retirde,
    Or from his heart have thrust my semblance out.
    The wanton Queene that never lov'd for love,
    False *Cleopatra*, wholly set on gaine:
    With all her slights did prove: yet vainly prove,
    For her the love of *Herod* to obtaine.
    Yet her allurements, all her courtly guile,
    Her smiles, her favours, and her smooth deceit:
    Could not my face from *Herods* minde exile,
20   But were with him of lesse then little weight.
    That face and person that in *Asia* late
    For beauties Goddesse *Paphos* Queene was tane:
    That face that did captive great *Julius* fate,
    That very face that was *Anthonius* bane.
    That face that to be *Egipts* pride was borne,
    That face that all the world esteem'd so rare:
    Did *Herod* hate, despise, neglect, and scorne,
    When with the same, he *Mariams* did compare.
    This made that I improvidently wrought,
30   And on the wager even my life did pawne:
    Because I thought, and yet but truly thought,
    That *Herods* love could not from me be drawne.
    But now though out of time, I plainly see
    It could be drawne, though never drawne from me:

Had I but with humilitie bene grac'te,
As well as faire I might have prov'd me wise:
But I did thinke because I knew me chaste,
One vertue for a woman, might suffice.
That mind for glory of our sexe might stand,
Wherein humilitie and chastitie   40
Doth march with equall paces hand in hand,
But one if single seene, who setteth by?
And I had singly one, but tis my joy,
That I was ever innocent, though sower:
And therefore can they but my life destroy,
My Soule is free from adversaries power.

    Enter DORIS.

You Princes great in power, and high in birth,
Be great and high, I envy not your hap:
Your birth must be from dust: your power on earth,
In heav'n shall *Mariam* sit in *Saraes* lap.   50

DORIS In heav'n, your beautie cannot bring you thither,
Your soule is blacke and spotted, full of sinne:
You in adultry liv'd nine yeare together,
And heav'n will never let adultry in.

MARIAM What art thou that dost poore *Mariam* pursue?
Some spirit sent to drive me to dispaire:
Who sees for truth that *Mariam* is untrue,
If faire she be, she is as chaste as faire.

DORIS I am that *Doris* that was once belov'd,
Belov'd by *Herod*: *Herods* lawfull wife: 60
Twas you that *Doris* from his side remov'd,
And rob'd from me the glory of my life.

MARIAM Was that adultry: did not Moses say,
That he that being matcht did deadly hate:
Might by permission put his wife away,
And take a more belov'd to be his mate?

DORIS What did he hate me for: for simple truth?
For bringing beautious babes for love to him:
For riches: noble birth, or tender youth,
Or for no staine did *Doris* honour dim?   70

Oh tell me *Mariam*, tell me if you knowe,
Which fault of these made *Herod Doris* foe.
These thrice three yeares have I with hands held up,
And bowed knees fast nailed to the ground:
Besought for thee the dreggs of that same cup,
That cup of wrath that is for sinners found.
And now thou art to drinke it: *Doris* curse,
Upon thy selfe did all this while attend,
But now it shall pursue thy children worse.

80   MARIAM   Oh *Doris* now to thee my knees I bend,
That hart that never bow'd to thee doth bow:
Curse not mine infants, let it thee suffice,
That Heav'n doth punishment to me allow.
Thy curse is cause that guiltles *Mariam* dies.

DORIS   Had I ten thousand tongues, and ev'ry tongue
Inflam'd with poisons power, and steept in gall:
My curses would not answere for my wrong,
Though I in cursing thee imployd them all.
Heare thou that didst mount *Gerarim* command,

90   To be a place whereon with cause to curse:
Stretch thy revenging arme: thrust forth thy hand,
And plague the mother much: the children worse.
Throw flaming fire upon the baseborne heads
That were begotten in unlawfull beds.
But let them live till they have sence to know
What tis to be in miserable state:
Then be their neerest friends their overthrow,
Attended be they by suspitious hate.
And *Mariam*, I doe hope this boy of mine

100   Shall one day come to be the death of thine.   *Exit* [DORIS].
MARIAM   Oh! Heaven forbid. I hope the world shall see,
This curse of thine shall be return'd on thee:
Now earth farewell, though I be yet but yong,
Yet I, me thinks, have knowne thee too too long.
                                    Exit [MARIAM].

CHORUS The fairest action of our humane life,
    Is scorning to revenge an injurie:
    For who forgives without a further strife,
    His adversaries heart to him doth tie.
      And tis a firmer conquest truely sed,
      To winne the heart, then overthrow the head.   110

If we a worthy enemie doe finde,
To yeeld to worth, it must be nobly done:
But if of baser mettall be his minde,
In base revenge there is no honor wonne.
    Who would a worthy courage overthrow,
    And who would wrastle with a worthles foe?

We say our hearts are great and cannot yeeld,
Because they cannot yeeld it proves them poore:
Great hearts are task't beyond their power, but seld
The weakest Lyon will the lowdest roare.   120
    Truths schoole for certaine doth this same allow,
    High hartednes doth sometimes teach to bow.

A noble heart doth teach a vertuous scorne,
To scorne to owe a dutie over-long:
To scorne to be for benefits forborne,
To scorne to lie, to scorne to doe a wrong.
    To scorne to beare an injurie in minde,
    To scorne a free-borne heart slave-like to binde.

But if for wrongs we needs revenge must have,
Then be our vengeance of the noblest kinde: 130
Doe we his body from our furie save,
And let our hate prevaile against our minde?
    What can gainst him a greater vengeance bee,
    Then make his foe more worthy farre then hee?

Had *Mariam* scorn'd to leave a due unpaide,
Shee would to *Herod* then have paid her love:
And not have bene by sullen passion swaide

> To fixe her thoughts all injurie above
> Is vertuous pride. Had *Mariam* thus bene prov'd,
140   Long famous life to her had bene allowd.

Act V. Scene 1

[*Enter*] NUNTIO.

NUNTIO When, sweetest friend, did I so farre offend
    Your heavenly selfe: that you my fault to quit
    Have made me now relator of her end,
    The end of beautie? Chastitie and wit,
    Was none so haples in the fatall place,
    But I, most wretched, for the Queene t'chuse,
    Tis certaine I have some ill boding face
    That made me culd to tell this luckles newes.
    And yet no news to *Herod*: were it new,
10 To him unhappy t'had not bene at all:
    Yet doe I long to come within his vew,
    That he may know his wife did guiltles fall:
    And heere he comes. [*Enter* HEROD.] Your *Mariam* greets you
        well.

HEROD What? lives my *Mariam*? joy, exceeding joy.
    She shall not die.

NUNTIO   Heav'n doth your will repell.

HEROD Oh doe not with thy words my life destroy,
    I prethy tell no dying-tale: thine eye
    Without thy tongue doth tell but too too much:
    Yet let thy tongues addition make me die,
20 Death welcome, comes to him whose griefe is such.

NUNTIO I went amongst the curious gazing troope,
    To see the last of her that was the best:
    To see if death had hart to make her stoope,
    To see the Sunne admiring *Phoenix* nest.
    When there I came, upon the way I saw
    The stately *Mariam* not debas'd by feare:
    Her looke did seeme to keepe the world in awe,
    Yet mildly did her face this fortune beare.

HEROD Thou dost usurpe my right, my tongue was fram'd
   To be the instrument of *Mariams* praise: 30
   Yet speake: she cannot be too often fam'd:
   All tongues suffice not her sweet name to raise.

NUNTIO But as she came she *Alexandra* met,
   Who did her death (sweet Queene) no whit bewaile,
   But as if nature she did quite forget,
   She did upon her daughter loudly raile.

HEROD Why stopt you not her mouth? where had she words
   To darken that, that Heaven made so bright?
   Our sacred tongue no *Epithite* affords,
   To call her other then the worlds delight.   40

NUNTIO Shee told her that her death was too too good,
   And that already she had liv'd too long:
   She said, she sham'd to have a part in blood
   Of her that did the princely *Herod* wrong.

HEROD Base picke-thanke Divell. Shame, twas all her glory,
   That she to noble *Mariam* was the mother:
   But never shall it live in any storie
   Her name, except to infamy ile smother.
   What answere did her princely daughter make?

NUNTIO She made no answere, but she lookt the while,   50
   As if thereof she scarce did notice take,
   Yet smilde, a dutifull, though scornefull smile.

HEROD Sweet creature, I that looke to mind doe call,
   Full oft hath *Herod* bene amaz'd withall. Go on.

NUNTIO She came unmov'd with pleasant grace,
   As if to triumph her arrivall were:
   In stately habite, and with cheerfull face:
   Yet ev'ry eye was moyst, but *Mariams* there.
   When justly opposite to me she came,
   She pickt me out from all the crue: 60
   She beckned to me, cald me by my name,
   For she my name, my birth, and fortune knew.

HEROD What did she name thee? happy, happy man,
   Wilt thou not ever love that name the better?
   But what sweet tune did this faire dying Swan
   Afford thine eare: tell all, omit no letter.

NUNTIO Tell thou my Lord, said she.

HEROD   Mee, ment she mee?
Ist true, the more my shame: I was her Lord,
Were I not made her Lord, I still should bee:
But now her name must be by me adord.
Oh say, what said she more? each word she sed
Shall be the food whereon my heart is fed.

NUNTIO Tell thou my Lord thou saw'st me loose my breath.

HEROD Oh that I could that sentence now controule.

NUNTIO If guiltily eternall be my death,

HEROD I hold her chast ev'n in my inmost soule.

NUNTIO By three daies hence if wishes could revive,
I know himselfe would make me oft alive.

HEROD Three daies: three houres, three minutes, not so much,
A minute in a thousand parts divided,
My penitencie for her death is such,
As in the first I wisht she had not died.
But forward in thy tale.

NUNTIO   Why on she went,
And after she some silent praier had sed:
She did as if to die she were content,
And thus to heav'n her heav'nly soule is fled.

HEROD But art thou sure there doth no life remaine?
Ist possible my *Mariam* should be dead,
Is there no tricke to make her breathe againe?

NUNTIO Her body is divided from her head.

HEROD Why yet me thinkes there might be found by art,
Strange waies of cure, tis sure rare things are don:
By an inventive head, and willing heart.

NUNTIO Let not my Lord your fancies idlely run.
It is as possible it should be seene,
That we should make the holy Abraham live,
Though he intomb'd two thousand yeares had bene,
As breath againe to slaughtred *Mariam* give.
But now for more assaults prepare your eares.

HEROD There cannot be a further cause of mone,
This accident shall shelter me from feares:
What can I feare? already *Mariams* gone.

Yet tell ev'n what you will.

NUNTIO   As I came by,
From *Mariams* death I saw upon a tree,
A man that to his necke a cord did tie:
Which cord he had designd his end to bee.
When me he once discern'd, he downwards bow'd,
And thus with fearefull voyce he cride alowd,
Goe tell the King he trusted ere he tride,
I am the cause that *Mariam* causeles dide.   110

HEROD Damnation take him, for it was the slave
That said she ment with poisons deadly force
To end my life that she the Crowne might have:
Which tale did *Mariam* from her selfe divorce.
Oh pardon me thou pure unspotted Ghost,
My punishment must needes sufficient bee,
In missing that content I valued most:
Which was thy admirable face to see.
I had but one inestimable Jewell,
Yet one I had no monarch had the like,   120
And therefore may I curse my selfe as cruell:
Twas broken by a blowe my selfe did strike.
I gaz'd thereon and never thought me blest,
But when on it my dazled eye might rest:
A pretious Mirror made by wonderous art,
I prizd it ten times dearer then my Crowne,
And laide it up fast foulded in my heart:
Yet I in suddaine choler cast it downe.
And pasht it all to peeces: twas no foe,
That robd me of it; no *Arabian* host,   130
Nor no *Armenian* guide hath usde me so:
But *Herods* wretched selfe hath *Herod* crost.
She was my gracefull moytie, me accurst,
To slay my better halfe and save my worst.
But sure she is not dead you did but jest,
To put me in perplexitie a while,
Twere well indeed if I could so be drest:
I see she is alive, me thinkes you smile.

NUNTIO If sainted *Abel* yet deceased bee,

140   Tis certaine *Mariam* is as dead as hee.

HEROD Why then goe call her to me, bid her now

     Put on faire habite, stately ornament:

     And let no frowne oreshade her smoothest brow,

     In her doth *Herod* place his whole content.

NUNTIO Sheel come in stately weedes to please your sence,

     If now she come attirde in robe of heaven:

     Remember you your selfe did send her hence,

     And now to you she can no more be given.

HEROD Shee's dead, hell take her murderers, she was faire,

150   Oh what a hand she had, it was so white,

     It did the whitenes of the snowe impaire:

     I never more shall see so sweet a sight.

NUNTIO Tis true, her hand was rare.

HEROD   Her hand? her hands;

     She had not singly one of beautie rare,

     But such a paire as heere where *Herod* stands,

     He dares the world to make to both compare.

     Accursed *Salome*, hadst thou bene still,

     My *Mariam* had bene breathing by my side:

     Oh never had I: had I had my will,

160   Sent forth command, that *Mariam* should have dide.

     But *Salome* thou didst with envy vexe,

     To see thy selfe out-matched in thy sexe:

     Upon your sexes forehead *Mariam* sat,

     To grace you all like an imperiall crowne,

     But you fond foole have rudely pusht thereat,

     And proudly puld your proper glory downe.

     One smile of hers: Nay, not so much: a looke

     Was worth a hundred thousand such as you,

     Judea how canst thou the wretches brooke,

170   That robd from thee the fairest of the crew?

     You dwellers in the now deprived land,

     Wherein the matchles *Mariam* was bred:

     Why graspe not each of you a sword in hand,

     To ayme at me your cruell Soveraignes head.

Oh when you thinke of *Herod* as your King,
And owner of the pride of *Palestine*:
This act to your remembrance likewise bring,
Tis I have overthrowne your royall line.
Within her purer vaines the blood did run,
That from her Grandam *Sara* she deriv'd,   180
Whose beldame age the love of Kings hath wonne,
Oh that her issue had as long bene li'vd.
But can her eye be made by death obscure?
I cannot thinke but it must sparkle still:
Foule sacriledge to rob those lights so pure,
From out a Temple made by heav'nly skill.
I am the Villaine that have done the deed,
The cruell deed, though by anothers hand,
My word though not my sword made *Mariam* bleed,
Hircanus Grandchild died at my command.   190
That *Mariam* that I once did love so deare,
The partner of my now detested bed,
Why shine you sun with an aspect so cleare?
I tell you once againe my *Mariams* dead.
You could but shine, if some *Egiptian* blows,
Or *Aethiopian* doudy lose her life:
This was, then wherefore bend you not your brows,
The King of *Juries* faire and spotles wife.
Denie thy beames, and *Moone* refuse thy light,
Let all the starres be darke, let *Juries* eye   200
No more distinguish which is day and night:
Since her best birth did in her bosome die.
Those fond Idolaters the men of *Greece*,
Maintaine these orbes are safely governed:
That each within themselves have Gods a peece,
By whom their stedfast course is justly led.
But were it so, as so it cannot bee,
They all would put their mourning garments on:
Not one of them would yeeld a light to mee,
To me that is the cause that *Mariams* gon.   210

For though they faine their *Saturne* melancholy,
Of sowre behaviours, and of angry moode:
They faine him likewise to be just and holy,
And justice needes must seeke revenge for blood.
Their *Jove*, if *Jove* he were, would sure desire,
To punish him that slew so faire a lasse:
For *Laedaes* beautie set his heart on fire,
Yet she not halfe so faire as *Mariam* was.
And *Mars* would deeme his *Venus* had bene slaine,
220   *Sol* to recover her would never sticke:
For if he want the power her life to gaine:
Then Physicks God is but an Empericke.
The Queene of love would storme for beauties sake,
And *Hermes* too, since he bestow'd her wit,
The nights pale light for angrie griefe would shake,
To see chast *Mariam* die in age unfit.
But oh I am deceiv'd, she past them all
In every gift, in every propertie:
Her Excellencies wrought her timeles fall,
230   And they rejoyc'd, not griev'd to see her die.
The *Paphian* Goddesse did repent her wast,
When she to one such beautie did allow:
Mercurius thought her wit his wit surpast,
And *Cinthia* envi'd *Mariams* brighter brow.
But these are fictions, they are voyd of sence,
The *Greekes* but dreame, and dreaming falsehoods tell:
They neither can offend nor give defence,
And not by them it was my *Mariam* fell.
If she had bene like an *Egiptian* blacke,
240   And not so faire, she had bene longer livde:
Her overflow of beautie turned backe,
And drownde the spring from whence it was derivde.
Her heav'nly beautie twas that made me thinke
That it with chastitie could never dwell:
But now I see that heav'n in her did linke,
A spirit and a person to excell.
Ile muffle up my selfe in endles night,
And never let mine eyes behold the light.

Retire thy selfe vile monster, worse then hee
That staind the virgin earth with brothers blood,   250
Still in some vault or denne inclosed bee,
Where with thy teares thou maist beget a flood,
Which flood in time may drowne thee: happie day
When thou at once shalt die and finde a grave,
A stone upon the vault, some one shall lay,
Which monument shall an inscription have.
And these shall be the words it shall containe,
Heere Herod *lies, that hath his* Mariam *slaine.*   [*Exeunt.*]

CHORUS   Who ever hath beheld with steadfast eye,
          The strange events of this one onely day: 260
          How many were deceiv'd? How many die,
          That once to day did grounds of safetie lay?
              It will from them all certaintie bereve,
              Since twice six houres so many can deceive.

          This morning *Herod* held for surely dead,
          And all the *Jewes* on *Mariam* did attend:
          And *Constabarus* rise from *Saloms* bed,
          And neither dreamd of a divorce or end.
              Pheroras joyd that he might have his wife,
              And *Babus* sonnes for safetie of their life.   270

          To night our *Herod* doth alive remaine,
          The guiltles *Mariam* is depriv'd of breath:
          Stout *Constabarus* both divorst and slaine,
          The valiant sonnes of *Baba* have their death.
              Pheroras sure his love to be bereft,
              If *Salome* her sute unmade had left.

          Herod this morning did expect with joy,
          To see his *Mariams* much beloved face:
          And yet ere night he did her life destroy,
          And surely thought she did her name disgrace.   280
              Yet now againe so short do humors last,
              He both repents her death and knowes her chast.

Had he with wisedome now her death delaide,
He at his pleasure might command her death:
But now he hath his power so much betraide,
As all his woes cannot restore her breath.
  Now doth he strangely lunatickly rave,
  Because his *Mariams* life he cannot save.

This daies events were certainly ordainde,
To be the warning to posteritie:
So many changes are therein containde,
So admirablie strange varietie.
  This day alone, our sagest *Hebrewes* shall
  In after times the schoole of wisedome call.

FINIS.

NOTES

ABBREVIATIONS

AS   *Astrophil and Stella*, in Ringler

Cerasano and Wynne-Davies   Cerasano and Wynne-Davies, *Renaissance Drama by Women*

Croft   *The Poems of Robert Sidney*, ed. P. J. Croft (Oxford: Clarendon, 1984)

Dunstan   Cary, Elizabeth, *The Tragedy of Mariam*, ed. A. C. Dunstan, Malone
                                Society (Oxford: Oxford University Press, 1914)

England   Euripides, *Iphigeneia in Aulis*, ed. E. B. England (London: Mac-
                                millan, 1891)

Garnier   *Two Tragedies by Robert Garnier*, ed. C. M. Hill and M. Morrison
                                (London: Athlone, 1975)

Herford and Simpson   *Ben Jonson*, ed. C. H. Herford and Percy and Evelyn Simpson,
                                11 vols. (Oxford: Oxford University Press, 1925–52)

Ringler   *The Poems of Sir Philip Sidney*, ed. W. J. Ringler (Oxford: Clarendon,
                                1962)

Riverside   *The Riverside Shakespeare*, ed. G. Blakemore Evans et al. (Boston:
                                Houghton Mifflin, 1974)

Weller and Ferguson   Cary, Elizabeth, *The Tragedy of Mariam, The Fair Queen of Jewry*, ed.
                                Barry Weller and Margaret W. Ferguson (Berkeley: University of
                                California Press, 1994)

Wright   Cary, Elizabeth, *The Tragedy of Mariam the Fair Queen of Jewry*, ed.
                                Stephanie J. Wright (Keele: Keele University Press, 1996)

The Tragedie of Iphigeneia

Tragedy by Euripides, *Iphigeneia he en Aulidi* (*Iphigeneia in Aulis*), first production dated
to *c.* 406 BC, in a version by Jane, Lady Lumley entitled *The Tragedie of Euripides called
Iphigeneia*.

   DATE: *The Tragedie of Iphigeneia* is conventionally dated to 1550 because this is
the date of John, Baron Lumley's translation of Erasmus' *Institution of a Christian
Prince*, also dedicated to Lady Lumley's father the Earl of Arundel. The family
owned a number of works by or edited by Erasmus, and the assumption is that
Lord and Lady Lumley compiled their translations as a pair. However, there are a
number of possible objections to this early date: Lady Lumley would only have

been twelve or thirteen when she completed *Iphigeneia*, not impossible in the sixteenth century, but rather prodigious; it predates the principal period of Lady Lumley's bookbuying, since of the six printed books with her signature on the title page to be found in the Lumley library, only Cicero's *Rhetoricorum ad Herennium libri quatuor* dates from before 1550 (Venice, 1546; the other works, largely pietistic and theological, date from between 1552 and 1567); if Lady Lumley consulted a Greek text (see Introduction, p. xxiv), her work must have been done after 1553, unless such a text was mysteriously removed from the Lumley library. Together with consideration of sources below, these factors suggest a date in the mid 1550s, still close enough to Lord Lumley's Erasmus to give it a clear relationship to that work.

SOURCES: The text used for the translation has not been determined, but it has been convincingly demonstrated from internal evidence that Lady Lumley knew and consulted Erasmus' Latin translation (first published 1506). Manuscripts of Euripides' *Iphigeneia* were in circulation by the mid fourteenth century, but the play did not become a popular choice for translation until the appearance of Erasmus' Latin version, with *Hekabe*, also translated by Erasmus. Thereafter, *Iphigeneia* became the most translated Greek tragedy in Europe in the sixteenth century; if Lady Lumley used Erasmus as a crib, she was not alone. The more pressing question is whether she used the Greek text at all, or simply translated Erasmus' Latin, as suggested by Frank Crane (see Further Reading below). Internal evidence is shaky either way because Lady Lumley is clearly not attempting the kind of exact translation which would allow us to be certain about what text she used. Her spelling of 'Iphigeneia' in Greek style may be significant, as may the fact that the play is bound in with translations of Isocrates (see below). Both Euripides and Isocrates are considered 'pure' Attic, good texts for beginners in Greek translation. There were a number of Greek texts of Euripides available, which Lady Lumley could have consulted. The Aldine edition of 1503 under the editorship of M. Musurus contained all the Greek texts except *Elektra*, and another complete edition of the plays was produced in Basle in 1537. As well, there were editions of selected plays, in Greek and Latin. There were also editions of Erasmus which included the Greek text as well as his Latin versions (Basle, 1524 and 1530). She might also have consulted a manuscript. However, none of these works is listed in the Lumley library catalogue of 1596 (copied in 1609); it lists only *Euripidis Hecuba Iphigenia tragediae graece* (Louvain, 1520), a Greek companion to Erasmus' Latin text. This copy belonged to Thomas Cranmer, and cannot have been available to the Lumleys until 1553 at the earliest.

OTHER SOURCES: There is no sign in the text that Lady Lumley knew Euripides' *Iphigenia in Tauris*, which was relatively neglected until the eighteenth century, or that she knew the harsher version of the sacrifice found in Aeschylus' *Libation-Bearers*. She might have known the story from Ovid's *Metamorphoses*, which depicts both Iphigeneia's sacrifice and Artemis' substitution of a deer for the princess. Lady Lumley might have consulted the Italian translation of *Iphigeneia in*

Aulis by Lodovico Dolce (Venice, 1551); at least one of his translations of classical drama was in the Lumley library (*Lodovice Dolce Thyeste Tragedia Tratta de Seneca*; Venice, 1543), and her knowledge of Italian is attested by her ownership of Guiccardini's *Descrittione di tutti I Paesi Bassi* (Antwerp, 1567). There is an English academic play in Greek, the only one to survive, *Iepthae*, by John Christopherson, which dramatizes Judges 11 with large additional doses of *Iphigeneia in Aulis* and *Hekabe*; this may attest to a vogue of which Lady Lumley's translation was a part. Christopherson was a Catholic humanist who became Master of Trinity College, Cambridge, in the mid sixteenth century, probably under Mary.

INFLUENCE: It is unlikely that Lady Lumley's translation was known outside the family; her work's resemblance to Lady Pembroke's and Elizabeth Cary's arises from common humanist influences, rather than from any direct connection. See Introduction, pp. xxi–xxii. Lady Lumley's reputation as a learned lady may have been mildly enabling for other women, especially in recusant circles.

BIOGRAPHY: Daughter of Henry Fitzalan, Earl of Arundel, and Catherine Grey; cousin of Lady Jane Grey, who was also a prodigy of Hellenic learning. Fitzalan family's position weakened when their only son died in 1556; the sister Mary Fitzalan married the Duke of Norfolk, but died in childbirth. Member of one of the great humanist households of England; her ambitious and powerful father owned the finest library in England, and his daughters presented scholarly exercises as New Year gifts to their father. Her husband John, first Baron Lumley, also encouraged learning and continued his father-in-law's book collection. Bore three children, all of whom died in infancy. Translated several dialogues by Isocrates and *The Tragedie of Iphigeneia*. Shared her husband's interest in medicine, as her notes on the medicinal eaglestone on the back page of *Iphigeneia* suggest. Continued to purchase and read books in Latin and Italian; central participant in acquisition of the Lumley library. Received dedication for astrological treatises by Robert Forster in 1569. Her death, perhaps in childbirth, occurred when she was only thirty-nine; the inability to get the requisite two barons to follow her funeral cortège suggests that her Catholicism had begun to isolate her.

FURTHER READING

Biographical sources

'Life of Henry Fitzalan, Earl of Arundel', BL MS Royal 17. A. IX, reprinted in the *Gentleman's Magazine* 154 (1833), P. 2, pp. 11–18, 118–23, 213–15, 495–500

The Lumley Library: The Catalogue of 1609, ed. Sears Jayne and Francis R. Johnson (London: Trustees of the British Museum, 1956)

Milner, Edith, *Records of the Lumleys of Lumley Castle* (London: George Fell, 1904)

Milson, John, 'The Nonesuch Music Library', in *Sundry Sorts of Music Books . . . presented*

> *to O. W. Neighbour on his 70th birthday*, ed. Chris Banks, Arthur Searle and
> Malcolm Turner (London: British Library, 1993)

Tierney, M. A., *The History and Antiquities of the Castle and town of Arundel* (London,
1834)

There is a reasonable summary of most of this evidence in Warnicke, *Women of the
English Renaissance and Reformation* (see below).

General reading

Beilin, Elaine V., *Redeeming Eve: Women Writers of the English Renaissance* (Princeton:
Princeton University Press, 1987)

Crane, Frank D., 'Euripides, Erasmus, and Lady Lumley', *Classical Journal* 39 (1944),
223–8

Foley, Helena, *Ritual Irony: Poetry and Sacrifice in Euripides* (Ithaca, N.Y.: Cornell
University Press, 1985)

Greene, David H., 'Lady Lumley and Greek tragedy', *Classical Journal* 36 (1941), 537–
47

Iphigenia At Aulis Translated by Lady Lumley, ed. Harold H. Child (London: Malone
Society, 1909)

Levin, Carole, 'Lady Jane Grey: Protestant queen and martyr', in *Silent but for the Word*,
ed. Margaret Patterson Hannay (Kent, Ohio: Kent State University Press,
1985), pp. 92–106

Purkiss, Diane, 'Blood, sacrifice, marriage and death: why Iphigeneia and Mariam
have to die', *Women and Writing*, Special Issue, ed. Marion Wynne-Davies,
forthcoming

Smith, Bruce R., *Ancient Scripts and Modern Experience on the English Stage, 1500–1700*
(Princeton: Princeton University Press, 1988)

Warnicke, Retha M., *Women of the English Renaissance and Reformation*, Contributions in
Women's Studies No. 38 (Westport, Conn.: Greenwood Press, 1983)

Wilkins, John, 'The state and the individual: Euripides' plays of voluntary self-sacrifice',
in *Euripides, Women and Sexuality*, ed. Anton Powell (London: Routledge, 1990),
pp. 177–93

TEXT: A unique authorial manuscript is now in the British Library, London (MS
Royal 15. A. IX Lumley), from which this text is taken, and is titled: *Isocrates orations
ad Nicoclem & c, translated out of Greeke into Latin by Jane ladie Lumley ... Euripides
tragedie called Iphygenia, translated likewise by hir out of greeke into English, and written with
hir owne hande.* As well as the Isocrates translations mentioned above, the MS also
contains a short extract from *Pandectae medicinae*, by Mattheus Silvaticus, which was
first published in the fifteenth century, and was most recently reprinted in 1541,

in Lady Lumley's hand; it concerns the eaglestone (*De lapide aquilae*), but has no clear relation with the play.

TEXTUAL NOTES

Emendations are the present editor's. The swung dash replaces a word in recording a punctuation variant.

17	walles] wallles	544	this? ~.
39	matter?] ~:	570	For] for
45	daughters: Phoebus,] ~~	604	But] but
45	maried,] ~:	624	Alas,] ~?
200	it? Howe] ~: howe	681	you,] ~.
209	For] for	694	For] for
294	miserye? For] ~ for	698	For] for
295	happie:] ~.	709	Helena?] ~.
306	remedie?] ~,	769	it was] is was
321	For] for	794	wordes,] ~.
385	comminge?] ~.	796	For] for
409	haven?] ~.	822	For] for
432	firste] fiste	823	barbarians] barbarias
439	But] but	845	selfe?] ~.
478	me?] ~.	850	you?] ~.
492	Leda] leda	862	you?] ~.

COMMENTARY

The Argument of the Tragadie

2 *Aulida*: Aulis, both the Greek and Latin accusative form of Aulis.

The names of the spekers

2 SENEX: Latin word for 'old man', used by Erasmus in his Latin translation; the Greek word is *presbutes*. This may point to Lady Lumley's use of Erasmus' Latin text, or it may suggest merely that her ideas of stock characters were drawn from drama in Latin.

8 *NUNCIUS*: Messenger in Latin, perhaps another sign that Latin dramatic conventions influenced Lady Lumley's approach to the play or that she depended on Erasmus.

Play

10 *course of the seven starres*: The Pleiades, known as the seven stars or seven sisters; the moment of their setting was a common marker of time, in ancient and early modern worlds, and their visibility in the sky is used to mark the season of maximum fertility (roughly 10 May to 11 November; see e.g. in the Hippocratic corpus, *Epidemics*, I.2.6, the time of maximum disease). Lady Lumley was interested in astronomy and in astrological medicine, as her notes at the end of the MS of *Iphigeneia* show. Nevertheless, this line is a mistranslation; the exchange might accurately be translated as follows: Agamemnon: What is that star that moves across the sky? Old Man: That is Sirius, near the seven Pleiades/ It's still the hour when he rides right in the midst of the heavens. Crane (see Further Reading above) argues that Lady Lumley's version of it is so far from the Greek that it proves she did not consult it. Yet Erasmus is so much closer to the Greek that one might just as well suspect that Lady Lumley did not consult him; she is much more likely to have made a guess at the Greek and got it wrong. (Erasmus gives: *Senex: Sirius ardens, qui Pleiadibus/ Septemgeminis vicinus adhuc/ Media rapidus fertur coelo.*) This may just conceivably be a sign that Lady Lumley began her translation from a corrupt manuscript rather than from Erasmus.

238 *the barbarians*: 'the' appears at the bottom of the verso of f.73 (as the catchword) but has been omitted from the top of the recto of f.74; the omission is clearly an error, and so the word has been retained.

314 *let me see your hande*: A request for reconciliation.

350 *Ulisses*: Here represented as a popular demagogue in the traditional late-medieval fashion, he is also portrayed as a dangerous self-fashioner.

366 *CHORUS*: Lady Lumley summarizes Euripides rather than translating. Her lack of interest in the choral odes may reflect her notion that drama was mostly valuable as a source of *sententiae*; see Introduction, pp. xxv–xxvi.

421 *strange house*: Iphigeneia hints that Agamemnon intends to give her in marriage, but dramatic irony points to her transition to the house of Hades.

434 *verie noble*: Agamemnon imagines Iphigeneia married to Hades.

440 *husbande*: Lady Lumley omits a long section in Euripides here about the lineage of the House of Atreus, perhaps because she wished to dissociate herself from its unpleasant associations.

473 *mariage*: In Euripides Agamemnon makes misogynistic complaints here which Lady Lumley does not translate. She also omits the succeeding choral ode, a vision of Troy and the Trojan wars.

555 *Nowe therfore*: Clytemnestra's speech to Achilles is greatly shortened from Euripides. Lady Lumley cuts all references to supplication, perhaps because she doesn't understand them or finds them demeaning in a queen. Compare Iphigeneia's speech at 696.

563 *troblesome thinge to have children*: In Euripides the Chorus comments more specifically on the agony of *motherhood*. Lady Lumley perhaps generalizes it to parenthood to make the phrase a more appropriate compliment for her father.

612 *Exit . . . Enter*: Lady Lumley's cuts in Euripides make the entrances and exits of the characters awkward. Orestes (ll. 619, 865) is a non-speaking part.

624–6 *Alas . . . miserie*: Modern editors attribute this speech to Clytemnestra, continuing the debate between her and Agamemnon; this makes much more sense of Agamemnon's next line.

666 *Helens*: Clytemnestra's sister.

816 *one noble man*: Lady Lumley is more misogynistic than Euripides here, who says only that *in war* it is better for women to die than men.

849 *teare your clothes*: Traditional sign of grief in ancient Greece (the Greek reads *met'amphi soma melanas ampiskhei peplous*).

873 *praie you not to hate my father*: Here and at 880 Iphigenia is warning Clytemnestra not to murder Agamemnon in revenge for her death, showing the kind of prophetic knowledge given by imminent death.

908–10 *Beholde yonder . . . owne blode*: These lines represent Iphigeneia as a Christian martyr and type of Christ. Erasmus hints at this too in the language he chooses: *Manus antibusque rivis/ Purpurante aspergine/ Cruroris irrigabit.*

920 *As we wente*: From here to the end is now generally regarded as a late interpolation in the text of Euripides' play, but this view was not current in the Renaissance. Modern texts of *Iphigeneia* lack this ending, which is of course precisely what gave the play its Christological significance.

The Tragedie of Antonie

Translation of the French tragedy *Marc-Antoine*, by Robert Garnier (Paris, 1578).

DATE: Dated very precisely in the epistle, 'At Ramsburie. 26 November 1590'.

SOURCES: Principal source is Garnier. Garnier's tragedies focus on war and rebellion; the dedication of *Marc-Antoine* speaks of 'les représentations Tragiques des guerres civiles de Rome' (the representations in tragedy of the civil wars of Rome) and of 'nos dissentions domestiques et les malheureux troubles de ce Royaume aujourd'hui despouillé de son ancienne splendeur et de la reverable majesté de nos Rois, prophanée par tumultuouses rebellions' (our local dissensions and the unlucky troubles of the realm today, despoiled of its ancient splendour and the revered majesty of our kings, profaned by tumultuous rebellions). Lady Pembroke may well have consulted Plutarch's *Life of Antony* too, either in a Latin translation, or in Thomas North's English rendering (1579) from the French translation of Amyot. The influence of Seneca's drama and also his maxims is apparent everywhere, as is the influence of Philip Sidney's *Defence of Poetry*, though the extent to which *Antonie* was part of an attempt to reform popular drama was at one time greatly exaggerated as a result of this connection. The work is also related to the DuPlessis-Mornay treatise on death originally published with it, which is less about death *per se* than about the stoical repression of worldly hopes and the futility of political ambition.

INFLUENCE: Samuel Daniel produced a sequel, *The Tragedie of Cleopatra* (1594), in direct response to Lady Pembroke's play and under her patronage. Her play is said to have influenced Shakespeare's *Antony and Cleopatra*. Henry Herbert may have been Shakespeare's patron very briefly in the early 1590s, and Lady Pembroke's sons were the dedicatees of the First Folio. Fulke Greville also produced an *Antony and Cleopatra*, which he destroyed when it seemed politically problematic in the light of the Essex rebellion. *The Tragedie of Antonie* also inaugurated a revival in Senecan tragedies, including *Philotas*, also by Daniel (printed 1605); Fulke Greville, Lord Brooke, *Mustapha* (*c.* 1594–5); Thomas Kyd's translation of Garnier's *Cornelia* (1594); Samuel Brandon's *The Tragicomoedi of the Vertuous Octavia* (1598); and William Alexander's *Darius* (1603), *Croesus* (1604) and *Julius Caesar* (1607). The Senecan dramas also influenced Ben Jonson's *Sejanus* (1603–4) and *Catiline* (1611), written for the public stage.

BIOGRAPHY: Born at Penshurst, daughter of Lady Mary Dudley, sister of Robert Dudley, Earl of Leicester, and sister-in-law of Lady Jane Grey, and Henry Sidney; briefly maid of honour to Elizabeth I. At fifteen married Henry Herbert, second Earl of Pembroke, twenty-five years her senior; bore him four children (1580–84). Set up court at Wilton House, near Salisbury, becoming one of the most widely praised patrons of the age, with numerous clients. Recipient of dedication of her brother Philip Sidney's prose romance *Arcadia*. Seems to have begun writing only upon his death; completed his translation of the Psalms, not printed in her lifetime but circulated in MS and an influence on poets such as Donne and Jonson; translated *The Tragedie of Antonie* from Robert Garnier's French original; also translated Philippe DuPlessis-Mornay's stoic *A Discourse of Life and Death*, and Petrarch's *Trionfo della Morte* in the 1590s; all these works on death and her work as her brother's literary executor gave her an additional public role as his chief mourner; she issued corrected editions of her brother's works, and composed an elegy for him. Apparently stopped writing when her husband died in 1601; rapidly lost her political influence and position as public woman of letters to her son, William Herbert, the new Earl. Died of smallpox in 1621.

BIOGRAPHICAL SOURCES: Other lives have been largely superseded by Hannay, *Philip's Phoenix* and Lamb, *Gender and Authorship in the Sidney Circle*.

FURTHER READING

Bergeron, David, 'Women as patrons of English Renaissance drama', in *Patronage in the Renaissance*, ed. Guy Fitch Lytle and Stephen Orgel (Princeton: Princeton University Press, 1981)

Bullough, Geoffrey (ed.), *Narrative and Dramatic Sources of Shakespeare*, vol. 5 (New York: Columbia University Press, 1966)

Crewe, Jonathan, *Hidden Designs: The Critical Profession and Renaissance Literature* (New York: Methuen, 1986)

Hannay, Margaret Patterson, *Philip's Phoenix: Mary Sidney, Countess of Pembroke* (New York and Oxford: Oxford University Press, 1990)

Kay, Dennis, ' "She was a queen, and therefore beautiful": Sidney, his mother and Queen Elizabeth I', *Review of English Studies* ns, 43 (1992), 18–39

Lamb, Mary Ellen, *Gender and Authorship in the Sidney Circle* (Madison: University of Wisconsin Press, 1990)

— 'The myth of the Countess of Pembroke: the dramatic circle', *Yearbook of English Studies* 11 (1981)

Luce, Alice, *The Countess of Pembroke's Antonie* (Weimar: Verlag von Emil Felber, 1897)

Schanzer, Ernest, '*Antony and Cleopatra* and the Countess of Pembroke's *Antonius*', *Notes and Queries* 201 (1956), 152–4

Sidney, Mary, Countess of Pembroke, *The Triumph of Death and Other Unpublished and Uncollected Poems by Mary Sidney Countess of Pembroke*, ed. G. F. Waller (Salzburg: Institut für Englische Sprache und Literatur, 1977)

Tricomi, A. H., 'Philip, Earl of Pembroke, and the analogical way of reading political tragedy', *Journal of English and Germanic Philology* 85 (1986), 332–45

Waller, Gary, *Mary Sidney, Countess of Pembroke* (Salzburg: Institut für Englische Sprache und Literatur, 1979)

Witherspoon, Alexander MacLaren, *The Influence of Robert Garnier on Elizabethan Drama* (New Haven, Conn.: Yale University Press, 1924)

TEXT: Printed in 1592 in a single volume with her translation of Philippe DuPlessis-Mornay's *Discourse of Life and Death*, as *Discourse of Life and Death written in French by Ph. Mornay. Antonius A Tragedie written also in French by Ro. Garnier.* The printer was William Ponsonby, who became the printer of choice for the Sidney circle and with whom Lady Pembroke printed her brother's revised works, suggesting that she saw *Antonie* as part of the collective project in which she and his circle were engaged. The play was published singly in revised form, again by Ponsonby, in 1595 under the title *The Tragedie of Antonie*; this edition is the base text here.

TEXTUAL NOTES

Emendations are the present editor's. See also p. 171.

Act II	*Act III*
259 workmanship,] ~.	342 thereby.] ~,
483 nothing [to]] nothing	
506 *dies.*] ~	

COMMENTARY

Act I

2 *round engin*: Wheel, hence fortune's wheel.

9 *Sisters wrong, my wife*: Antonie's wife Octavia is Octavius' sister.

28 *Triumph of me*: I.e. triumph over me.

30 *use his victorie*: I.e. exercise his victory over me.

39–41 *Have Caesar fortune . . . the earth*: I.e. Caesar can have good luck, and the Gods for his friends, since love and the fates have given him the whole world.

50 *Thracian wolfe*: I.e. Caesar can throw him to the wolves to be eaten.

53–5 *Antonie . . . never Cupids fire*: Antonie is suggesting that Cupid alone could never have caused his passion.

67–8 *Baies . . . mirtles*: Laurel victory wreaths and lovers' plants respectively.

110 *Nilus*: Garnier has *Tu ne veux que revoir les Canopides ondes* (110); Canopus was an island in the mouth of the Nile notorious for its luxury. Lady Pembroke swaps a precise reference for a vague one.

149 *The boyling tempest*: Cf. Horace, *Odes*, II.9, *Non semper imbres*.

154 *the morning beames*: Garnier has a specific reference: '*Tousjours du marchand, qui traverse/ Pour le proufit jusqu'au Levant*' (. . . always of the merchant, who crosses/ For profit as far as the Levant). It is interesting that Lady Pembroke excised this reference to trade. On the importance of Oriental trade, see Lisa Jardine, *Worldly Goods* (London: Macmillan, 1996).

Act II

12 *him*: Salmoneus, named in Garnier, who imitated Zeus's lightning with thrown torches. See Virgil, *Aeneid*, VI.585ff.

14–16 *cursed banquet . . . from his course returne*: The sun turned away in horror when Atreus fed his brother Thyestes on Thyestes' children. Cf. Seneca's tragedy *Thyestes* on the subject.

50 *Priams sonne*: Paris.

67 *The fearfull dragon*: Probably the Nile crocodile.

85 *Lament we*: For this chorus, cf. Seneca, *Agamemnon* 664ff., and *Hercules Oetaeus*, 184–208.

92 *wood-musiques Queen*: The nightingale, named as Philomela by Garnier, was pursued by Tereus, husband of her sister Procne, who when she refused him raped her and cut out her tongue to prevent her revealing the crime. She managed to tell her sister through embroidery, and Procne killed Tereus' son and served him to his father (cf. II.14). Philomela became a nightingale, and is supposed always to say Tereus, the name of her assailant.

109 *the bird in death*: The swan is traditionally only capable of song just before it dies;

Cycnus was a friend of Phaeton who mourned him so much he changed into a swan. Cf. Ovid, *Metamorphoses*, II.367ff.

127 *she*: Niobe, who boasted that she was a better mother than Leto (see note on IV.76).

194–210 *My face too lovely . . . Blasting his former flourishing renowne*: This self-accusation, a key part of the sympathetic portrayal of Cleopatra, is Garnier's as well as Lady Pembroke's; he also borrows from Plutarch the idea that she is motivated by jealousy of Octavia rather than by political considerations (Plutarch, *Antony*, 53).

226 *the Sunne*: In the 1578 edition of Garnier (*M. Antoine, tragedie*; Paris: Mamert Patisson) an additional four lines appear here which Lady Pembroke does not translate.

304 *from that lodging parte*: I.e. die, and cross the 'joyles' Stygian lake to the Elysian fields.

368 *Carian Queene*: Artemisia.

477–82 *The Allablaster . . . fetters, dartes*: Garnier and Sidney break into the clichés of Petrarchanism, obliterating Cleopatra's otherness.

507 *O sweete*: For this song, cf. Tibullus, *Elegies*, I.viii.20–23, 25–6, and Lucan, *Pharsalia*, X.11–12.

522–7 *visiting each yeare . . . busie reapers*: The Nile's annual floods brought rich alluvial soil to Egypt and were the basis of its wealth.

Act III

73–4 *For nothing . . . state represents*: These lines are italicized in Garnier, to signify that they are a quotation from Dante, *Divine Comedy*, *Inferno*, canto V, where they are spoken by Francesca, doomed to suffer eternally because of her immoderate and excessive love for Paolo, which makes them especially appropriate.

85 *Mutina*: The war of 43 BC, in which the consuls (l. 86) Hirtius and Pansa were killed opposing Antony (cf. Dio Cassius 46.38–9).

89 *thy unkle*: Julius Caesar, whose slayers were defeated by Antony.

101 *Lucill*: Lucilius gave himself up to Antony at Philippi in an effort to save Brutus, which so impressed Antony that they became friends (Plutarch, *Antony*, 25).

120 *rowling bowle*: In Garnier, *boule*, or bowling ball, from the French game *boules*. Lady Pembroke makes no attempt to anglicize it.

137 *as heire*: Caesar adopted Octavius, who was his nephew.

139 *allied in bloud*: Antony was part of the Julian clan, like Octavius.

169–72 *Sleepeles Suspicion . . . not away*: Unidentified quotation.

203–4 *Gaule . . . fields of Thessalie*: Site of Antony's victories, and Pharsalia and Philippi.

221 *Scipio*: Probably P. Cornelius Scipio Africanus Major (who won the battle of Zama, 202 BC), but perhaps his son (who razed Carthage, 146 BC).

279–86 *It was not fortunes . . . was conceiv'd*: Also an unidentified quotation.

339 *th'Assirian kinge*: Usually identified as Sennacherib.

347 *Hercules*: Garnier mentions Omphale by name, who made Hercules dress as a woman and spin to humiliate him. Hercules' enslavement by Omphale was his punishment for sacrilege rather than a result of her captivity. Lady Pembroke plays with the story to create a neater inversion of hierarchy. Later Cleopatra stresses Antony's own descent from Hercules, making the parallel clearer (V.64).

387 *Alas, with*: For this chorus, cf. Seneca, *Agamemnon*, 589–92, 598–600. This stoical meditation on death reminds us of Lady Pembroke's other recent elegiac works; see Introduction, pp. xxxii–xxxiv.

428 *triple-barking*: Because Cerberus, dog-guardian of the realm of Pluto, had three heads.

477 *Psammetiques*: Psemmeticus: Lady Pembroke does not anglicize the name, suggesting it was unfamiliar to her.

Act IV

57 *Sonnes of mother earth*: The giants bred by Gaia to exact revenge on the gods for the imprisonment of the Titans.

66–9 *For no one . . . to stand*: Another unidentified quotation; the revolt of the giants was a popular topic.

76 *his two children*: Phoebus and Phoebe, named for Apollo and Diana, the children of Leto (also Latona).

150–87 *Then to the end . . . one brest*: The following debate on mercy and justice is based on the one between Seneca and Nero in Seneca's *Octavia*.

395–6 *blushing hue . . . Tyrian shell*: The shell is the murex, which gives purple dye; the image is not just of the multitudinous seas incarnadine with Antony's blood, but of the spillage of imperial power and of the sea mourning an emperor.

414 *Olive*: Athene won Athens from Poseidon by giving the inhabitants an olive tree, judged more useful than his salt spring.

416–19 *temple dore . . . Janus shall make fast*: The doors of Janus' temple in Rome were closed only when Rome was at peace; they were shut in 29 BC for the first time for two hundred years.

Act V

25 *Sisters*: The moirae, or fates; Garnier names Atropos, who cuts the thread, and Clotho, who spins it; the third is Lachesis.

105 *Phaetons sisters*: Wept so much for their brother that they turned into trees.

137 *O Goddesse*: Cf. Horace, *Odes*, I.30, and Catullus, 36. There is also an allusion to Virgil, *Aeneid*, Book I, in which Venus protects the shipwrecked Aeneas by inspiring Dido with love for him. Cleopatra does not seem to see the irony.

161 *the winged race*: Cf. Virgil, *Aeneid*, IV.653–8.

169 *What say I*: Cf. Ariosto, *Orlando Furioso*, XXIV.78ff.

208 *Fainting on you, and forth my soule may flow*: It remains unclear whether Cleopatra simply collapses over Antony's body or actually kills herself and expires.

The Tragedie of Mariam

Original play by Elizabeth Cary.

DATE: Philip Cary was knighted in 1604/5, and married his wife, Elizabeth, in 1609. This would date the play to after 1609, but it has been suggested that Elizabeth Cary would not have addressed his wife as 'Mistris'. An alternative dedicatee is Henry and Philip's sister, Elizabeth, wife of Sir John Saville, but in the family context addressed by her maiden name and title. John Davies of Hereford refers to *Mariam* when he congratulates Elizabeth Cary on her evocation of 'the scenes of Syracuse and Palestine' in *The Muse's Sacrifice or Divine Meditations* (1612); plainly he knew of *Mariam*'s existence. If an early date of *c.* 1603–4 is correct, *Mariam* is a continuation of Elizabeth Cary's schoolroom exercises, possibly a conscious imitation and Protestantization of Senecan tragedy. If Michael Drayton or John Davies was her tutor, either might have acted as a conduit from the Sidney circle to her, encouraging her to write this particular kind of play as part of the fashion for Senecan tragedy. For this reason, too, an early composition date is likely.

SOURCES: Principal source is Josephus' *History of the Jewish People*, probably in Thomas Lodge's English translation of 1602; some attach significance to the fact that Lodge alludes to his conversion to Catholicism in his poem *Prosopopeia* (1596), but we should be wary of reading *Mariam* as a Catholic play. Elizabeth Cary may also have known another version of Mariam's life in Joseph Ben Gurion's *Compendious and Most Marvellous History of the Jewes Common Weale*, translated by Peter Morwyn (1558 and subsequently). There is no evidence that she knew Lodovico Dolce's *Marianna* (1565). Many other plays deal with the stories of various tyrannical Herods; indeed the various Herods were the very type of stage tyrants, from the mystery plays onward. Elizabeth Cary is unlikely to have known either Nicholas Grimald's *Archipropheta* (*c.* 1546), or George Buchanan's *Baptistes sive Calumnia* (1541–4, published 1577), both of which deal with the more familiar Herods and Salomes of the New Testament in terms of politics and tyranny. Elizabeth Cary is said in the *Life* (see Further Reading below) to have translated Seneca's *Epistles*, which may also have been an influence. Straznicki and Rowland detect the influence of Montaigne, perhaps in Florio's translation, perhaps in French. She may also have known the other Senecan or closet dramas being produced in learned circles at this time; for a list of the principal instances, see the headnote on *The Tragedie of Antonie*, above.

INFLUENCE: *Mariam*'s influence has not yet been demonstrated, though it has been suggested that it left a mark on *The Second Maiden's Tragedy*, anonymous (possibly by Middleton) (1611). Other comparisons between Elizabeth Cary and male canonical writers such as Shakespeare are predicated more on the gender roles represented than on any scholarly notion of influence.

BIOGRAPHY: Daughter of Lawrence Tanfield, a lawyer who later became

Lord Chief Baron of the Exchequer, and Elizabeth Symondes, daughter of a major gentry family of Norfolk. Elizabeth Symondes Tanfield showed some interest in both court drama and writing, and her daughter received a solid humanist education, girls' style. Married to Henry Cary, soon to become Viscount Falkland (1620), at the age of fifteen; lived with Henry's mother for some years, in some dissension. Received dedications from (among others) Michael Drayton and John Davies, who compared her with Lady Pembroke. Wrote a (lost) tragedy set in Syracuse, before *The Tragedie of Mariam*. Gave birth to eleven children; eldest was Lucius Cary, who was Edward Hyde, Earl of Clarendon's hero of the Civil War. Visited Ireland with her husband in 1622. Formally received into the Catholic Church soon after her return, in November 1626; this ended her marriage and her public position as patron of major writers, but at the time it may have seemed that she had chosen the winning side, since hers was one of a wave of conversions among aristocratic and gentry women specifically targeted by the Jesuits, and since the conversion was declared during the ascendancy of Queen Henrietta Maria's Catholic faction. That this was a miscalculation is signified by the fact that she received only one more dedication, unauthorized by the author, from the printer of John Marston's *Collected Works* in 1633. Wrote several devotional works, including lives of women saints in verse; none survives. Also wrote a dramatic history of the life of *Edward II*, published only in 1680 with late additions designed to make it relevant to the Exclusion Crisis. Elizabeth Cary translated a work of Counter-Reformation debate, Jacques Davy du Perron's *Replie*, printed at Douai (1630); it is dedicated to Henrietta Maria, which may indicate that she entered Henrietta's circle, as may her burial in Henrietta's private chapel after her death in 1639.

BIOGRAPHICAL SOURCES: Most editions of *Mariam* (see below) attempt a biography, usually dependent on the *Life* by her daughter, reproduced in full in Weller and Ferguson's edition; there is some useful material on Elizabeth Cary's factional alliances in Schleiner, *Tudor and Stuart Women Writers*.

FURTHER READING

Callaghan, Dympna, 'Re-reading Elizabeth Cary's *The Tragedie of Mariam, Faire Queene of Jewry*', in *Women, 'Race', and Writing*, ed. Hendricks and Parker

Cary, Elizabeth, *The History of the Life, Reign and Death of Edward II*, in *Renaissance Women: The Plays of Elizabeth Cary and the Poems of Aemilia Lanyer*, ed. Diane Purkiss (London: William Pickering, 1994)

Cary, Elizabeth, *The Tragedie of Mariam*, ed. A. C. Dunstan, Malone Society (Oxford: Oxford University Press, 1914), reissued with a supplement by Marta Straznicki and Richard Rowland (Oxford: Oxford University Press, 1992)

Cary, Elizabeth, *The Tragedie of Mariam*, in Weller and Ferguson, with the life of Elizabeth Cary by her daughter

Ferguson, Margaret, ' "Running On With Almost Public Voice': The case of "E.C." ',

Tradition and the Talents of Women, ed. Florence Howe (Urbana: University of Illinois Press, 1991), pp. 37–67

Katz, David, *Philosemitism and the Readmission of the Jews to England 1603–1655* (Oxford: Clarendon, 1982)

Knott, John Ray, *Discourses of Martyrdom in English Literature 1563–1694* (Cambridge: Cambridge University Press, 1993)

Purkiss, Diane, 'Blood, sacrifice, marriage and death: why Iphigeneia and Mariam have to die', *Women and Writing*, Special Issue, ed. Marion Wynne-Davies, forthcoming

Raber, Karen L., 'Gender and the political subject in *The Tragedy of Mariam*', *Studies in English Literature* 35 (1995), 321–43

Shannon, Laurie, '*The Tragedie of Mariam*: Cary's critique of the terms of founding social discourses', *English Literary Renaissance* 24 (1994), 135–53

Shapiro, James, *Shakespeare and the Jews* (New York: Columbia University Press, 1996)

Straznicki, Marta, ' "Profane Social Paradoxes": *The Tragedie of Mariam* and Sidneian closet drama', *English Literary Renaissance* 24 (1994), 104–34

Wright, Stephanie, 'The canonization of Elizabeth Cary', in *Voicing Women: Gender and Sexuality in Early Modern Writing*, ed. Kate Chedgzoy, Melanie Hansen and Suzanne Trill (Keele: Keele University Press, 1996)

TEXT: Printed 1613 by Thomas Creede for Richard Hawkins; Stationers' Register entry, 17 December 1612. Numerous surviving copies; some minor press variants, listed in full by Weller and Ferguson. No manuscript has as yet been located, but the recent discovery of a manuscript of Elizabeth Cary's *Edward II* (Northants Record Office, Finch-Malton MS 1; probably not authorial) might encourage further searches, since as Greg remarks it is probable that *Mariam* was presented in manuscript at or around composition date and may have circulated more widely among Elizabeth Cary's friends (Dunstan and Greg, preface to Malone edition, p. ix). In the absence of an MS or of a printing which we can be certain was overseen by her, editors have found many reasons to amend the text of *Mariam*, some justified, some perhaps overzealous. Elizabeth Cary was not lucky with her printer – there are a number of clear printer's errors, including several turned letters – and possibly she was not fortunate in her scribe either, but some of the text's eccentricities may be her own. The base text for this edition is the British Library copy designated A by Dunstan, shelfmark 162. c. 28.

TEXTUAL NOTES

Emendations are the present editor's. See also p. 171.

The names of the Speakers

5 *Doris*] *Salome*
7 SILLEUS] *Sillius*
16 BU[TLER]] *Bu.*

The Argument

2–3 daughter] daughrer

Act I. Scene 1

35 lovlyest] lowlyest (Dunstan's emendation)
47 mind] maide

Act I. Scene 2

12 famed] fain'd
44 *Herod*] *Mariam*
53 MARIAM] *Nun:*
104 seeke] leeke

Act I. Scene 3

47 suspitions] suspitious

Act I. Scene 4

2 *Mariam: Herods* spirit] *Mariam Herods* ~:
16 all eyes] allyes
40 *Constabarus*] *Contabarus*

Act I. Scene 5

37 whome] home

Act I. Scene 6

51 beastes swim] beastes, swine
56 Water-bearing] Waters-bearing
90 vow] vowd
127 If] Of
132 cheerfull] chreefull

Act II. Scene 1

73 *Graphinas*] *Graphina*

Act II. Scene 2

39 overpast] operpast
48 safety] safely
66 feare] leare
75 Believe] believe
93 lie] live

Act II. Scene 3

1 You] Your

Act II. Scene 4

92 *They fight.*] I, I, they fight,
97 Very] very

Act III. Scene 1

3 can make] cane mak
23 beautie.] ~,

Act III. Scene 2

37 not] no
39 doomed] done
41 I] he

42 our] his
81 bids] bides

Act III. Scene 3

14 bred.] ~:
35 hypocrite] hypcorite

Act IV. Scene 1

4SD *Enter* NUNTIO.] *at the end of l. 5*
24 geese] griefe

Act IV. Scene 2

3 *Caesar*] *Cæsar*;
30 your] you
37 *Salome*] *Salom*
42 *Salome*] *Salom.*

Act IV. Scene 4

3 I?] ~:
35 They] they
46 wert] never wert
56 heav'nly] heavy
70 guiltles] guiltles
71 locke] looke
81 her?] ~:
81 You] you
87 love] bove

Act IV. Scene 5

2 causeles] caules

Act IV. Scene 6

20 our] your
23 Where] Were
26 die] ~:
58 she] he

Act IV. Scene 7

7 repell] refell
26 Doubt] doubt

Act IV. Scene 8

4 As] At
51 In] I
106 scorning] scorniug

Act V. Scene 1

38 darken] darke
54 Go on.] *Nun.* Go on,
55 She] she
57 cheerfull] cheeful
99 eares.] eares,
103 will.] ~:
108 he] she
153 Her] her
167 much: a] ~ ~:
190 died] did

Several lines are two syllables short (I.1.10, III.2.18, IV.7.68).

SELECTED VARIANTS

I follow Weller and Ferguson's designation of copies, which in turn follows Dunstan and Greg for the copies in the UK: A, B and C (British Library), D, E and F (National Library of Scotland), G and M (Bodleian Library), Dyce Collection at the Victoria

Act IV. Scene 4

29 I would] would (unique to D)

Act IV. Scene 7

153 a new A, D, Y, BP; anew B, C,
E, F, G, M, Dyce, Wo, Eton,
NY, EC, Ho, Of, Hu, N

Act V. Scene 1

211/ On the verso of H4 copies read
213 either 'faine' or 'fame' in both
lines; one might be a
printing-house emendation, but
we cannot know which. About

half the extant copies have
'fame' for faine here and at line
213. Faine makes better sense
at 211, since Herod is criticizing
this notion of Saturn, and at
213, where Herod is doubting
the properties of the gods since
they have not justly struck him
down. Dunstan gives faine/
faine, as do Weller and
Ferguson; Wright gives fame/
fame.
faine A, D, F, G, Dyce, Wo, Y,
Ho, N
fame B, C, E, M, Eton, NY,
EC, BP, Of, Hu

COMMENTARY

To Dianaes earthlie deputesse

This dedicatory sonnet and the accompanying list of characters appear only in the Huntington Library and Houghton Library copies; the Eton copy contains a manuscript list, in an unidentified hand, divided into male and female characters as if to help in allocating reading parts, and containing Silleus' man and Herod's soldiers.
Dedication *Mistris Elizabeth Carye*: There are two Elizabeth Carys (apart from the author): the wife of her husband's brother Philip, whom he married in 1609, and her husband's sister Elizabeth, married to Sir John Savile in 1586. The dedicatee is probably the latter; see p. 179.
1–4 *Phoebus . . . his Sister*: Phoebus is Apollo; his sister is Diana, so this addresses Henry Cary and his sister. Henry is absent; this probably refers to his imprisonment after fighting in the Netherlands in 1604–8, but may simply mean one of his frequent sojourns at court.
11 *Sicily*: Elizabeth Cary dedicated a previous work on Sicily to Henry Cary; this is probably the tragedy referred to by John Davies (see headnote), as Syracuse is in

Sicily. Davies was her handwriting tutor; his mention of the plays does not necessarily suggest that they circulated widely.

The Argument

2–3 *daughter*: Can mean 'grand-daughter', as it does here.

Act I. Scene 1

2 *Romes last Hero*: Julius Caesar, who wept when he saw Pompey's severed head (Plutarch, *Caesar*). Mariam later apostrophizes Caesar.

30 *I quickly . . . I abhord*: I.e. I learned to ignore Herod, but not to be adulterous.

47 *mind*: 'maide' in 1613 is an error, probably suggested by the proximity of 'servant' in l. 49.

67 *I*: With the sense of 'Aye'.

75 *But teares . . . your bankes*: Mariam's address of her tears as a river recalls the images of Niobe and Phaeton's sisters in *Antonie*.

Act I. Scene 2

3 *murthers*: Many editors emend to 'murderers' (or old-spelling 'murthrers'), but if left unemended, the line could be read as a rebuke, i.e. 'you're crying, and it can't be for Herod; it must be for the brother he killed'.

12 *Judas*: Judah's, not Judas Iscariot, the betrayer of Jesus.

28 *blood is red*: Esau sold his birthright to Jacob for a mess of pottage, coloured red (Genesis 25:29ff.); Esau itself means 'red'. The passage also equates violence with the red blood of lust.

38 *double oyle*: Oil (in Christianity, chrism) was used to anoint both priests and kings.

55 *If*: Emended to 'Of' and 'In', by some editors, but the line makes sense as it stands as 'Herod would not love Doris now, even if he fell out of love with me'. The syntactical awkwardness might imply a dramatic pause and then the resumption of a different line of thought.

77 *Felicitie*: Not a woman, but happiness or fortune. Alexandra later suggests that Antony is fortune's lover, meaning that he is specially favoured by her (92).

104 *seeke*: The printer probably mistook a long s for an 'l' (leeke).

119 *mart of Beauties*: A market of beauties is Alexandra's reduction of Mariam to a commodity – and one more valuable than Cleopatra because not made up – which contrasts with Mariam's passionately virtuous response.

Act I. Scene 3

13 *raine*: Rein; the sense is 'give your tongue its head'.
22 *collor*: Rage, choler, but with an additional sense of colour, rhetorical colouring.

Act I. Scene 4

14–15 *When I . . . Silleus*: Salome's plight – pledged to one man having fallen in love with another – anticipates the situation of Beatrice-Joanna in Thomas Middleton and William Rowley's *The Changeling* (1622).
33 *But shame is gone, and honour wipt away*: See *Othello*, I.iii.95–6. Salome also recalls Emilia at I.4.45 (*Othello*, IV.iii.92–103).
49 *Ile be the custome-breaker*: Early feminist readings took this as agreeably rebellious; if so, Elizabeth Cary is equating protofeminism with promiscuity, lying and murder.
54 *the futures sake*: I.e. for the sake of Silleus.

Act I. Scene 5

4 *pray*: Prey, that is, Salome is Silleus's prey.

Act I. Scene 6

25 *forfeited haples fate*: Wright, Weller and Ferguson, and Cerasano and Wynne-Davies all emend to 'forfeited *to* haples fate', meaning that Constabarus has forfeited his life, but it is perfectly possible that 'haples fate' is Salome's self-description.
32 *Use make*: Most editors emend to 'use makes', but this makes nonsense of the succeeding warning. The sense is 'my habit makes my anger uncontrollable'.

Act II. Scene 1

2 *right*: With the sense of 'rite' also.
5 *How oft have I . . . implor'd*: Resembles Mariam's first line.
73 *let*: Hinder, i.e. that concern should not prevent you from smiling.

Act II. Scene 2

10 *A poore reward were thankes for such a merit*: I.e. thanks are a poor reward for such a favour.
20 *Each hath to what belongs to others right*: I.e. each has a right to what belongs to others.
26 *Jesses Sonne*: David, whose friendship with Jonathan was proverbial for fidelity. This speech reads like a rhetorical exercise on *Amicorum communia omnia*, the first of

Erasmus' *Adages*. Elizabeth Cary may have incorporated a schoolroom exercise into her play.

97–8 *Octavious . . . Julions*: 'Julion' is Julius Caesar. This reference is another sign that the stories of the first and second triumvirates were on Elizabeth Cary's mind, evidence of the influence of the Sidney circle's Senecan drama on *Mariam*.

Act II. Scene 3

2 *scope*: Often emended to 'stoop', but the line makes sense as: bow your walls and your space/height to Doris.

Act II. Scene 4

41 *painted sepulcher*: See Matthew 23:27, where the scribes and Pharisees are likened to whitened sepulchres full of bones.

106 *Sterne enmitie to friendship can no art*: I.e. enmity knows no means to become friendship.

Act III. Scene 2

41 *for Herods sake*: Salome claims to divorce Constabarus out of loyalty to Herod.

64 *slite*: Sleight of hand, cunning, with a quibble on slight, slender.

Act III. Scene 3

58 *To be commandresse of the triple earth*: I.e. to command all three parts of the empire ruled by the triumvirate.

69 *The fattall axe*: Allusion to the sword of Damocles, but the transposition from sword to axe fits the context of seventeenth-century judicial execution of nobles and royalty and prefigures Mariam's end.

76 *Alexanders*: Mariam's son, mentioned at I.2.62ff. Some editors emend to Alexandra, but it seems unlikely that Sohemus would give supreme power to a woman.

79 *Davids Tower*: This name was given by the Crusaders to a structure built by Herod; an interesting anachronism.

89 *darknes palpable*: See Matthew 28:45, the death of Christ, and also the plagues of Egypt (Exodus 10:21); proleptic of Mariam's death.

94 *table*: Tables, on which the law of modesty is written; alludes to the tablets of the ten commandments.

Act IV. Scene 1

8 *darke taper*: The sun, which will be made redundant by Mariam's beauty and the light it casts.

16 *Josualike the season*: Herod picks up the image of Joshua making the sun stand still used by Sohemus at III.3.89ff.

24 *geese*: Dunstan first suggested this emendation; it refers to the story of the Capitoline geese, which awakened the Romans when the Gauls attempted a surprise attack. Explanations of 'griefe' (1613 edition), offered by other editors, seem distinctly implausible: Weller and Ferguson suggest Coriolanus' grief over his mother's pleas for the city.

Act IV. Scene 3

43–5 *As I . . . heartie truth*: The quatrain here is incomplete; the first line is probably the missing one, since the syntax is awkward.

Act IV. Scene 4

17–18 *painted . . . white*: Painted is a synonym for deceptiveness, and a highly gendered one; 'white' means fair-seeming. A Renaissance proverb said 'the white devil is worse than the black'.

32 *Caedar*: A soft wood within a hard bark; the meaning is that its condition cannot be guessed from the outside.

90 *the fairest lam*: Image of Christ.

Act IV. Scene 5

20 *I will follow thee*: I.e. even though I know you were wrong.

Act IV. Scene 6

19 *You never did her hatefull minde offend*: Constabarus is speaking of Salome and explaining that the sons of Babus are not responsible for her hatred.

39 *Teare massacring Hienas*: These animals were believed to attract prey by feigning tears.

49–50 *since a flood no more . . . second flood*: Constabarus is saying that since there can be no second flood, women are an alternative means of chastisement.

63 *Chams*: Cham, or Ham, who was black, was cursed to be a servant for ever because he had brought his brothers to see their father naked; Elizabeth Cary uses this as a metaphor for God's curse on Eve. Race becomes a metaphor for sex.

Act IV. Scene 7

45 *A Crimson bush*: Crimson because painted; bushes were spread with sticky lime to catch birds. The comparison is awkward, to say the least.

57 *on the brow . . . hangs a Fleece*: Herod compares Mariam's hair to the Golden Fleece; like Cleopatra, she is Petrarchanized.

74 *false as powder*: Usually glossed as gunpowder, in which case it may actually allude to the Gunpowder Plot; powder as synecdoche for treason. But Elizabeth Cary may mean facepaint.

125 *his sonne*: Solomon.

130 *The humble Jewe*: Esther, married to king Ahasuerus.

Act IV. Scene 8

89 *Gerarim*: Garizim, which in Deuteronomy 11:29 is named as the place to set the blessing for obtaining God's commandments. Elizabeth Cary may have confused Garizim with its twin peak, Mount Ebal, named as the place for setting the course of disobedience.

Act V. Scene 1

65 *dying Swan*: Another image (see note to I.1.75) which seems to glance back at *Antonie*.

69 *made her Lord*: I.e. had I not been her king, I would still be her husband.

105 *A man*: The butler; this story is not in Josephus, but introduced by Elizabeth Cary to strengthen the parallels between Mariam and Christ.

222 *Physicks God*: Apollo.

231 *Paphian*: Venus, who represents the lavishness of Mariam's beauty, but also the waste of it in death.

249 *vile monster*: Cain.

GLOSSARY

acknow recognize, acknowledge

affected liked

afore before

after-livers posterity

albee albeit

allablaster alabaster

amitie friendship

anon, anone at once, soon

apt prepared for

aspects appearance, expression

attaint touch, hit, strike

attend expect

aught anything

awnciters ancestors

azur'd blue

bad ordered

baies bays, laurel wreath

baites temptations

bane (1) destruction; (2) discord

bate lessen, abate

beamy radiant

beldame old woman

beseeming to suit, befit

besottes makes a fool of

betide unfortunate

blab reveal secrets

blackamore black African

blast brief gust

blows whore

booted benefited

bootles unprofitable

brand torch

brickle brittle

bringing giving birth to

brinish salty

bristled dried out

broile fight, battle

build depend upon

catiffe a coward or villain

chamberer one who visits ladies' chambers, and thinks only of love

charet, charette chariot

chaunce fortune

chide argue, wrangle, scold

choller one of the four bodily humours, believed to cause irascibility

color disguise, cloak

combine marry

commodite well-being, profit

compast circumscribed

complotted planned together

comune talk, discuss

consul Roman magistrate

contende fight, oppose

councell advice

covenante agreement

coz'ning deceiving, cheating

crafte plan, skill

culd chosen

curiace part of armour

curtlax curtal-axe, broad sword

cuts clips

dart spear

dastard coward

desart desert

design'd assigned

disastred destroyed

distaffe staff around which wool was wound

divine predict

doudy whore

drest reprimanded

durst dare

ebon black

ediles Roman officials responsible for the city's games

egging encouraging

empeach hinder

empericke quack

empt empty

enlaced joined together

ensue succeed

entertaine receive

enwalles to enclose within a wall

ephod a sleeveless garment worn by priests in ancient Israel

erst previously, before

expedition swift action

fain (1) eager, willing; (2) feign

fauchion a sword

felicitie good fortune personified

filde defiled

file smooth or polish

fingred stolen

foile sword

fond foolish

forbeare put up with

forborne treated with mercy for former kindness

freezed stiff, rigid

fumish short-tempered

giddy inconstant

grandam grandmother

grave engrave

haples hapless, unfortunate

hard near

hearses portcullis

hit succeed

humor disposition, mood

immured imprisoned

impackt packed up

improvidently without care and attention

indude supplied

inly inwardly

justly exactly

lam lamb

larmes alarmes

leare to regard with disdain, envy or mistrust

leaves pages

lenitie leniency

lewdly wickedly

lighten strike

liquorishe desirous

list choose

mangle cut

manqueller man-killer

marry oath, from 'By Mary'

mart market-place

mary marrow

meede reward

meete, mete apt, fitting

minish diminish

mirtle Myrtle, tree sacred to Venus

mo more

moisted moistened

morion helmet

move propose

moytie half, part

muffle cover

murther murder

mynions favourites

naughtie wicked

notarie legal secretary

nowne own

ope open

overlive outlive

paines efforts

paintings cosmetics

pasht smashed

passe an end

pates heads

peculiar privately owned

pell mell confused

perforce with force or violence

perruque wig

person body

phisnomy physiognomy, the face as an index of character

picke-thanke sycophantic

pill steal

pitched pitch-black

plaguie resembling the plague

plaine complain

play plaything

portion fate, lot

powder make-up, cosmetics

practise plot

prate talk, chatter

prejudicate prejudiced

preparatives preparations

president precedent

prising seizing, grabbing

prively privately

prove test

quaile fade, wither

quicke living

quondam once, previously (Latin)

racke torture

raile utter abuse

rampiers ramparts

ranging freedom of desire

rare exceptional

rate criticize

rebate blunt

recur'd restored

redoubting revering, in apprehension of

repine complain

requite return, repay

retorted reversed

ruth, ruthe pity

sable black

saith says, it is said

seale verification

seelie harmless, common, pitiful

seld seldom

semblant appearance

sepulcher tomb, often used to indicate a corrupt interior beneath a calm exterior

shades ghosts

shake disturb

shamefaste modest

slite trick

smart suffer

sot fool

state position

sticke hesitate, delay

stickler moderator at a tournament or match who separated combatants

still quiet

stonie without thought or feeling

straw strew

style name

sue plead, woo

sute, swte petition, plea

table portrait

taper candle

target shield

tarie, tary delay, linger, wait

tasked burdened

temper moderation, self-control, composure

thorne to prick

timeles untimely

traffique low trade

training alluring

trothe truth

try test

tuition protection

twit aggravate, taunt

ulcer ulcerate

unev'n unjust

unfained true

unshamefaste immodest

vaunt praise, exult

vaunt-courier a precursor or forerunner

wafted carried

waienge weighing, hence assessing, judging

wanne white, pale

warped changed, altered, twisted

weedes clothes

weight balance

wherfore why

whilome previous

whist hush

withall in spite of all

witte intelligence, knowledge

wittely intelligently, rather than humorous

wrack ruin, destruction

wreake avenge

ysop hyssop, a herb associated with purification in Jewish ceremonies

LIST OF HISTORICAL,
GEOGRAPHICAL AND
MYTHOLOGICAL NAMES

ABEL Biblical; son of Adam and Eve, murdered by his jealous brother Cain.

ABRAHAM Biblical; father of Isaac, ancestor of the Hebrew nation and, through Ishmael, of other Semites. His life is an example of outstanding faith in God.

ACHERON Greek; a river in the underworld.

ACHITOPHEL Biblical; counsellor for David who deserted to his son Absalom and then hanged himself when his advice was ignored.

ACTIAN, ACTIUM Geographic; area off the west coast of Greece where the fleets of Antony and Cleopatra were defeated by Octavius in 31 BC.

ADAM Biblical; first man and father of humanity.

ALCEST Greek; wife of Admetus, in whose place she agreed to die. Hercules rescued her from death.

ALCIDES *see* Hercules.

ALECTO Greek; one of the three furies.

ALEXANDRIA Geographic; city on the north coast of Egypt, near the western mouth of the Nile, founded by Alexander the Great in 331 BC.

ALEXAS Roman; servant of Cleopatra who turned against Antony.

AMASIS successful King of Egypt.

ANTONIE Marcus Antonius (*c.* 82–30 BC). Roman general and statesman, and close friend and officer of Caesar who, with Octavius and Lepidus, ruled the Roman world. The lover of Cleopatra.

ANTIPODES Roman; the place located on the opposite side of the world.

ANUBIS Egyptian; in Egyptian religion, the jackal-headed god who conducted the souls of the dead to the area of immortal life.

APIS Egyptian; sacred bull worshipped by Egyptians.

APOLLO *see* Phoebus.

ARTEMISIA built the mausoleum, one of the seven wonders of the ancient world, at Halicarnassus for her husband Mausolus.

ASUERUS Biblical; Ahasuerus, the Persian King. After his wife refused to show herself to his banquet guests, he married Esther, a Jewish maiden.

ATE Greek; the personification of error or blind folly.

ATREUS Greek; mythical King of Mycenae, one of the sons of Pelops, husband of Aerope, father of Agamemnon and Menelaus, and brother of Thyestes. After Pelops was cursed, each generation of the family came to disaster.

AVERNUS Roman; lake; one of the entrances to the underworld.

BACCHUS Roman god of wine and pleasure.

BELLONA Roman goddess of war.

BETHSABE Biblical; Bathsheba, wife of the Hittite Uriah, who was murdered to enable David to marry her.

BOREAS Greek; the north wind.

CAIN Biblical; slew his brother Abel; he and his descendants were marked on the forehead so that they would be recognized instantly and permanently exiled from humanity.

CAMILL Marcus Furius Camillus, traditionally credited with freeing Rome from the Gauls (390 BC).

CARTHAGE North African city, and rival to Rome.

CAUCASUS mountains in Asia.

CEYX in Greek mythology, husband of Alcyone. They were both changed into birds, either because he was drowned and the gods reunited them, or because of their impiety.

CHARON ferryman who took the souls of the dead across the river Styx in Hades.

CILICIA country in the south-east of Asia minor.

CINTHIA, CYNTHIA see Diana.

CLEOPATRA 69–30 BC, Queen of Egypt, famous for her beauty.

CLOTHO Greek; one of the three fates – the 'spinner', who held the distaff.

CRASSUS Marcus Licinius Crassus (115–53 BC), ruled Rome with Julius Caesar and Pompey. He was murdered by Parthians.

CUPID Roman god of love.

CYBEL Near Eastern goddess who fell in love with the shepherd Attis. After his infidelity, she drove him mad, and he castrated himself.

DAVID Biblical; youngest son of Jesse, of the tribe of Judah, and second King of Israel.

DIANA Roman goddess of the moon, chastity, woodland and hunting. She is often known by the alternative designations Artemis, Phoebe and Cynthia.

EDOMITES Biblical; inhabitants of Edom, supposedly descended from Esau and so the enemies of Jacob's descendants who lived in Israel.

ENIPEUS river near to the battle at Pharsaly.

ESAU Biblical; the elder of Isaac's twin sons. His antagonism with his twin Jacob led to Edom and Israel's animosity.

EUMENIDES also furies. The avenging spirits which punished wrongs. They were typically depicted as three female figures with snakes in their hair, brandishing whips, firebrands and scorpions.

EUPHRATES river in south-west Asia.

FURIES see Eumenides.

GARAMANTE tribe in North Africa.

GAULE present-day France. Taken by Julius Caesar, 59–60 BC.

GLAUQUES Glauce was a marine nymph.

HAM Biblical; second son of Noah; after his banishment his children were said to be the origin of the nonwhite races; hence Egyptians and Egypt.

HECTOR Greek; son of Priam and leader of the Trojan armies at the siege of Troy.

HERCULES also Heracles, Alcides. The son of Jupiter and Alcmene and the greatest mythological hero, who became renowned for his strength and endurance having successfully completed twelve heroic labours. Named after his grandfather Alcaeus.

HERMES Greek; messenger god, known for his intelligence and wit.

HIRCANIE a district on the southern shore of the Caspian Sea, adjacent to Media and Parthia; summer living place of the Parthians.

HIRCANUS Biblical; last legitimate ruler of Maccabean descent, ruled Judea 142–63 BC. Usurped by Herod from Idumaea, south of Judaea.

IBERIA Spain and Portugal.

IDUMEAN Biblical; a person inhabiting Idumaea or Edom. A descendant of Esau.

ISIS Egyptian goddess, connected with the moon; wife of Osiris.

IXION Greek; King who attempted to seduce Zeus' wife Hera; father of the Centaurs.

JACOB Biblical; the younger of Isaac's twin sons: *see* Esau.

JANUS Roman god with two faces, whose temple in Rome had its doors closed in peace and open in war.

JOSHUA Biblical; military leader who swore peace with the Gibeonites but then subjected them to servitude. Conqueror of Jericho with divine help.

JOVE *see* Jupiter.

JUDAH fourth son of Jacob; also one of the twelve tribes of Israel; with tribe of Benjamin forms kingdom of Judaea.

JUPITER Roman; king of the gods who expressed an insatiable sexual appetite and was best known for administering divine judgements through the use of thunderbolts. Commonly referred to as Jove as well as being designated Zeus, in Greek mythology.

LEDA Greek; a beautiful woman ravished by Jupiter.

LEPIDUS ruled Rome in second triumvirate with Octavius and Antony.

LIVIA wife of Octavius Caesar.

LUCIUS Lucius Antonius, conspired with Antony's wife Fulvia against Octavius, but later surrendered and was pardoned, and became governor of Spain.

MAEGAERA one of the three furies.

MARCELLUS Marcus Claudius Marcellus took Syracuse (212 BC).

MARS Roman god of war and lover of Venus.

MASSAGETES people of Massagetae, in central Asia.

MEDE the Medes lived in Media, a mountainous country south-west of the Caspian Sea later absorbed into the Persian empire by Cyrus the Great.

MERCURIUS, MERCURY also Hermes. Messenger of the gods, as well as patron of travellers, thieves and lawyers.

MIRRHA or Myrrha, who fell in love with her father and seduced him. She was changed into the myrrh tree.

MITHRIDATE King of Pontus during three wars against the Romans, defeated by Pompey. Made himself proof against all poison by taking it incessantly.

MUTINA town famous for its successful resistance to Pompey in 78 BC and to Antony in 43 BC.

NEPTUNE god of the sea, who built the walls of Troy.

NILUS the river Nile.

NIOBE wife of Amphion; when her children were killed, she wept so much she was changed into a stone fountain on Mount Sipylus.

NISA the area where Bacchus, or Dionysos, grew up.

NUMIDIANS North African nomads.

OBODAS weak King of Arabia who let Silleus run his affairs.

OCTAVIUS Gaius Octavius, renamed Julius Caesar Octavianus after his adoption by Caesar (63 BC–AD 14). Ruled Rome with Antony and Lepidus. Later called Augustus Caesar, the first of the Roman emperors.

OPHIR in the Old Testament, a source of gold.

ORESTES in Greek mythology, he murdered his mother and was consequently driven mad by the furies as a punishment.

PALLAS also Minerva, Athena. She sprang, motherless, from the head of Zeus (Jupiter) to become the goddess of war, wisdom, justice and the liberal arts, carrying a reflective shield to which was fixed the snaky head of the gorgon, Medusa.

PAPHIAN see Venus and Paphos.

PAPHOS on Cyprus, the site of a temple dedicated to Venus.

PARIS son of Priam, King of Troy; his abduction of Helen, wife of Menelaus, caused the Trojan War when the Greeks invaded Troy to get her back.

PARTH, PARTHIANS semi-nomadic military people who fought against Rome.

PELUSIUM city in lower Egypt lost to Octavius, supposedly with Cleopatra's help.

PHAETON the son of Apollo, the sun god, who ignored warnings not to ride his father's chariot. When he lost control, he inflicted a scar in the sky (the Milky Way) and plummeted to Earth; Jupiter destroyed him with a thunderbolt during his descent, and thus prevented the destruction of the Earth.

PHAROS lighthouse on Pharos at Alexandria, one of the seven wonders of the world.

PHARSALY site of battle between Pompey and Julius Caesar, in which Antony led the left wing.

PHASAELUS Herod's brother who killed himself when captured by Parthians.

PHILIPPI site of the defeat in 42 BC of the republican forces of Brutus and Cassius by those of Antony and Octavius.

PHILOMELA was pursued by Tereus, husband of her sister Procne, who raped her and cut out her tongue to prevent her revealing the crime. She managed to tell her sister through embroidery, and Procne killed Tereus' son and served him to his father. Philomela became a nightingale.

PHOEBE see Diana.

PHOEBUS Phoebus Apollo, god of the sun, poetry, music, archery, prophecy and healing.

PHOENIX mythical Arabian bird. A symbol of resurrection.

PHRAATE Phraates, King of Parthia and Media, or the city said by Plutarch to be a great Median city.

PLEGETHON river in the underworld.

PLUTARCH *c.* AD 46–120, Greek biographer, moral philosopher and historian.

PLUTO Roman god of the underworld.

PROCONSUL governor of a Roman province.

PROCULEIUS Octavius' captain; *see* Octavius.

PROMETHEUS Titan; in Greek myth, he restored fire to the earth from the sun after Jove had taken it from man, and was punished by being chained to a rock with a eagle gnawing his liver.

PSAMMETIQUES also Psemmeticus. King of Egypt; returned from banishment to defeat his enemies and become sole ruler of Egypt.

PTOLOMIES Ptolemies; Macedonian Greek dynasty that ruled Egypt 323–30 BC. Cleopatra was the last of the line.

PYRRHUS King of Epirus 319–272 BC, he defeated the Romans but failed to take advantage of his victory.

ROMULUS mythical founder of Rome, with his twin Remus.

SAMNITE people of Samnium, central Italy. Particularly warlike, they were finally subdued by the Romans in 290 BC.

SARA wife of Abraham in the Old Testament.

SCYTHES people of Scythia, in North Asia. A nomadic tribe.

SENNACHERIB King of Assyria (704–681 BC); overthrown by a rebellion because of his excesses.

SION the fortress of the pre-Israelite city of Jerusalem taken by David and made his capital. A place of sacred ceremony.

SOL Latin for the sun.

SOLOMON Biblical; the third King of Israel (*c.* 961–922 BC), famous for his wisdom.

STYGIAN in Greek myth, the river Styx encircled Hades, and carried the souls of the dead to the underworld.

TANTALUS in Greek myth, the mythical King of Phrygia, tormented by Hades after he angered the gods.

THRASE a northern province of Greece, associated with fierce mountain tribes.

THYESTES Greek; brother of Atreus who suffered from the curse of their father Pelops. Subject of a tragedy by Seneca.

THYRE Thyrus negotiated with Cleopatra for Octavius. Antony grew jealous.

TIBER river on which Rome stands.

TITAN in Greek myth, the children of heaven and earth who rebelled against the gods and were eventually overthrown by Jove; later, used for the sun.

TRITON in Greek myth, sea figure, half man, half fish.

TYRUS Tyre, a rich Phoenician trading-port sacked by Alexander the Great.

ULISSES also Odysseus. The king of Ithaca, whose legendary journey was the subject of Homer's epic poem, *The Odyssey*. This tale famously recounts the many incidents which hampered the return voyage of Ulysses and his crew such as the alluring song of the sirens and the difficult passage through Scylla and Charybdis, the encounter with the lotus-eaters, and the transformation of his men into swine by the goddess, Circe.

VENUS also Aphrodite. Goddess of erotic love and beauty who won the Golden
    Apple in the Judgement of Paris – an event which eventually precipitated
    the Trojan War.

READ MORE IN PENGUIN

RENAISSANCE DRAMATISTS

The *Renaissance Dramatists* series provides scrupulously prepared texts with original spelling and punctuation, edited by leading scholars with extensive explanatory notes. The General Editor is John Pitcher.

Published or forthcoming:

The Spanish Tragedie by Thomas Kyd, ed. Emma Smith
includes the anonymous *The First Part of Jeronimo*

Plays and Poems by George Chapman, ed. Jonathan Hudston
includes *All Fooles*, *Bussy D'Ambois*, *The Widdowes Teares* and a selection of poems

Three Tragedies by Renaissance Women, ed. Diane Purkiss
includes *The Tragedie of Iphigeneia*, by Jane, Lady Lumley; *The Tragedie of Antonie*, by Mary, Countess of Pembroke; and *The Tragedie of Mariam*, by Elizabeth Cary

Volpone and Other Plays by Ben Jonson, ed. Lorna Hutson
includes *Every Man in his Humour*; *Sejanus, His Fall*; *Volpone, or the Foxe*; and *Epicoene, or the Silent Woman*

The Malcontent and Other Plays by John Marston, ed. David Pascoe
includes *The History of Antonio and Mellida*; *Antonios Revenge*; *The Malcontent*; *The Dutch Courtezan*; and *Parasitaster, or the Fawne*

A New Way to Pay Old Debts and Other Plays by Philip Massinger, ed. Richard Rowland
includes *The Roman Actor*, *Believe as you List*, *The Maid of Honour* and *A New Way to Pay Old Debts*

The Complete Plays by Christopher Marlowe, ed. Frank Romany

Visit Penguin on the Internet
and browse at your leisure

◆ preview sample extracts of our forthcoming books
◆ read about your favourite authors
◆ investigate over 10,000 titles
◆ enter one of our literary quizzes
◆ win some fantastic prizes in our competitions
◆ e-mail us with your comments and book reviews
◆ instantly order any Penguin book

and masses more!

'To be recommended without reservation ... a rich and rewarding on-line experience' – Internet Magazine

www.penguin.co.uk

READ MORE IN PENGUIN

In every corner of the world, on every subject under the sun, Penguin represents quality and variety – the very best in publishing today.

For complete information about books available from Penguin – including Puffins, Penguin Classics and Arkana – and how to order them, write to us at the appropriate address below. Please note that for copyright reasons the selection of books varies from country to country.

In the United Kingdom: Please write to *Dept. EP, Penguin Books Ltd, Bath Road, Harmondsworth, West Drayton, Middlesex UB7 ODA*

In the United States: Please write to *Consumer Sales, Penguin Putnam Inc., P.O. Box 999, Dept. 17109, Bergenfield, New Jersey 07621-0120.* VISA and MasterCard holders call 1-800-253-6476 to order Penguin titles

In Canada: Please write to *Penguin Books Canada Ltd, 10 Alcorn Avenue, Suite 300, Toronto, Ontario M4V 3B2*

In Australia: Please write to *Penguin Books Australia Ltd, P.O. Box 257, Ringwood, Victoria 3134*

In New Zealand: Please write to *Penguin Books (NZ) Ltd, Private Bag 102902, North Shore Mail Centre, Auckland 10*

In India: Please write to *Penguin Books India Pvt Ltd, 210 Chiranjiv Tower, 43 Nehru Place, New Delhi 110 019*

In the Netherlands: Please write to *Penguin Books Netherlands bv, Postbus 3507, NL-1001 AH Amsterdam*

In Germany: Please write to *Penguin Books Deutschland GmbH, Metzlerstrasse 26, 60594 Frankfurt am Main*

In Spain: Please write to *Penguin Books S. A., Bravo Murillo 19, 1° B, 28015 Madrid*

In Italy: Please write to *Penguin Italia s.r.l., Via Benedetto Croce 2, 20094 Corsico, Milano*

In France: Please write to *Penguin France, Le Carré Wilson, 62 rue Benjamin Baillaud, 31500 Toulouse*

In Japan: Please write to *Penguin Books Japan Ltd, Kaneko Building, 2-3-25 Koraku, Bunkyo-Ku, Tokyo 112*

In South Africa: Please write to *Penguin Books South Africa (Pty) Ltd, Private Bag X14, Parkview, 2122 Johannesburg*

READ MORE IN PENGUIN

A CHOICE OF CLASSICS

Armadale Wilkie Collins

Victorian critics were horrified by Lydia Gwilt, the bigamist, husband-poisoner and laudanum addict whose intrigues spur the plot of this most sensational of melodramas.

Aurora Leigh and Other Poems Elizabeth Barrett Browning

Aurora Leigh (1856), Elizabeth Barrett Browning's epic novel in blank verse, tells the story of the making of a woman poet, exploring 'the woman question', art and its relation to politics and social oppression.

Personal Narrative of a Journey to the Equinoctial Regions of the New Continent Alexander von Humboldt

Alexander von Humboldt became a wholly new kind of nineteenth-century hero – the scientist–explorer – and in *Personal Narrative* he invented a new literary genre: the travelogue.

The Pañćatantra Visnu Sarma

The Pañćatantra is one of the earliest books of fables and its influence can be seen in the *Arabian Nights*, the *Decameron*, the *Canterbury Tales* and most notably in the *Fables* of La Fontaine.

A Laodicean Thomas Hardy

The Laodicean of Hardy's title is Paula Power, a thoroughly modern young woman who, despite her wealth and independence, cannot make up her mind.

Brand Henrik Ibsen

The unsparing vision of a priest driven by faith to risk and witness the deaths of his wife and child gives *Brand* its icy ferocity. It was Ibsen's first masterpiece, a poetic drama composed in 1865 and published to tremendous critical and popular acclaim.

READ MORE IN PENGUIN

A CHOICE OF CLASSICS

Sylvia's Lovers Elizabeth Gaskell

In an atmosphere of unease the rivalries of two men, the sober tradesman Philip Hepburn, who has been devoted to his cousin Sylvia since her childhood, and the gallant, charming whaleship harpooner Charley Kinraid, are played out.

The Republic Plato

The best-known of Plato's dialogues, *The Republic* is also one of the supreme masterpieces of Western philosophy, whose influence cannot be overestimated.

Ethics Benedict de Spinoza

'Spinoza (1632–77),' wrote Bertrand Russell, 'is the noblest and most lovable of the great philosophers. Intellectually, some others have surpassed him, but ethically he is supreme.'

Virgil in English

From Chaucer to Auden, Virgil is a defining presence in English poetry. Penguin Classics' new series, Poets in Translation, offers the best translations in English, through the centuries, of the major Classical and European poets.

What is Art? Leo Tolstoy

Tolstoy wrote prolifically in a series of essays and polemics on issues of morality, social justice and religion. These culminated in *What is Art?*, published in 1898, in which he rejects the idea that art reveals and reinvents through beauty.

An Autobiography Anthony Trollope

A fascinating insight into a writer's life, in which Trollope also recorded his unhappy youth and his progress to prosperity and social recognition.

READ MORE IN PENGUIN

A CHOICE OF CLASSICS

Leopoldo Alas	**La Regenta**
Leon B. Alberti	**On Painting**
Ludovico Ariosto	**Orlando Furioso** (in 2 volumes)
Giovanni Boccaccio	**The Decameron**
Baldassar Castiglione	**The Book of the Courtier**
Benvenuto Cellini	**Autobiography**
Miguel de Cervantes	**Don Quixote**
	Exemplary Stories
Dante	**The Divine Comedy** (in 3 volumes)
	La Vita Nuova
Machado de Assis	**Dom Casmurro**
Bernal Díaz	**The Conquest of New Spain**
Carlo Goldoni	**Four Comedies (The Venetian Twins/The Artful Widow/Mirandolina/The Superior Residence)**
Niccolò Machiavelli	**The Discourses**
	The Prince
Alessandro Manzoni	**The Betrothed**
Emilia Pardo Bazán	**The House of Ulloa**
Benito Pérez Galdós	**Fortunata and Jacinta**
Giorgio Vasari	**Lives of the Artists** (in 2 volumes)

and

Five Italian Renaissance Comedies
(Machiavelli/**The Mandragola;** Ariosto/**Lena;** Aretino/**The Stablemaster;** Gl'Intronati/**The Deceived;** Guarini/**The Faithful Shepherd**)
The Poem of the Cid
Two Spanish Picaresque Novels
(Anon/**Lazarillo de Tormes;** de Quevedo/**The Swindler**)

A CHOICE OF CLASSICS

Francis Bacon	**The Essays**
Aphra Behn	**Love-Letters between a Nobleman and His Sister**
	Oroonoko, The Rover and Other Works
George Berkeley	**Principles of Human Knowledge/Three Dialogues between Hylas and Philonous**
James Boswell	**The Life of Samuel Johnson**
Sir Thomas Browne	**The Major Works**
John Bunyan	**The Pilgrim's Progress**
Edmund Burke	**Reflections on the Revolution in France**
Frances Burney	**Evelina**
Margaret Cavendish	**The Blazing World and Other Writings**
William Cobbett	**Rural Rides**
William Congreve	**Comedies**
Thomas de Quincey	**Confessions of an English Opium Eater**
	Recollections of the Lakes and the Lake Poets
Daniel Defoe	**A Journal of the Plague Year**
	Moll Flanders
	Robinson Crusoe
	Roxana
	A Tour Through the Whole Island of Great Britain
Henry Fielding	**Amelia**
	Jonathan Wild
	Joseph Andrews
	The Journal of a Voyage to Lisbon
	Tom Jones
John Gay	**The Beggar's Opera**
Oliver Goldsmith	**The Vicar of Wakefield**
Lady Gregory	**Selected Writings**

READ MORE IN PENGUIN

A CHOICE OF CLASSICS

William Hazlitt	**Selected Writings**
George Herbert	**The Complete English Poems**
Thomas Hobbes	**Leviathan**
Samuel Johnson/ James Boswell	**A Journey to the Western Islands of Scotland** and **The Journal of a Tour of the Hebrides**
Charles Lamb	**Selected Prose**
George Meredith	**The Egoist**
Thomas Middleton	**Five Plays**
John Milton	**Paradise Lost**
Samuel Richardson	**Clarissa**
	Pamela
Earl of Rochester	**Complete Works**
Richard Brinsley Sheridan	**The School for Scandal and Other Plays**
Sir Philip Sidney	**Selected Poems**
Christopher Smart	**Selected Poems**
Adam Smith	**The Wealth of Nations** (Books I–III)
Tobias Smollett	**The Adventures of Ferdinand Count Fathom**
	Humphrey Clinker
	Roderick Random
Laurence Sterne	**The Life and Opinions of Tristram Shandy**
	A Sentimental Journey Through France and Italy
Jonathan Swift	**Gulliver's Travels**
	Selected Poems
Thomas Traherne	**Selected Poems and Prose**
Henry Vaughan	**Complete Poems**